18th Century Hair & Wig Styling

History & Step-by-Step Techniques

by Kendra Van Cleave

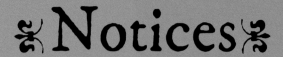

Notices

Copyright © 2014 by Kendra Van Cleave

All rights reserved. The written instructions, photographs, designs, patterns, and projects in this volume are intended for the personal use of the reader and may be reproduced for that purpose only. Any other use, especially commercial use, is forbidden under law without the written permission of the copyright holder. No part of this publication may be reproduced or transmitted, partly or as a whole, without prior written content of the author/publisher.

First Printing, 2014

ISBN 978-0-692-22043-6

www.18thCenturyHair.com

Every effort has been made to ensure that all the information in the book is accurate. However, due to differing conditions, tools and individual skills, the author/publisher cannot be responsible for any injuries, losses, and other damages which may result from the ideas, information, or advice in this book.

    The application and quality of hair products and tools is beyond the control of the author/publisher, who cannot be held responsible for any problems resulting from their use. Always follow the manufacturer's instructions and if in doubt, seek further advice.

    All reasonable efforts have been made to identify and contact image copyright holders but in some cases these could not be traced. If you hold or administer rights for materials published here, please contact us. Any errors or omissions will be corrected in subsequent editions.

Acknowledgments

I would like to thank:
- Tara Maginnis, for inadvertently sparking the idea for this book;
- The readers of my blog and other costumers online, for their encouragement for this project and participation in market research;
- Judy Grivich, for teaching me the method of making rolls with glue, and giving me permission to include it in this book;
- The Bibliothèque Nationale de France; the Bunka Gakuen University Library; Google and their library partners; and museums, libraries, and archives worldwide for making research materials available online;
- The Getty Museum, Lewis Walpole Library, Library of Congress, Los Angeles County Museum of Art, National Gallery of Art, Rijksmuseum, Wellcome Library, and Yale Center for British Art for making publication-quality digital images of their collections available for commercial use; and the Metropolitan Museum of Art for using a broad definition of scholarly publishing in their open access image program;
- Catherine, Leia, Lisa, and Trystan for their editorial assistance;
- The models, for their beauty and patience: Angela, Bridget, Catherine, Cathie, Cynthia, Diana, Francis, Jenn, John, Karen, Katherine, Katie, Liam, Linda, Sarah, Tara, Teresa, and Trystan;
- The critters: Winston and Olive for "entertaining" the models during photo shoots, and Albert and Sadie for keeping the photo backdrop in good condition;
- And most of all my husband, Michael Fleming, for taking many of the photos, dedicating a month of his life to editing them and creating all of the graphics, technical and design advice, making an amazing ship model, encouragement, putting up with the world's largest hairball tumbleweeds floating through the house, and love.

The following fabulous people supported this book project by donating funds for printing and art licensing. This book would not have happened without your support. You have my eternal gratitude!

Katherine Adrian	Sahrye Cohen	Wendy Farrell	Heather Hamill
Angela Bacci	Diana Collins	Fashion Resource Center	Kirsten Hammerstrom
Susan Bailey	Danine Cozzens	Amanda Lerum Faulkner	Karen Hanuschuk
Catherine Balint	Tatiana Crawford	Anne Fenimore	Richard Harper
Constance Barbarino	Betty Creegan	Natalie Ferguson	Lisa Deutsch Harrigan
Trystan L. Bass	Alison Cumming	Stacy Ferguson	Emmalia Harrington
Anna Beard	Colleen M. Danyluk	Allison Foreman	Cathy Hay
Yves Borkholz	Kathleen M. Danyluk	Johanna Frank	Debrah Henslet-The
Gailynne Bouret	Loren Dearborn	Garet Gardina	Helen Hester
Bridget Bradley-Scaife	Sarah Dickinson	Aylwen Gardiner-Garden	Elizabeth R. Hobbs
Kim Byrnes	Sharon Doig	Agnes Gawne	Heather Hofshi
Marguerite Bystrom	Mary Dotson	Lina Gissberg	Amie Holloway
Cédric Canac	Jane Xavier Dougherty	Veronica Gonzalez-Rubio	Christina Holmertz
Maureen Caoilfhionn	Jessica Dove	Sarah Lorraine Goodman	Kim Holte
Katherine Caron-Greig	Laetitia Durand	Karen Green	Mela Hoyt-Heydon
Cameron Clark	Aubry Bennett Eary	Judith Grivich	Claire Hummel
Suzi Clarke	Elisa Edgren	Nicole Grohs	Jess Hutchison
Francis Classe	Caroline Eliades	Maija Hallikas-Manninen	K. Janke

Supporters continued...

Donna Jefferis
Cathy Jin
Christina Johnson
Kathryn Johnson
Bobbie Kalben
Amy Karow-Thara
Jana Keeler
Yvette Keller
Tracey King
Elizabeth Klimek
Athene Kovacic
Ginger Lane
Elizabeth Langford
Claudia Laughter
Jennifer Lemus
Miriam Lewis
J. Leia Lima
Cecil Longino
Cindy Lu
Thena MacArthur
Tara Maginnis
Jennifer Malik
Saara Malmi
Crystal Marinelli
Pamela McCrae
Meilin
John Mendola
Natalie Meyer
Shelley Monson
Sara Mueller
Kelly Mulry
Kimberly Mumford
Sheryl Nance-Durst
Sharon Nevin
Rebecca Noble
Kathleen Noll
Johanna Nybelius
Jennifer Old
Merja Palkivaara
Cheryl Adams Palmer
Laura Parker
Betsy Hanes Perry
Noelle Pettit
Wendy Pfile
Victoria Platt
Amber Pohle
Heather Pritchett

Jay E Ragan
Shefali Raigne
Céline Raillat
Elizabeth Reed
Kayla Roca
Christine Rodriguez
Athena Roehnert
Tricia Roush
Jenny Schmelia
Gregory Seelye
Cynthia Settje
Taylor Shelby
Alena Shellenbean
Abigail Shelly
Gloria Sheu
Mackenzie Sholtz
Marthe Sikkerbol
Chelsea Skellenger
Michael Slack
Barbara Smith
Josie Smith
Rita Smith
Debbie Stern
Emily Stringham
Perian Sully
Holly Taylor
Lynne Taylor
Rebecca Thelin
Jennifer Thompson
Randi Thompson
Jennifer Tifft
Lani K Tucker
Chris Underwood
Katie Van Camp
Tyson Vick
Christina Walley
David Walters
Ryan Weir
Michael Owen Wells
Katy Werlin
Jenny-Rose White
Toni Whyte
Wendy Wildermoth
Jane A. Wong
Laina Worth
Kim Yasuda
Kaitlyn Yaworski

Haley Zerr

Table of Contents

Acknowledgments 1
Introduction 5

Part I: History

Sources 8

Historical Overview 9
- Hairstyling & Wig Vocabulary 11
- How's & Why's of Wigs 13
- Techniques 17
- Powder & Pomatum 21
- Stylistic Changes 24
- What Did They Call It? 27
- Hair Colors 29

Women's Styles: Year-by-Year 30
- High Front Styles (1700s-1710s) 31
- Simple Parted Styles (1720s-1730s) 34
- Simple Pulled-Back Styles (1740s) 38
- Simple Pulled-Up Styles (1750s - late 1760s) 42
- High Styles (late 1760s - late 1770s) 47
- High & Wide Styles (late 1770s - early 1780s) 52
- Bushy Styles (early 1780s - 1780s) 57
- Simple Short & Long Styles (1790s) 62

Men's Styles: Year by Year 66
- Popular Wigs of the Eighteenth Century ..67
- Full-Bottomed Styles (1700s-1710s) 69
- Bob Styles (1720s-1730s) 71
- Queue Styles (1730s-1740s) 73
- Buckle/Queue Styles (1740s-1770s) 76
- High Buckle/Queue Styles (1770s) 80
- Bushy Styles (1780s - mid-1790s) 84
- Simple Styles (1790s) 88

Part II: Techniques

Introduction 94

Supplies 96

Working With Human Hair 97

Working With False Hair 98
- Purchasing False Hair & Wigs 98
- Styling False Hair 102
- Making Your Own Weaving Hair 102
- Curling Synthetic Hair 103
- Straightening Synthetic Hair 105
- Making Basic Hairpieces 106
- Buckles (Rolls) 108

Raising Hair & Wigs 113

Wig-Specific Techniques 115
- Wig Basics 115
- Adding Extra Hair 118
- Changing a Hairline 119
- Enlarging a Wig 123
- Making it All Look Smooth 124
- Wearing False Hair & Wigs 124

Wig Care 127

Ornamentation 128

Powdering 129

Part III: Finished Styles

Introduction 132

Women
- Marie-Adélaïde (1700s-1710s) 134
- Elizabeth (1720s-1730s) 139
- Clarissa (1730s-1740s) 144
- Summer (1740s) 148
- Madame de Pompadour (1750s) 152
- Derby (1760s) 158
- Madame Du Barry (late 1760s - mid-1770s) 163
- Miss Nettlethorpe (1770s) 170
- Euridice (1770s) 176
- Lady Betty (1770s) 185
- Dorothée (1770s) 195
- Marine Royale (1770s) 202
- Queen Charlotte (late 1770s-early 1780s) 211
- Lilac (late 1770s-early 1780s) 219
- Marie-Antoinette (late 1770s-early 1780s) 228
- Pearl (late 1770s-early 1780s) 237
- Plume (1780s) 247
- Georgiana (1780s) 253
- Balloon (1780s) 257
- Star (mid- to late 1780s) 262
- Matilda (1790s) 268
- Adela (1790s) 273

Men
- King George (1750s-1770s) 276
- Joseph (1770s) 280
- Captain Robert (1780s) 285

Shopping Resources 290

Sources & Further Reading 291

Illustration Credits 297

Introduction

This book is intended to be a resource for people who are interested in learning more about, and/or would like to recreate, eighteenth-century hairstyles: fashion historians, film and theater costumers, living history reenactors, recreational costumers, and more. Creating a complete historical look requires more than just clothes – cosmetics, accessories, and hairstyles can change a "costume" to "just stepped out of the past." At the same time, fashion cannot be analyzed fully without understanding the technical aspects of fashion production and consumption, while accurate dating is only improved by the study of the detailed specifics of stylistic changes. All of these statements are of particular import when dealing with the eighteenth century, when hairstyles were a particularly featured part of an ensemble — so much so that at the end of the period, fashion magazines devoted multiple paragraphs to descriptions of hair and headdress, yet only a sentence or two to clothes.

The scope of this project includes both women's and men's hairstyles worn in France, Great Britain, and the North American colonies. This geographic focus was chosen because of French and British dominance in eighteenth-century fashion, and also because the vast majority of theatre, film, and historical reenactment is set in these areas. The fashionable elites of many European and North American countries followed the leads of France and England, although this was still an era of distinct regionalism. Those who are interested in learning more about the different styles worn in other areas are encouraged to conduct further research including and beyond the sources suggested on pages 291-296.

While the hairstyles studied and reproduced in this book are primarily those worn by the middle and upper classes, I have tried to include some information on lower classes when possible. Many of the finished hairstyles can be made appropriate for the middle or lower classes by modification – for example, lowering the height of a style, or decorating it more conservatively.

In **Part 1: History**, I offer an overview of the history of hair in the eighteenth-century: its role in the larger context of eighteenth-century fashion and society, the why's and how's of wigs and powder, the techniques used to make and style wigs and hair, and an analysis of changing fashions. The focus of this research is on the hair of adult, white Europeans and Americans. Due to space considerations, I have not been able to add much information about the hair of people of non-white ancestry, but I have included sources for these topics in the bibliography on beginning on page 291. Similarly, I was unable to include information on the hairstyles worn by children.

In **Part 2: Techniques**, I give you all of the tips and tricks I have learned over the years for creating historical hairstyles, including working with false hair and wigs. My goal with this book is to teach you how to take modern, commercially available wigs, hairpieces, and hair and turn them into styles that will give a historically accurate look. This book will *not* teach you how to make a wig from scratch in the modern (ventilating – tying each hair on individually) or historical (weaving hair into wefts by hand) methods. If you would like to know more about either of these advanced methods, I have included sources on page 294. Instead, I would like to put *good* historical hair and wig styles into the hands of those who do not have the time or resources to become a specialized wig professional or hair stylist, modern or historical. While I use modern tools and products, I do follow the eighteenth-century approach of using false pieces and wigs to create fashionable styles – something that we modern wearers often need even more, as we usually have different haircuts and lifestyles than those who lived in the past.

In **Part 3: Finished Styles,** I provide step-by-step instructions for creating 25 eighteenth-century hairstyles based on real historical examples. The majority of these styles are for women. This is because female styles tend to generate the most interest among one of the primary markets for this book (historical reenactors). For men, I have chosen to focus on three variations of the queue (ponytail) style. It was the most popular male wig/hair style from the 1730s through the 1790s, and is the most frequently seen today on stage and screen as well as in reenactments. This style did change subtly over time, with a number of variations available within a given era; these details can be gleaned from the historical overview section and then applied to the finished styles. I have chosen to demonstrate the simpler female styles on a model's natural hair, but all of them could be made as a wig. Similarly, many of the wigs (both male and female) demonstrated could be accomplished using natural hair. It is my hope that you will experiment with the different techniques and approaches, and mix and match those that work best for you and the head of hair with which you are working.

Throughout the book, I have tried to select images that will show the range of hairstyles worn in this period, but also to focus on those styles that were most popular. No doubt I will have missed some specific trends or variations, so I encourage you to do your own additional research.

> *"Sr Durand, called Legout, Coëffeur, [Paris] ... makes and sells wigs with straight and side buckles, ringlets, cords, &c.; cushions mounted on brass wire; combs trimmed with hair, forming the knot called* cachepeigne *[hidden comb]; high, frizzy, or ratted chignons..."*
>
> —
>
> *L'Avantcoureur,* 1769.

Part I: History

Sources

Elisabeth-Louise Vigée Le Brun, French (1755-1842). *Portrait of Marie-Gabrielle de Gramont, Duchesse de Caderousse*, 1784. Oil on wood panel, 41 3/8 x 29 7/8 inches (105.1 x 75.9 cm). The Nelson-Atkins Museum of Art, Kansas City, Missouri. Purchase: William Rockhill Nelson Trust, 86-20. Photo: John Lamberton.

To present accurate and detailed information about the history of hair and wigs across the eighteenth century, my research draws on a number of sources, including published works of history and the records left by eighteenth-century hairdressers and wearers. Most modern histories tend to include the topic of hair and wigs as a portion of a larger work – either a survey of hairstyles across a longer period, or a study of the broader topic of fashion in the eighteenth century. As a result, generalities are created and passed on, leading to an indistinct understanding of the topic and, sometimes, inaccurate information being accepted as fact. To try to combat this problem, I have reviewed a large number of eighteenth-century documents to find information from the period: fashion magazines, hairdressing and wigmaking manuals, newspaper articles, personal diaries and correspondence, and works of art (drawings, paintings, sculpture, and fashion plates). A detailed list of these sources is on pages 294-296. I hope that this book will help to clarify some previously muddied topics, and correct some commonly accepted errors.

The main visual sources of my research are works of art: paintings, drawings, fashion plates, and sculptures. It is important to note that artists frequently idealized their subjects, and so hairstyles may be presented that are more perfect than reality. However, we can turn this to our advantage by noting that idealized images help us create an understanding of the period's desired beauty archetype(s).

Another point to understand is that artists often persuaded their sitters to include some elements of fantasy in their attire for dramatic or symbolic purposes. What is portrayed may have been the creation of the artist, not what was ever worn outside of the studio. Yet at the same time, art could and did set fashion. As an example, French painter Elisabeth Vigée-Le Brun provides an example of both, recalling in her memoirs,

> "I could not endure [hair] powder. I persuaded the handsome Duchess de Grammont-Caderousse to put none on for her sittings. Her hair was ebony black, and I divided it on the forehead, disposing it in irregular curls. After the sitting, which ended at the dinner hour, the Duchess would not change her headdress, but go to the theatre as she was. A woman of such good looks would, of course, set a fashion : indeed, this mode of doing the hair soon found imitators, and then gradually became general."[1]

Moreover, whether or not an artist aimed to accurately depict the sitter's daily appearance, fashion (including hairstyle and headdress) carries with it meaningful references – an unspoken language easily readable to contemporary viewers. Eighteenth-century observers were able to interpret signs and symbols that may no longer be apparent to us. Thus, I have tried to consider some of the symbolism of hair and wigs in the following analysis, and to highlight when a style shown in a piece of art was likely to have been influenced by some element of fantasy. All of this illustrates how we must view art with a careful, critical eye when looking to study fashions.

1. Louise-Elisabeth Vigée-Le Brun, *Memoirs of Madame Vigée Lebrun*, trans. Lionel Strachey (New York: Doubleday, 1903), 22.

Historical Overview

Fashion – both the specific looks worn by people across the social spectrum, as well as the processes by which they acquire and wear items of apparel and other aspects of personal appearance – cannot be untied from its social, political, and economic context. The eighteenth century is an era particularly identified with hairstyles, in part because they became such potent symbols of the aristocracy and the *ancien régime* (the old order) during the French Revolution.

Across Western Europe and the North American colonies, French and English fashions had the greatest sway due to these countries' political and cultural influence.[2] France was arguably the more dominant force until the end of the period, when English styles captured the cultural zeitgeist. At the same time, this century is one of the last in which distinct regional styles can be identified. While London and Paris fashions were copied outright in the provinces and in other countries, or at least wielded heavy influence, unique styles specific to particular countries and regions can also be found.

When reviewing the fashions worn in France and Great Britain, one finds relatively similar silhouettes and garments – the differences lay more in terms of formality.[3] French culture was ceremonial and hierarchical, with the court serving as the center of high society, and artifice in appearance was the norm. The formal clothing worn in France dominated Western European fashion for most of the century. Although Britain too had a monarchy, its culture was more focused on convenience and country living (riding, hunting, and shooting), which required more casual clothing. Over the course of the century, the Enlightenment – the intellectual movement focused on social and political reform through reason and science – effected great change on the societies of Western Europe and their colonies. There was a growing interest in humanity's "state of nature" and a desire to return to what were considered more "natural" ways of living, along with growing support for republicanism (*i.e.*, representational government). Both of these trends opposed the luxury of French court models. England, with its constitutional monarchy and focus on rural life, became increasingly fashionable as a symbol of this new way of living, and its comparatively informal styles were influential across much of Western Europe in the last few decades of the century.

The fact that the majority of North American colonists were from Great Britain meant that they were very likely to follow British fashions – reading British publications, purchasing goods from Britain, etc. Modified versions of the fashions worn in London and Paris were adopted in the colonies, such as the high hairstyles of the late 1760s and 1770s.[4] A letter in the *New York Journal or General Advertiser* from 1767 complained about the increasingly elaborate hairstyles of that period: "It is now the Mode to make the Lady's Head of twice the natural Size, by

> *"The first thing to be done, in Paris, is always to send for a Taylor, a Peruke maker and Shoemaker, for this nation has established such a domination over the Fashion, that neither Cloaths, Wigs nor Shoes made in any other Place will do in Paris."*
>
> — John Adams, 1782

---

2. Aileen Ribeiro, *The Art of Dress: Fashion in England and France, 1750 to 1820* (New Haven, Conn.: Yale University Press, 1995), 30.
3. *Ibid.*, 35.
4. Kate Haulman, "A Short History of the High Roll," *Common-Place* 2, no. 1 (October 2001): http://www.common-place.org/vol-02/no-01/lessons/

means of artificial Pads, Boulsters, or Rolls."[5] The American Revolution (1775-1783) interrupted this flow to some degree, while at the same time casting fashionable English styles as politically disloyal, but nonetheless Americans continued to follow British modes.[6] However, although the dress of many in the large Eastern coastal cities *could* rival the English elite, Americans were by and large less likely to be quite as fashion-forward. Historian Viola Hopkins Winner argues, "Hair styles of American women, as with styles in general, tended not to go to the extremes found in high society in England and in France."[7] Until the 1760s, portraits of American women often to depict them wearing styles that are about a decade out of style in England. Whether that means some American women were wearing older styles, or that Americans (and American artists) were simply more conservative in their choices for a formal portrait, is debatable. A Boston newspaper noted in 1770 that American women were about two years behind their London counterparts: "I have for some time past taken notice of a *growing* disorder among the Ladies (*heads*) [hairstyles] in this metropolis, and thought before now to have seen some *cure* proscribed for it. It seems about two years ago, the same distemper reigned epidemical in England…"[8]

 The French Revolution (1789-1799) was a watershed moment in the political, social, and cultural history of Europe, with significant effects on fashion. The origins of the aesthetic trends popularized during and after the revolutionary period – informality and equality of appearance – can be traced back as far as the middle of the century to the philosophy of the Enlightenment. Nonetheless, the changes in clothing, hair, and makeup wrought by the Revolution were still striking. Gone was the artifice and formality that had characterized most of the century, leaving in its place comparatively narrower silhouettes, lighter fabrics, and more "natural" looks in terms of cosmetics and hair.[9]

 In eighteenth-century Europe, the desire for fashionable hairstyles extended across the class spectrum. By contrast, in the American colonies, the middling sorts (tradesmen, servants, apprentices) were less likely than the same classes in Europe to wear wigs or formal styles. This contrast can be seen clearly in an incident that took place in 1784, when John and Abigail Adams visited Paris.[10] They hired Parisian servants for their temporary household, but also brought two Americans (one man, one woman) from home. The Parisian servants ridiculed their American counterparts, both male and female, for their hairstyles, until the American servants were obliged "to have their hair dressed. Esther [the American maid] had several crying fits upon the occasion, that she should be forced to be so much of a fool; but there was no way to keep them from being trampled upon but this; and, now that they are à la mode de Paris, they are much respected."[11]

 Having one's hair styled, or "dressed" as it was called in the period, was essential to facing the world, even in one's own home. English writer Fanny Burney reported that when she visited the house of a married couple, the wife was unable to see them as her hair was not yet dressed: "She was extremely unhappy she could not wait upon us, but had all her hair combed out [*i.e.,* unstyled], and was waiting for the man to dress it, who had disappointed her ever since two o'clock."[12] When Abigail Adams visited London in 1784, she was surprised to find both ladies and gentlemen less formally attired than in the United States; however, having one's coiffure styled was still a requirement:

---

5. Quoted in *The Wigmaker in Eighteenth-Century Williamsburg: An Account of His Barbering, Hair-Dressing, & Peruke-Making Services, & Some Remarks on Wigs of Various Styles* (Williamsburg, VA: Colonial Williamsburg, 1971), 6.
6. Kate Haulman, *The Politics of Fashion in Eighteenth-Century America* (Chapel Hill, NC: University of North Carolina Press, 2011), 5.
7. Viola Hopkins Winner, "Abigail Adams and the Rage of Fashion," *Dress* 2001: 67.
8. "To the Printer of the Massachusetts Spy," *Massachusetts Spy*, 5-8 November 1770 (Vol 1, Issue 41): 1.
9. The term "natural" will consistently be surrounded by quotation marks in this book as a reminder that what was considered natural during the eighteenth century was, of course, a product of that specific time and culture. The hairstyles that were regarded as "natural" during this period were still constructed and artificial, they just conformed to a different aesthetic.
10. John Adams was then a diplomat on behalf of the fledging United States. He would later serve as president from 1797 to 1801.
11. Abigail Adams to Mrs. Cranch, 5 September 1784, in vol. 2 of *Letters of Mrs. Adams: the Wife of John Adams* (Boston: C.C. Little and J. Brown, 1840), 52.
12. Frances Burney, between April and July 1777, in vol. 2 of *The Early Diary of Frances Burney, 1768-1778: With a Selection from her Correspondence, and from the Journals of her Sisters Susan and Charlotte Burney* (London: George Bell and Sons, 1889), 181.

Hairstyling & Wig Vocabulary

ACCOMODAGE (fr): to style a hair or a wig; a finished hairstyle (frequently, but not always, masculine)

BOUCLES (fr), **BUCKLES** (eng): structured rolls of hair, generally worn on the sides of the head

CAUL (eng/fr): base of a wig – a fitted cap to which wefts of hair are sewn

CHIGNON (eng/fr): the back half of a woman's hairstyle, from the crown to the nape of the neck

COIFFEUR (eng/fr), **FRISEUR** (fr): hairdresser

COIFFURE (eng/fr), **HEAD DRESS** (eng), **HEAD** (eng): women's finished hairstyle, with or without hats and accessories

CUSHION (eng), **TOCQUE** (fr): pad on which women's high hairstyles of the late 1760s – early 1780s were styled

FRIZZLE (eng), **FRISER** (fr): to make narrow, tight curls creating a frizzy texture

HALF-WIG (eng), **DEMI-PERRUQUE** (fr): a wig that only covers the back half of the head, from the crown to the nape of the neck

QUEUE (fr/eng): the hanging tail on many men's hairstyles or wigs

PERRUQUE (fr), **PERUKE** (eng), **PERIWIG** (eng), **TETE** (eng): wig; "tete" is usually a woman's wig

PERRUQUIER (fr), **PERUKE-MAKER** (eng): wigmaker

PIPE (eng): clay roller used for making curls

TAPER, **TAPET** (fr): to rat the hair; ratted hair

TOUPEE (fr), **TOUPET** (eng/fr), **FORETOP** (eng), **FOREPART** (eng): top and sides of a wig (usually masculine) or hairstyle, from the front hairline to the crown and ears

WEFT (eng): a length of hair woven onto threads. Rows of wefts are sewn to a caul in order to make a wig

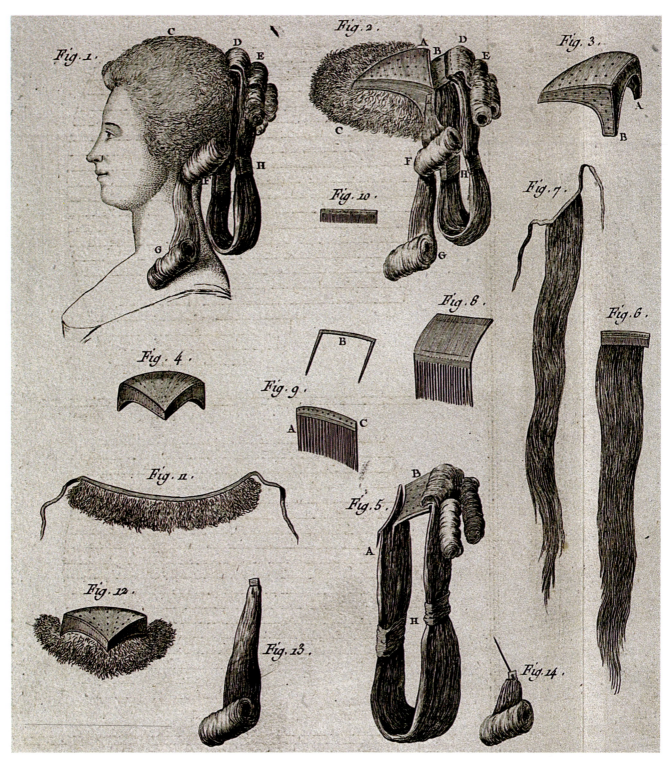

An example of the numerous false hairpieces that could be used to create the so-called "natural" female styles of the mid-1780s.

Bénard, Robert. Detail from *Wigs and Wig Accessories for Women, Left; Two Patterns of Wigs for Men, Right* ["Perruquier, Coeffure de Femme et Mesures pour les Nouvelles Perruques d'Hommes," *Recueil de Planches de l'Encyclopedie par Ordre de Matières*, Vol. 4. Paris: Chez Panckoucke; 1785]. Engraving. Wellcome.

"'T is true, you must ... have your hair dressed... [to be] thought dress[ed] sufficient to go into company."[13]

HOW'S & WHY'S OF WIGS

The wearing of wigs by men was ubiquitous in Great Britain and France throughout the eighteenth century. In her study of eighteenth-century British portraiture, historian Marcia Pointon notes, "Once it became customary for gentlemen to wear wigs, to appear without one was to expose oneself as eccentric, exceptional or deviant."[14] The wearing of a wig was a requirement for a man to appear in polite society. When James Boswell's wig was stolen from his room at an inn, he noted, "I was obliged to go all day in my night-cap and absent myself from a party of ladies and gentlemen who went and dined with the Earl on the banks of a lake."[15] In the end, he traveled twenty-five miles away simply to purchase a replacement. To be shown dis-wigged, at least in portraiture, was equated with a loss of dignity, or an extremely intimate situation. Pointon notes, "Men who wear their own hair and who appear in public places, that is in portraits, without a wig are defined by that absence."[16]

On the other hand, women rarely wore whole wigs. Instead, they hired professional hairdressers who added false hair to their natural hair. While they were expected to augment their own hair with false hair, padding, powder, and ornaments, women's hair was supposed to remain "natural" by avoiding the total fabrication of men's wigs.[17] Of course, this did not preclude a woman from wearing a wig; she simply tried to integrate her own hair in order to conceal that fact.

Wigs as a fashion item were introduced in the 1620s for the same reasons they are worn in any era: to cover baldness and provide extra hair to those who did not have enough of their own for the current styles.[18] Certain fashion leaders helped promote the wearing of wigs, among them King Louis XIII of France (1610-43), who had let his own hair grow long, and then began to bald prematurely at the age of 23. Louis XIV of France (1643-1715) had long, luxuriant hair, which caused courtiers to wear long wigs to emulate him; Louis himself began wearing a wig after 1670. The fashion spread to England during the period of the Restoration of Charles II (1660s), when Britain re-opened itself to continental styles.

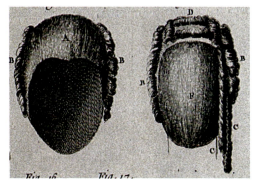

Top: **man's wig.**
Bottom: **ladies' full wigs.**
Both images are originally from Diderot's Encyclopédie.

—

Top: Bénard, Robert. Detail from *Various Styles of Wigs*. Engraving, 1762. Wellcome.

Bottom: Bénard, Robert after J.R. Lucotte. Detail from *A Variety of Wigs*. Engraving, 1762. Wellcome.

Wigs for men were pervasive in France and Britain from the late seventeenth century until the 1790s, with a brief trend for natural hair in England in the 1760s.[19] In 1673, an independent wigmakers' guild was created in France; by the late 18th century, the number of

---

13. Adams to Mrs. Cranch, 24 July 1784, in vol. 3 of *Letters of Mrs. Adams*, 174.
14. Marcia R. Pointon, *Hanging the Head: Portraiture and Social Formation in Eighteenth-Century England* (New Haven, Conn.: Yale University Press, 1993), 117.
15. Quoted in Pointon, *Hanging the Head*, 120.
16. Pointon, *Hanging the Head*, 107.
17. *Ibid.*
18. Janet Arnold, *Perukes & Periwigs* (London: H.M.S.O., 1970), 5-7.
19. Anne Buck, *Dress in Eighteenth-Century England* (New York: Holmes & Meier, 1979), 30.

A man's eighteenth-century wig. The queue (the long hair in back) is tied in a wig bag, which is decorated with a pinked cockade.

—

Wig. Silk, metal, linen, leather, horsehair, 1780-1800. MMA. Brooklyn Museum Costume Collection at The Metropolitan Museum of Art, Gift of the Brooklyn Museum, 2009; Caroline A. L. Pratt Fund, 1974.

French master wigmakers had more than quadrupled.[20] Wigs were primarily an elite style in the seventeenth century, but by the early 1700s, the fashion had grown to include most any man who could afford it. Historian John Styles studied advertisements for runaway tradesmen in Britain across the century. He found that "during the middle years of the eighteenth century large numbers of plebian men were able to acquire wigs and evidently considered them a sufficiently important element in their attire to wear them when they absconded."[21] While traveling through England in 1748, Swedish botanist Pehr Kalm commented,

> "I believe there is scarcely a country where one gets to see so many Peruques as here… It did not, therefore, strike one as being at all wonderful to see farm-servants, clod-hoppers, day-labourers, farmers, in a word, all labouring-folk go through their usual every-day duties all with Peruques on the head. Few, yea, very few, were those who only wore their own hair. I had to look around a long time in a church or other gathering of people, before I saw anyone with his own hair."[22]

---

20. Michael Kwass, "Big Hair: A Wig History of Consumption in Eighteenth-Century France," *American Historical Review* 111, no. 3 (June 2006): 635.
21. John Styles, *The Dress of the People: Everyday Fashion in Eighteenth-Century England* (New Haven, Conn.: Yale University Press, 2007), 86.
22. Pehr Kalm, *Kalm's Account of His Visit to England: On His Way to America in 1748*, trans. Joseph Lucas (London: Macmillan and Co., 1892), 52.

Across the Channel, the *Tableau de Paris* of 1782 noted all of the various types of ordinary men who wore wigs: schoolmasters, choirmasters, public scribes, law court ushers, shop boys, legal clerks, servants, cooks, and kitchen boys.[23] They were worn in capital cities and provincial towns. Aumale, France (population 2,000) had one master wigmaker in 1710, and seven in 1789.[24]

By contrast, in the American colonies, the wearing of wigs by men was more commonly restricted to the upper classes.[25] One (probably European) observer noted of 1740s Maryland, "'Tis an odd Sight, that except some of the very elevated Sort, few Persons wear Perukes, so that you would imagine they were all sick, or going to bed… Methinks, 'ts very ridiculous."[26] A study of advertisements in the *South Carolina Gazette* for runaway white male indentured servants – the lowest of the social order among whites – from 1732-52 shows that only 10.5 percent of the advertisements noted that the fugitive was wearing a wig.[27]

Two rough drunks are among those who wear wigs (rather haphazardly!) in this London street scene.

—

Grignion, Charles after William Hogarth. Detail from *Canvassing for Votes*. Etching and engraving, 1757. NGA.

Why did wigs become such a ubiquitous item of dress in this period? There are two theories accepted by scholars. The first is that the wearing of wigs was a product of conspicuous consumption. Historian Lynn Festa explains: "Many fashionable items are uncomfortable to wear. Indeed, the expenditure, inconvenience, and uselessness of fashion in part create its symbolic value. Only those possessed of leisure and wealth could afford the hours it took to dress a head, not to mention the price of a 'pound of hair and two pounds of powder.'"[28] (On the other hand, it should also be mentioned that wearing a wig, which was usually sent off to the wigmaker to be styled, was actually *more* convenient than sitting in a chair for hours having one's own hair dressed.) The second theory is based on the link between wigs and personal identity. Over time, specific wig styles began to be associated with various professions, and thus considered *de rigeur* for men of the middling and upper classes. Wearing a wig was a way of proclaiming your "corporate identity" – the groups with which you identified (*e.g.*, your social class, profession) – in an era when group identity was considered far more important than personal individuality (contrary to our modern outlook).[29] To this day, British lawyers and judges wear a version of the full-bottomed wig, fashionable in the late seventeenth and early eighteenth centuries, as a mark of their profession. There were over 200 named wigs associated with different social classes, professions, etc. Furthermore, wigs were a literal symbol of masculinity and the power associated with that gender. Marcia Pointon argues, "It was universally recognized that masculine authority was vested in the wig."[30]

Because of the social statement made by wigs, men frequently did not make any effort to mask the fact that they were wearing one. Charlotte Papendiek, who served Queen Charlotte of England, later recalled (with the benefit of hindsight), "Wigs were not then what they are now, a covering made to imitate the hair, but real fright-

---

22. Kwass, "Big Hair": 635.
24. *Ibid.*: 637.
25. *Wigmaker in Eighteenth-Century Williamsburg*, 11-13. Kate Haulman clarifies, "No man of rank [in the American colonies] preferred natural hair until late in the century" (*Politics of Fashion*, 64).
26. Quoted in *Wigmaker in Eighteenth-Century Williamsburg*, 13.
27. Shane White and Graham White, "Slave Hair and African American Culture in the Eighteenth and Nineteenth Centuries," *Journal Of Southern History* 61, no. 1 (February 1995): 62.
28. Lynn Festa, "Personal Effects: Wigs and Possessive Individualism in the Long Eighteenth Century" *Eighteenth-Century Life* 29, no. 2 (Spring 2005): 54.
29. *Ibid.*, 62.
30. Pointon, *Hanging the Head*, 110.

Note the differences in hairlines among the two men: on top is the American artist himself, whose more naturalistic hairline may indicate that he is wearing his own hair, or that he has brushed his hair into the front of the wig. His father-in-law, merchant Richard Clarke, has a more obvious line around the edge of his wig.

—

Copley, John Singleton. Detail from *The Copley Family*. Oil on canvas, 1776/7. NGA.

ful wigs. Mr. Papendiek [her husband] looked older, his fine forehead was hidden, and his beauty greatly diminished by this horrid wig."[31] Many portraits of the period show an obvious line where the wig lays on the forehead. On the other hand, the hair along the hairline could be brushed into the wig to create a more natural-looking appearance. Similarly, there were half-wigs that only covered the back half of the head, meant to be worn with the man's natural hair showing in front.[32]

In England, the wearing of wigs began to fall out of favor first with the lower classes in the 1770s. When a London mob attacked peers on their way to the House of Lords as part of an anti-Catholic protest in 1780 (an event called the Gordon Riots), they specifically tore off the aristocrats' wigs as a means of removing symbols of authority. Over the course of that decade, the cultural changes that would lead to the French Revolution meant that a "natural" appearance was becoming fashionable throughout the Western world. Despite their professional connotations, wigs were also strongly associated with the aristocracy, a group with which few wanted to identify.[33] Thus, younger men began to wear their own hair, dressed and powdered into the same styles as those worn by wearers of wigs. In 1786, Eliza de Feuillide (Jane Austen's fashionable cousin) agreed with her cousin Phylly that a suitor's penchant for wigs was reason enough to refuse him, although she did suggest, "Would it not be possible for You to prevail on your admirer to relinquish a part of Dress so little suited to your Taste?"[34]

---

31. Charlotte Louise Henrietta Papendiek, *Court and Private Life in the Time of Queen Charlotte: Being the Journals of Mrs. Papendiek, Assistant Keeper of the Wardrobe and Reader to Her Majesty* (London: R. Bentley & Son, 1887), 284.
32. Pointon, *Hanging the Head*, 107.
33. Festa, "Personal Effects": 79.
34. Deirdre Le Faye, *Jane Austen's "Outlandish Cousin": The Life and Letters of Eliza de Feuillide* (London: British Library, 2002), 71.

A servant dresses her mistress's hair while attendants look on.

―

Troy, Jean-François de. Detail from *Before the Ball*. Oil on canvas, 1735. Getty.

TECHNIQUES

Hair styling (and cosmetics application) had a particularly important function in this period. The *lever* (male) and *toilette* (female) were daily ceremonies in which important persons were dressed (including hair styled and cosmetics applied) – or re-dressed – before a select audience. While the ritual was created by King Louis XIV of France and is associated with royalty, the aristocracy and even members of the bourgeois classes held their own morning dressing ceremonies before limited audiences.[35] The tradition spread to England, where it was called the "toilet" or "levy."[36] Most people performed two toilettes, one in which they dressed privately, and another public toilette at which their dressing was restaged for the benefit of friends, tradespeople, and hangers-on.[37] Mrs. Delaney recounted how her brother observed the toilette of an Englishwoman renowned for her very long hair: he "was admitted to madame Montandre's toilette, who was attended by her two filles-de-chambre [chambermaids]… When she had frizzed and set the forepart [the front of her hair] her two damsels divided the hind hair, and in the same instant braided it up, which she twisted round her head before she put on her cap…"[38]

It took an immense amount of time to have one's hair dressed. Many women reported spending time reading, writing, and visiting while having their hair styled. Englishwoman Mary Hamilton complained that she was under her hairdresser's hands for nearly three hours: "What a waste of time! however I always read so I need not say that. She has been putting my hair into fashionable order, cutting, curling, dressing it."[39] When it became modish for men to wear their natural hair near the end of the century, they too had to endure such discomfort. Henry Angelo later recalled that when he was at the British court,

---

35. Kimberly Chrisman-Campbell, "Dressing to Impress: The Morning Toilette and the Fabrication of Femininity," in *Paris: Life & Luxury in the Eighteenth Century* (Los Angeles: J. Paul Getty Museum, 2011), 53-74.
36. Tita Chico, *Designing Women: The Dressing Room in Eighteenth-Century English Literature and Culture* (Bucknell University Press, 2005), 55-56.
37. Chrisman-Campbell, "Dressing to Impress," 54.
38. Mrs. Delaney to Mrs. Dewes, February 4, 1758, in vol. 2 of *The Autobiography and Correspondence of Mrs. Delany* (Boston: Roberts Brothers, 1879), 47.
39. Mary Hamilton, 3 January 1785, in *Mary Hamilton Dickenson, Mary Hamilton, Afterwards Mrs. John Dickenson, at Court and at Home* (London: J. Murray, 1925), 261.

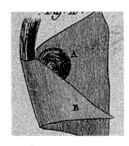
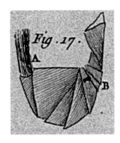
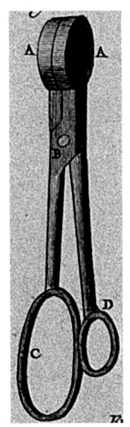
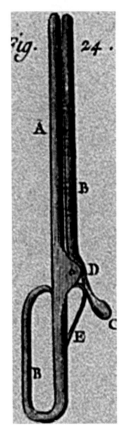

Top: hair arranged for papillotes ("butterfly" curls); papillote curl wrapped with tissue paper, ready to be heated.

Bottom: flat iron, used to heat wrapped papillotes; rounded curling irons.

—

Bénard, Robert after J.R. Lucotte. Detail from *Hair and Wig-Dressing Equipment*. Engraving, 1762. Wellcome.

"The head-dress was so essential, that many a night (I then sported four curls on each side), previous to going to bed, my time has been long employed, plaistering each curl with a mixture of powder and pomatum ; I had then to roll them up, separately, preparatory to the hairdresser's visit the next day, to add his embellishments in improving the boucles *pendents bien poudré* [hanging well powdered], with marechal powder (scented, coulour, pink)."[40]

Most hairdressers of the era were male; in England, French coiffeurs were the most fashionable. This gave rise to many suspicions and jokes about what was really going on when half-dressed married ladies spent time alone with purportedly salacious Frenchmen. One writer in the *Lady's Magazine* complained, "I will not marry a woman who suffers a French barber to breathe in her face every day, handle her hair, and take a thousand impertinent liberties with her.... What woman of any delicacy, indeed, can admit such persons, especially at a time when she is, probably half dressed?"[41]

Hair was frequently curled, waved, or frizzed before styling to create texture. Curls were set by one of the following methods: rag curls (wet hair wrapped around small pieces of fabric and allowed to dry), papillote curls (curled hair wrapped in paper and then set with heated tongs), or heated tongs (with the hair wrapped around it, like a modern curling iron). Styling was accomplished with combs, held with pins, and dressed with pomade. Women's coiffures were generally augmented with separate lengths of false hair, buckles (rolls), and ringlets. They could also wear full wigs.

When height was desired, hair was raised over "rolls" (small pads made of wool, tow, hemp, cut hair, or horsehair) or "cushions" (the same, but taller, wider, and sometimes with a dip in the top; these were also made of wire). Mary Frampton later recalled the hairstyles of the late 1770s and early 1780s:

"At that time everybody wore powder and pomatum; a large triangular thing called a cushion, to which the hair was frizzed up with three or four enormous curls on each side; the higher the pyramid of hair, gauze, feathers, and other ornaments was carried the more fashionable it was thought…"[42]

---

40. Henry Angelo, vol. 2 of *Reminiscences with Memoirs of His Late Father and Friends, Including Numerous Original Anecdotes and Curious Traits of the Most Celebrated Characters that Have Flourished During the Last Eighty Years* (London: Henry Colburn and Richard Bentley, 1830), 380.
41. Mrs. Grey, "The Matron: Number II," *The Lady's Magazine; or Entertaining Companion of the Fair Sex, Appropriated Solely to their Use and Amusement*, February 1774: 70.
42. Mary Frampton, *The Journal of Mary Frampton: From the Year 1779, Until the Year 1846. Including Various Interesting and Curious Letters, Anecdotes, &c., Relating to Events which Occurred During that Period* (London: S. Low, Marston, Searle, & Rivington, 1885), 2-3.

A hairdresser attaches a cushion to a client's head before dressing her hair. Note the rolls of false hair, as well as the hairpins, on the table, and the false hair the client's lap.

Detail from *The Village Barber*. Etching, 1778. LoC.

A 1780 hairdressing manual offered the following styling instructions for wearing one of these supports:

> "These Cushions should be pinned very tight on, or tied; the Hair comb'd smooth, or frized backwards, to appear craped in the Front; very little should be put in the Body of the Hair of the Toupee, as the Cushion will not pin on so Neat, if there is too much frize, the best Way of pinning your Hair over a Tocque is to turn the Points, as tho' you were going to make a Curl, pin it down with a double, or single Pin, when you have pin'd your Toupee Hair up, you must put a String across your long Hair, and do it up smooth, or what Way you like, then your hind Curls to cover the Cushion, and hide all Faults, are to be put on, those may be comb'd before you put them on, and may be made as long, or full as you please : The Side-Curls are to be done next, and may be fastened with one Pin, bent backwards after it is worked into the Curls."[43]

Unfortunately there are few specifics recorded about the exact shape of these cushions. The *Encyclopédie Méthodique*'s description of the late 1780s version (see the accompanying illustration on page 12) is frustratingly cryptic: "a cushion called *toque*, which each does in his own way, & the best of which have a more or less triangular shape, which is

---

43. William Moore, *The Art of Hair-Dressing and Making It Grow Fast, Together, with a Plain and Easy Method of Preserving It; with Several Useful Recipes, &c.* (Bath, England: J. Salmon, 1780), 33-4.

Historical Overview 19

also more or less high."⁴⁴ Visual imagery is similarly limited. *The Village Barber*, an English satirical print (pictured on the previous page), provides a rare glimpse of a high 1770s cushion – in this case a solid form made of coarse material. It is heart shaped, curving up and out in front, dipping on top, with the back curving out and then in. It is placed on the back of the crown of the head, with the hair down around it, ready to be styled up and over the cushion.

The more elaborate the hairstyle, the longer it was worn – at most, several weeks, although most were probably worn for shorter periods of time. Mary Frampton later recalled sleeping in the elaborate hairstyles of the 1770s-80s: "Such was the labour employed to rear the fabric that night-caps were made in proportion to it and covered over the hair, immensely long black pins, double and single, powder, pomatum and all ready for the next day."⁴⁵ Eighteenth-century standards of hygiene were very different from our own, and regular hair washing was not seen as important, especially considering the degreasing effects of hair powder. However, even these practices came under scrutiny during the period, and what were probably exaggerated complaints still point to an underlying problem: "Let any person consider what smell is likely to come forth when the head is opened; where powder, pomatum, and the perspiration of the head, has been denied an airing for three months together."⁴⁶

Wigs were made by hand by wig makers, a process that included weaving the loose hair into wefts on a small loom, and then sewing them to a fitted cap called a "caul." The highest quality wig hair was human, but cheaper alternatives included horse, goat, and other animals. Curls were set by wrapping the hair on paper clay rollers called "pipes" and then heating them in an oven or drying them in front of a fire (a process called "sweating"). Wigmakers also restyled and powdered wigs and provided shaving services.

As wig wearing became an everyday occurrence, many men opted to cut their own hair short or even to shave their heads, which improved the fit and stability of the wig.⁴⁷

Weaving a weft of hair on a reproduction eighteenth-century hair loom.

---

44. Vol. 6 of *Encyclopédie Méthodique, Arts et Métiers Mécaniques*, ed. Charles Panckoucke (Paris: Chez Panckoucke, 1785), s.v. "Perruquier - Barbier - Baigneur - Étuviste (Art du)," 270.
45. Frampton, *Journal*, 3.
46. *A Dissertation upon Head Dress; Together with a Brief Vindication of High Coloured Hair, and of Those Ladies on Whom It Grows; the Whole submitted to the Connoisseurs in Taste, Whether Antient*[sic] *or Modern, of What Nation or Kingdom Soever* (London: J. Williams, 1767), 39.
47. Arnold, *Perukes & Periwigs*, 13.

POWDER & POMATUM

To style hair, and to make powder stick to the hair, "pomatum" (*pommade* in French) was used. This was usually some combination of animal fat and other ingredients used to make it smell nice. A 1768 French hairdressing manual recommended the following recipe for beef pomatum:

"Take some beef marrow, and remove all the bits of skin and bone, put it in a pot with some hazel nut oil, and stir it well with the end of a rolling pin, adding more of the oil from time to time until it is thoroughly liquefied, and add a little essence of lemon. This pomatum will keep for 3 or 4 months..."[48]

Both men and women had begun powdering their hair and wigs in the seventeenth century. It was originally used as a degreaser, just like modern-day dry shampoos.[49] White haired wigs became fashionable in the 1710s, partially because the hair was rare and therefore expensive. The dyes and bleaches available at the time were destructive to the hair (causing fading and breakage), and so as a cheaper alternative to white hair, people began to use powder to color their wigs and hair.[50]

Our modern sensibility associates white/grey hair with age. While that association existed in the eighteenth century, there was also the more prevailing idea that white/grey hair set off a "fine" complexion, with very pale skin, darkened eyes, and rouged cheeks. In order for women to carry off powder, it was thought that a relatively substantial amount of cheek rouge was required. Even some men can be seen in eighteenth-century images with clearly heightened color on their cheeks. The Lady's Magazine complained in 1771, "Very few English women with their own natural complexions look well in [hair] powder; it requires that quantity of rouge the French women constantly wear to give it a sufficient relief."[51] Grey hair was considered attractive in a way that our modern culture does not. The Yverdon *Encyclopédie* defined the color *grisaille* as "a beautiful blend of white & brown hair" and further noted that "*Grisaille* wigs are expensive."[52]

Most sources point to the wearing of hair powder by both men and women across the century. An examination of art from the period shows that it was nearly ubiquitous in French, and less commonly depicted in British and American, portraits until late in the century. By the 1770s, British portraits frequently portray powder at equivalently high rates to that seen in France, but it is not until the 1780s that powdered hair appears very often in American images. Whether these

Many 18th century portraits show men with obvious white powder on the collar and shoulders. Clearly, this was both an inevitable side effect and one that was worthy of showing off.

—

Pratt, Matthew. *William Henry Cavendish Bentinck, 3rd Duke of Portland*. Oil on canvas, c. 1774. NGA.

---

48. Legros, *L'Art de la Coëffure des Dames Françoises, avec des Estampes, ou Sont Représentées les Têtes Coeffés* (Paris: Antoine Boudet, 1768), 16-17.
49. Catherine Lanoë, *La Poudre et le Fard: Une Histoire des Cosmétiques de la Renaissance aux Lumières* (Seyssel: Champ Vallon, 2008), 63.
50. Morag Martin, *Selling Beauty: Cosmetics, Commerce, and French Society, 1750-1830* (Baltimore: Johns Hopkins University Press, 2009), 13.
51. Quoted in Norah Waugh, *The Cut of Women's Clothes, 1600-1930* (New York: Theatre Arts Books, 1968), 119.
52. Vol. 22 of *Encyclopédie, ou Dictionnaire Universel Raisonné des Connoissances Humaines*, ed. Fortuné Barthélemy de Félice (Yverdon, 1773), s.v. "Grisaille," 382.

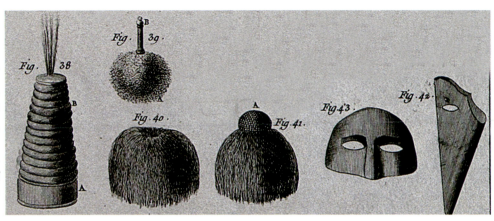

Various powdering tools: powder bellows (far left), three powder puffs, and two powdering masks (far right).

—

Bénard, Robert after J.R. Lucotte. Detail from *Hair and Wig-Dressing Equipment*. Engraving, 1762. Wellcome.

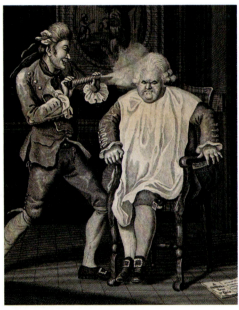

A barber powders his client's wig with a hand-held powdering bellows. The client wears a protective wrap over his clothes.

—

Caldwell, James after John Collet. Detail from *An Englishman Seated in a Parisian Coiffeur's Salon Having his Hair Dressed by a Mischievous Frenchman*. Engraving, 1770. Wellcome.

trends correlate with daily life is debatable; it may be that there was a greater desire in Britain and America to appear "natural" in portraiture.

Hair powder was made from a variety of materials, from the poorest quality in corn and wheat flour to the best in finely milled and sieved wheat starch. It was usually white, but it could also be brown, grey, orange, pink, red, blue, or violet. The *London Evening Post* reported in 1777 that "the hair dressed with light yellowish powder" was fashionable for ladies.[53] Meanwhile, Englishman John Crosier noted that in 1782, "Much aversion as people in general have to red hair, the appearance thereof was so much admired that it became the fashion, for all the Beaus, and Bells wore red powder…"[54]

Powder was applied with a bellows (the powderee being covered with a cone-shape face mask and fabric smock), with a puff used for touch-ups. A knife was used to remove the paste made from the combination of powder and pomatum. A description of the process of powdering taken from a 1780 hairdressing manual shows that the powder could be worked throughout the hair, not just applied at the end of the style:

> "The best Method I ever found to fill the Hair is to lay a good deal of Powder in it, and comb it well thro' opening the Hair in Layers as you put in the Powder, then take soft Pomatum, and do the same, combing it from Root to Point, as you put it in, after you have put Pomatum in once, take more Powder and comb in, then add more Pomatum 'till you find it sufficiently filled. For a Fortnight after, you will find a small Quantity will do, except the Hair is comb'd out of the Frize; if you put the Pomatum in the Hair first, you will find it unequally powdered and striped, and a great Difficulty to mix the Powder in."[55]

---

53. *London Evening Post*, May 22, 1777.
54. Quoted in C. Willett Cunnington and Phillis Cunnington, *Handbook of English Costume in the Eighteenth Century* (Boston: Plays, 1972), 381.
55. Moore, *Art of Hair-Dressing*, 26-7.

The well-to-do had a "wig closet" (a small room) used for powdering, but wigs could also be sent to the wig-maker for powdering (and restyling).

Thus far, my research shows that wigs featuring powder usually had a consistent level of powdering and color all over the wig. I have found only three images that show powder only applied around the face, and not on the rest of the hair – but note that these are a few among thousands, so it must have been quite unusual (see right, as well as Madame de Villeneuve-Flayosc on page 60, and Sir John Ligonier on page 73).

Just like the wearing of wigs, powdering began to decline in the 1780s, but was still fashionable enough that in 1795 England taxed it to raise money for the war against the French. Eliza de Feuillide reported from France in 1780, "Powder is universally worn, & in very large quantities, no one would dare appear in public without it, The Heads in general look as if they had been dipped in a mealtub...''; yet only five years later Englishwoman Betsy Sheridan advised, "I hope you wear no powder, all who have fine hair go without and if you have not quite enough [hair] 'tis but buying a few curls."[56] By the 1790s, the social changes wrought by French Revolution ended the use of wigs and hair powder except among the very old and/or conservative. The *Sporting Magazine* reported in 1798 that classically-inspired hairstyles "have banished hair powder, a change certainly to the advantage of female beauty."[57]

Unusually, this American has powdered the front and sides of her hair, but her long ringlets and chignon are unpowdered.

—

Earl, Ralph (1751-1801). *Esther Boardman*. Oil on canvas, 1789. Image copyright (C) The Metropolitan Museum of Art. Image source: Art Resource, NY.

---

56. Quoted in Le Faye, *Jane Austen's "Outlandish Cousin,"* 46; Betsy Sheridan, 1785, in *Betsy Sheridan's Journal: Letters from Sheridan's sister, 1784-1786, and 1788-1790* (New Brunswick, N.J.: Rutgers University Press, 1960), 58.
57. "New Fashions," *The Sporting Magazine*, October 1798, 3.

STYLISTIC CHANGES

In the early 1700s, men wore long, elaborate wigs. Women's styles echoed men's in terms of height on top, but otherwise were comparatively simpler.

—

Largilliere, Nicolas de. Details from *Family Portrait*. Musée du Louvre, Paris, France. Erich Lessing / Art Resource, NY.

Men began the eighteenth century wearing styles that were quite ornate. Wigs were very long, usually halfway down the back, and curly; on top, they were generally parted in the center, sometimes with curls built up on top of the head. Male hair grew comparatively less ostentatious in the 1720s with the bob wig, a shorter, simpler curly style. The silhouette grew even closer to the head in the 1730s with the fashion for queue wigs: the front hair shorter and brushed back, one or more buckles (rolls) at the sides of the face, and a long tail in back.

In the first decade of the century, women's hairstyles were curly and high on top, generally worn with the high *fontange* headdress.[58] One memoirist later recalled this fashion as "ridiculous… It was a structure of wire, ribbons, hair and geegaws more than two feet high which placed the head in the middle of the body. It shook with every movement and was extremely uncomfortable."[59] By the 1710s, however, women's hair began to be dressed simpler, generally with soft curls pulled back into a bun or braid at the back, and later the crown, of the head. This remained the mode until the 1750s, when the more constructed *tête de mouton* (literally "sheep's head") coiffure became fashionable in France. It featured rows of distinct curls across the top of the head, generally with the back hair pulled up smoothly.

Women's hair began to rise in the later 1760s, initially in an egg shape, continuing into the 1770s when huge hot-air-balloon-shaped coiffures were all the rage. Master coiffeur Léonard Autier recalled dressing Queen Marie-Antoinette's hair:

Both genders wore simple silhouettes in the mid-century.

—

Louis Carrogis, called Carmontelle. Details from *Monsieur and Madame Blizet with Monsieur Le Roy the Actor*. Watercolor and gouache on paper, c. 1765. NGA.

"The dauphine… has a head seventy-two *pouces* [70 inches or 177.8 centimeters] tall from the bottom of her chin to the summit of her coiffure… My happy ideas were realized: the pyramidal coiffure of Marie-Antoinette created a sensation at the Opéra. People crushed each other in the parterre…to see this masterpiece of learned audacity."[60]

False hair was essential to fill out these styles, and women bought and wore everything from braids, curls, and hanks of hair to full wigs. A 1770 hairdressing manual noted:

"If the hair is not remarkably thick, it will

---

58. Also called "*frelange*" in French and "commode" in English.
59. Saint-Simon, *Memoires*, 1713, quoted in Waugh, *Cut of Women's Clothes*, 114.
60. Quoted in Desmond Hosford, "The Queen's Hair: Marie-Antoinette, Politics, and DNA," *Eighteenth-Century Studies* 38, no. 1 (Fall 2004): 187.

not dress full, unless supported by wool, which, after the first day, will be distinguished through the hair, and appear very ill. This last inconvenience… hath brought artificial toupees [either a full wig, or a hairpiece that covers just the top and sides of the hair] into repute, which are made to appear as the natural hair, and to suit it under all the different accidents to which it is subject."[61]

A decade later, another manual advised, "Tetes [wigs] are made like the Hair and should be brought exact where it grew that they may be the more Natural; the Fronts are not to be seen to appear like a Wig…"[62] Women's coiffures grew large enough to make it difficult to fit into a carriage – or at least so the satirists claimed. Lady Clermont noted from Paris that "all young people…sit at the bottom of their coaches as they have not room if they sit on the seat," while Englishwoman Mrs. Delaney complained, "I hear nothing but balls and high heads - so enormous that nobody can sit upright in their coaches, but stoop forward as if they had got the children's collick."[63]

In this period, women's hair began to be accessorized with more than the usual hats, ribbons, and feathers. Headdresses were created that could incorporate decorative accessories, which made allegorical or political references. Initially, the majority of these were named after the popular theater – actresses like Saintval, Cléophile, and Beaumesnil, or dramas and operas like *Iphigénie*, *Tarare*, and *Figaro*.[64] Later, hairstyles represented current events, such as the *pouf à la Victoire* (with laurel branches, representing French military victory in the American War of Independence), and the *coiffure à la Belle Poule* (featuring the French ship that had won an important naval battle against the English).[65]

Although men's wigs often echoed women's head dress in this period, frequently with a high curved shape on top of the usual *queue* styles, they never reaching the extravagances of women's hair. However, masculine styles did grow high enough that the wearing of hats became difficult; the *chapeau bras* (literally "arm hat") was developed in this era specifically to be carried under the arm, not worn on the head.

The growing interest in "natural" dress brought about by the Enlightenment created what was considered to be a more organic hair style that dominated the

Women's hairstyles grew ostentatiously high in the 1770s. Masculine styles remained relatively constant.

—

Wheatley, Francis. Details from *The Oliver and Ward Families*. Oil on canvas, c. 1778. YBA.

In the 1780s, both men's and women's hair grew bushy and wide.

—

Gainsborough, Thomas. Detail from *Mr and Mrs William Hallett ("The Morning Walk")*. Oil on canvas, 1785. Bought with a contribution from The Art Fund (Sir Robert Witt Fund), 1954 (NG6209). National Gallery, London, Great Britain. © National Gallery, London / Art Resource, NY.

---

61. Peter Gilchrist, *A Treatise on the Hair* (London: 1770), 21.
62. Moore, *Art of Hair-Dressing*, 35.
63. Quoted in Kimberly Chrisman-Campbell, "French Connections: Georgiana, Duchess of Devonshire, and the Anglo-French Fashion Exchange," *Dress* 2004 31: par. 11; Mrs. Delaney to Mrs. Port, 21 December 1775, in *Autobiography and Correspondence*, 189.
64. *Modes et Révolutions : 1780-1804 : 8 février-7 mai 1989*, Musée de la Mode et du Costume, Palais Galliera (Paris: Paris-Musées, 1989), 47.
65. Hosford, "Queen's Hair": 188.

Hairstyles of the 1790s were relaxed versions of the same cuts worn in the previous decade.

―

Mosnier, Jean Laurent. Details from *Margaret Callander and Her Son James Kearney*. Oil on canvas, 1795. YBA.

1780s and early 1790s. The hair was cut shorter to form a large curly or frizzy halo around the head, which was wider than tall. Eliza de Feuillide reported from France in 1780, "The hair is cut in shades, not worn high at all. It was with reluctance, I conformed to the mode in this article, as my hair was very long on my arrival, & I was obliged to have it cut to half its length; but what will not All powerful Fashion effect...."[66] The chignon (back hair) was left long, like a man's queue, and could be left straight, curled in ringlets, or braided, and either hung down the back or looped up. Women's styles could still be very large, and cushions, false hair, and wigs continued to be used to fill out the natural hair. In keeping with this more "natural" look, powdering began to fall out of favor, although it still appears frequently in paintings and fashion plates. This same social shift meant that wigs began to go out of fashion for younger men, although those who wore their own hair had it dressed in the exact same styles.

In the 1790s, the influence of the French Revolution led to simpler coiffures. Most women in France, England, and America wore restrained versions of the 1780s style, with naturalistic curls worn close to the head and hanging down. The most fashionable and extreme French men *and* women sported the "crop," a short, tousled style. It conjured images of both sides of the political spectrum: as the *coiffure à la victime* and *sacrifié*, it evoked the image of hair disheveled as though cut by the guillotine; and as the *coiffure à la titus* or *brutus*, it referenced the classical Greek and Roman cultures that inspired the revolutionaries. Younger Englishmen, and even a few fashion-forward English women, did adopt the crop, although it was a controversial statement that conjured both fears and excitement about the French Revolution. Mary Frampton later recalled of 1791, "At this time in England it was only strong party men approaching to revolutionists, and calling themselves patriots, who wore no powder in their hair, and cut off their queues."[67] However, by the early 1800s such tensions had passed, and variations of the crop would become the prototypical hairstyle worn by nineteenth-century Western European men regardless of national origin.

Powder fell definitively out of fashion in France with the Revolution of 1789; in England, the tax on hair powder of 1795 soon brought about its abandonment.

Of course, just as in any era, not everyone wore the most up-to-date fashion. In particular, because of the tradition of wearing wigs, men frequently wore "fossilized" styles – that is, a fashionable style would become considered representative of a particular class or profession, and thus would continue to be worn for decades to come. Similarly, many women maintained the hairstyles of their youth and early middle age, long into their senior years.

---

66. Quoted in Deirdre Le Faye, *Jane Austen's "Outlandish Cousin": The Life and Letters of Eliza de Feuillide* (London: British Library, 2002), 46.
67. Frampton, *Journal*, 51.

WHAT DID THEY CALL IT?

Modern historians have tended to try to find historical terms for the changing styles worn by women in this period. However, a close reading of eighteenth-century sources proves that in contrast to the names given to specific men's wig styles, most feminine hairstyles that we would view as distinct did not have encompassing names. Instead, fashion magazines and other sources gave completely different names to what modern viewers would see as slight variations on the same style; other times, they will simply call it a "coiffure," "*frisure*," or "head dress." Thus, styles that to all intents and purposes looks exactly the same to us will have different names – see, for example, the "*Cleopatre*" on page 53 and the "*Euridice*" on page 176, both from the same fashion plate. Meanwhile, overarching styles do not appear to have had distinct names – they are simply the hairstyle of the day.

Unfortunately, modern costume historians have misapplied eighteenth-century terminology, giving rise to inaccurate understandings. It was impossible to research every term used to refer to a specific hairstyle, but an analysis of the popularly used terms "*pouf*," "hedgehog," and "*tête de mouton*" yielded the following information:

"*Pouf*": some fashion historians have referred to the very tall hairstyles of the late 1770s as the "*pouf*," which then supposedly had multiple variations like the *pouf à l'asiatique* or *pouf à la victoire*.[68] These terms do exist in the period, but the *pouf* itself referred to a puffy hat or cap, not the hairstyle worn underneath. The *Gallerie des Modes* includes multiple descriptions of its fashion plates that serve to clarify this term: "*Coëffure en racine droite* [perhaps a reference to dramatist Jean Racine?], topped with a *pouf* of gauze…" (1778); "Hat *en pouf*, with a band, accompanied by a string of pearls…" (1779); "*pouf* of Italian gauze" (1778).[69] The high styles of the 1770s do not appear to have had any particular overarching name, although different names are certainly

The description of this plate reads, "Pouf in a new taste in striped gauze ornamented with flowers with a string of pearls." Clearly, the "pouf" described is the fabric cap, not the hairstyle.

Publisher: Esnauts et Rapilly, French, 18th century. Detail from *Gallerie des Modes et Costumes Français, 29e. Cahier de Costumes Français, 7e Suite des coeffures à la mode en 1780. ee.169 "Pouf d un nouveau gout..."* French, 1780. Hand-colored engraving on laid paper. 41.9 x 26.7 cm (16 1/2 x 10 1/2 in.). Museum of Fine Arts, Boston. The Elizabeth Day McCormick Collection, 44.1459. Photograph © 2014 Museum of Fine Arts, Boston.

---

68. The *Trésor de la Langue Française* traces this misusage to Edmond de Goncourt, vol. 2 of *La Maison d'Artiste* (Paris: Charpentier, 1881); Stéphane, *L'art de la Coiffure Féminine, son Histoire à Travers les Siècles* (Paris: La Coiffure de Paris, 1932); and Maurice Leloir, *Dictionnaire du Costume et de ses Accessoires, des Armes et des Etoffes des Origines à nos Jours* (Paris: Gründ, 1961). The misuse of the term appears to have been revived in Caroline Weber, *Queen of Fashion: What Marie Antoinette Wore to the Revolution* (New York: H. Holt, 2006).
69. *Galerie des modes et costumes français, dessinés d'après nature, 1778-1787*, ed. Paul Cornu (Paris, É. Lévy, 1912), plate 3 (1778); *Ibid.*, plate 64 (1779); *Ibid*, plate 40 (1778).

Hérisson d'un nouveau goût orné de plumes fleurs et rubans avec des glands

An example of the true hérisson *("hedgehog") hairstyle: the hair is pulled smoothly up from the forehead and sides of the face with about 1' of extra height, and left sticking straight up in a spiky manner. The coiffure is described: "Hedgehog of a new taste ornamented with feathers flowers and ribbons with tassels."*

―

Esnauts et Rapilly, French, 18th century. Detail from *Gallerie des Modes et Costumes Français. 6e. Cahier de Modes Françaises pour les Coëffures despuis 1776. F.31 "Nouvelle Coëffure dite la Frégate la Junon..."* French, 1778. Hand-colored engraving on laid paper. Museum of Fine Arts, Boston. The Elizabeth Day McCormick Collection, 44.1290. Photograph © 2014 Museum of Fine Arts, Boston.

applied to individual variations.[70]

"*Hérisson*" (literally translated as "hedgehog"): many costume historians have referred to women's bushy styles of the 1780s as the *hérisson*. However, an examination of eighteenth-century fashion plates shows that in the period, this term was applied exclusively to a style worn from about 1776 to 1785, where the front hair was styled high and spiky, sticking straight up, like the spines of a hedgehog. A ribbon usually bisected the hair horizontally. The bushy styles typical of the 1780s do not appear to have had any particular overarching name, although different names are certainly applied to individual variations. In their first years, they were frequently called the *coiffure à l'enfant*. A French courtier recorded, "Since the lying in [after childbirth] of the Queen, the hair of Her Majesty has fallen out & art is continually occupied in repairing the gaps that form on this august head... She has no more than a flat chignon, ended by a buckle *en boudin* [sausage], much like the abbot's wig, & already several women of the court, eager to conform to the taste of their Sovereign, have sacrificed their beautiful hair. This hairstyle is called *à l'enfant*."[71] According to royal hairdresser Léonard's memoirs, it was he who first designed the style for the queen.[72] However, a very similar style can be seen on the English models in Thomas Gainsborough's paintings, beginning around 1777 (see, for example, Mary Heberden on page 53). Furthermore, there were many other "*à la*" ("in the style of") terms that were used for these same hairstyles later in the decade.

"*Tête de mouton*" (sheep's head): this style, featuring rows of small curls across the front of the head and fashionable in the 1750s-1760s, *was* a term used in the period. However, it seems to only refer to the front portion of a woman's hair, and does not encompass the chignon in back (which was generally worn pulled up smoothly and called the "*chignon relevée*"). As early as 1721, the *Dictionnaire Universel François et Latin* defines "moutonne" as "a coiffure which has long been worn by women. It is a tress of very bushy and curled hair, which one applies on the front [of the head]."[73] In 1765, the *Critical Review* mentioned, "The fact is, that *mouton lacè* was a tuft of false hair, which the ladies of those

---

70. Similarly, Kate Haulman ("Short History of the High Roll"; *Politics of Fashion*) calls the high styles of the 1770s the "high roll." While "roll" or "high roll" was one of the names for the padding worn to raise the hair, there are many other terms used interchangeably, and "high roll" was not used in such a way as to indicate it being considered a proper noun.
71. Louis Petite de Bachaumont, 26 June 1780, vol. 15 of *Memoirs Secrets* (London: J. Adamson, 1781), 227-8.
72. Léonard Autié, *Recollections of Léonard: Hairdresser to Queen Marie-Antoinette* (New York: Sturgis & Walton Company, 1909), 192-196.
73. *Dictionnaire Universel François et Latin, Contenant la Signification et la Définition...* (Paris: Delaulne, Foucault, Clousier, Nyon, & Gosselin, 1721), s.v. "moutonne," 528.

[Shakespeare's] times laced to their natural hair. That kind of false hair is now called a tête de mounton[sic] ... or the front curls of a woman's head."[74]

HAIR COLORS

Eighteenth-century people had definite opinions about which hair colors were desirable and which were not. Wigs could be purchased in whichever color the wearer preferred, and natural hair color could be changed by dyeing or, more frequently, powdering. Among the most popular colors were black, white, grizzle (an iron-grey mix of black and white hair), brown, and flaxen (light blonde). Less popular, but still worn, were milk white, "light natural," yellowish, "pale" (probably a near-white color), chestnut, auburn, "piss-burnt" (probably a yellowish- or reddish-brown color), and grey. Red was nearly always avoided, except for brief fads for red powder in the 1780s and 1790s. Lady Sarah Lennox complained of her niece, "Emily is a fine, tall, large woman with a Lennox complexion, but *red* or *auburn* hair…"[75] Meanwhile, Marie-Antoinette was teased while dauphine for her strawberry-blonde hair; Madame du Barry, mistress of the king, disparagingly nicknamed her "*la petite rousse*" (the little redhead).[76]

It is important to note that the application of white powder over dark hair produces shades of light to dark grey, not the paper white seen in films and costume wigs. White powder applied over very light hair produces a heightened, matte white or blonde effect. This effect was sometimes deemed blue-ish in the period. One English story included the following exchange: "'But what hast thou done to thy hair, child!' said I, ' is it blue?' [Answered the daughter] '…what gives my hair that bluish cast is the grey powder, which has always that effect upon dark-coloured hair, and sets off the complexion wonderfully.'—' Grey powder, child!' said I, with some surprize: 'Grey hairs I knew were venerable; but till this moment I never knew that they were genteel.'–'Extremely so, with some complexions,' said my wife; ' but it does not suit with mine, and I never use it.'"[77]

A young Frenchwoman has powdered her hair to a fashionable grey color. This coiffure, or at least the front, was indeed called the **tête de mouton.**

—

After Jean-Marc Nattier. Detail from *Portrait of a Young Woman*. Oil on canvas, 1750/60. NGA.

---

74. Review of *The Plays of Shakespeare*, by Samuel Johnson, *The Critical Review, or Annals of Literature* (1765): 403.
75. Lady Sarah Lennox to Lady Susan O'Brien, March 5, 1780, in T*he Life and Letters of Lady Sarah Lennox, 1745-1826, Daughter of Charles, 2nd Duke of Richmond…* (London: J. Murray, 1901), 306.
76. Marie Jeanne, Countess du Barry, *La Du Barry: De Lettres et Documents Inédits Tires de la Bibliotheque Nationale, de la Bibliotheque de Versailles, des Archives Nationales, et de Collections Particulieres*, eds. Edmond de Goncourt & Jules de Goncourt (Paris: Bibliothèque-Charpentier, 1903), 12.
77. *The World* 18 (3 May 1753): 108-9.

Women's Styles: Year-by-Year

In order to organize this section, I have separated styles into general eras based on arbitrarily selected dates. It is important to remember that fashions nearly always change gradually, and while some people will be seen in the newest style, others will continue to wear recently popular (or even completely out of date) hairstyles. This is particularly true in portraits depicting older women, who tend to be seen in the styles that were popular during their young adulthood and middle age. In the same vein, portraits of American women painted before the 1760s sometimes to depict them wearing styles that are about a decade out of style in England and France. Whether that means American fashion lagged behind Europe during this period, or that American artists and/or subjects were simply more conservative in their choices for a formal portrait, is debatable.

I have given basic biographical information when available as context. All ages listed are approximate.

WOMEN: GENERAL TRENDS

Powdering

A study of art (paintings, drawings, fashion plates, etc.) across the eighteenth century yields the following trends:

Note that what is depicted may not necessarily match what is worn in daily life.

Great Britain:
- 1700s-1760s: occasional
- 1770s-1780s: popular, but not ubiquitous
- 1790s: more likely to be worn by older and/or conservative women

France:
- 1700s-1710s: occasional
- 1720s-1780s: nearly ubiquitous
- 1780s-1790s: more likely to be worn by older and/or conservative women

American colonies/United States:
- 1700s-1770s: occasional
- 1780s: popular, but not ubiquitous
- 1790s: more likely to be worn by older and/or conservative women

HIGH FRONT STYLES
Fashionable: 1700s–1710s

Primary style:
- Full on top in soft ringlets, usually with a center part
- Two tendril curls lie on the outermost corners of the top of the forehead, both pointing inwards
- Close to the head on the sides
- Hair arranged in a bun or braided bun on the back of the head
- One or more long hanging curls at the nape of the neck

Also worn in France, late 1710s:
- Hair is straight or wavy
- Pulled tightly into a curly arrangement at the crown
- A few short tendril curls at the ears and/or neck

An American lady's hair is curly and high on the forehead, with a center parting. The rest of the hair is straight and drawn to the back of the head. Long ringlets hang on her left shoulder.

—

Duyckinck, Gerrit (attrib. to). Detail from *Mrs. Augustus Jay*. Oil on wood, c. 1700. MMA. Gift of Edgar William and Bernice Chrysler Garbisch, 1970.

Marie-Louise (age 13), princess of Savoy and queen of Spain, wears her hair straight up on top with a center part, ending in two curls on either side. The rest of the hair is waved and pulled back into a bun on the back of the head, with long ringlets hanging down from the nape of the neck, twisted with pearls. Two tendril curls lie on either side of her forehead.

—

Garavaque, Jean. Detail from *Portrait of Marie-Louise Gabrielle de Savoie, wife of King Philip V of Spain*. Marble, c. 1701. Louvre Museum (artwork in the public domain; photograph provided by Wikimedia Commons user Jastrow, PD).

This Englishwoman's hair is curled and high on top, with a center part. Two tendril curls lie at either side of the forehead. Long ringlets start at the nape of the neck and drape over the shoulders.

—

Attributed to Benjamin Arlaud. Detail from *Portrait of a Lady Called Elizabeth Knight*. Gouache and watercolor on vellum, 1701-19. YBA.

A French drawing shows the high fontange headdress (see page 24) worn with two slightly different coiffures. Both feature curly fullness, with height on top. The drawing on the right has forehead tendril curls, as well as a ringlet hanging behind the ear. The fontange itself consists of a cap on the back of the head, with two or three layers of pleated fabric that stand up (and lean forward) on top.

—

Picart, Bernard. Detail from *Vijf Vrouwenhoofden in Verschillende Standen, met Fontange*. Print, 1703. Rijksmuseum.

Queen Anne (age 37) of Great Britain's hair is styled in long sausage ringlets and pulled back. Shorter curls are on the top of the head with two curls on the forehead.

Boit, Charles. Detail from *Anne Stuart (1665-1714), Koningin van Engeland. Echtgenote Van George van Denemarken*. Enamel on copper, 1703-27. Rijksmuseum.

Lady Essex Mostyn was the wife of an English baronet and Member of Parliament (MP). Despite being dressed in artistic draperies, her hairstyle is fashionable: short and curled on top with a center part. The rest is styled close to the head, with long ringlets falling over her shoulders.

Smith, John after Sir Godfrey Kneller. Detail from *The Hon. Lady Essex Mostyn*. Mezzotint, 1705. YBA.

Arabella (age 44) was a celebrated English singer and lutenist. Her hair is curled into short sausage curls on top, with the rest drawn back. Long ringlets fall over the shoulders.

Smith, John after Sir Godfrey Kneller. Detail from *Mrs. Arabella Hunt*. Mezzotint, c. 1706. YBA.

The duchess Marie (age 55) was a prominent member of the French court. Although much of her hair is covered by her hood, we can still see that it is waved, dressed on high on top, and center parted, with the same characteristic tendril curls on the forehead that are seen in other images from this era.

Drevet, Pierre after Hyacinthe Rigaud. Detail from *Duchesse de Nemours*. Engraving, 1707. NGA.

Three British ladies wear the fontange headdress, consisting of a cap, high pleated lace on top supported by wire, and long lace streamers hanging over the shoulders. All three wear their hair close to the head, without the height seen previously, and arranged at the back of the head, presumably in a bun.

Ricci, Marco. Detail from *Rehearsal of an Opera*. Oil on canvas, c. 1709. YBA.

Although the top of this American woman's hair does not have the height seen in the British and French images of the same era, it still follows a similar silhouette: center part, shorter curls on top (now at the sides of the face), and long curls at the nape of the neck.

American 18th Century. Detail from *Young Woman with a Butterfly*. Oil on canvas, c. 1710. NGA.

This Frenchwoman's hair is waved, styled close to the head, and powdered to a light grey color. One small, short ringlet is just visible over her left shoulder. She wears a flat black cap, trimmed with gold, perched at an angle.

Louise Elisabeth (age 17) was a prominent member of the French court. She is painted as the Roman goddess of flowers. Her hair is waved, raised on top, with the rest pulled back or hanging in ringlets. Tendril curls lay on her forehead.

A French lady's hair is curled and pulled loosely up to the top of the head, where it is styled in two bunches of high, short curls. Long ringlets fall from the nape of the neck. Two tendril curls are on each side of the forehead.

French 18th Century. Detail from *Portrait of a Woman*. Oil on canvas, c. 1711. NGA.

Largillière, Nicolas de (school of). Detail from *Portrait of a Woman, According to Tradition, Marie-Louise Elisabeth d'Orléans, Duchesse de Berry, as Flora*. Oil on canvas, 1690-1740. Rijksmuseum.

Picart, Bernard. Detail from *Hoofd van Grijzende Vrouw met Opgestoken Haar*. Chalk on paper, c. 1712. Rijksmuseum.

This American wears her hair parted in the center, with the front hair tucked behind her ears. On the sides, the hair is curly. Ringlets hang from the nape of the neck. A tiny bun is perched on top of her head.

The hair of this Frenchwoman is waved and drawn up to the crown of the head, where it is arranged in a small group of curls. A ribbon is tied around the crown arrangement.

This is likely one of the daughters of King George II of England. Her hair may be powdered. It is waved slightly and drawn up to the crown of the head, where it is arranged in a bun. There is the barest suggestion of a center part.

Detail from *Lady with an Arrow*. Oil on wood panel, 1713-18. Brooklyn Museum (artwork in the public domain; photograph provided by the museum via Wikimedia Commons, PD).

Watteau, Antoine. Detail from *A Man Reclining and a Woman Seated on the Ground*. Red, black, and white chalk on laid paper, c. 1716. NGA.

Detail from *Portret van een Meisje, Vermoedelijk een Dochter van George II, Koning van Engeland*. Miniature on ivory, 1715-1725. Rijksmuseum.

SIMPLE PARTED STYLES
Fashionable: 1720s-1730s

- Soft, curly fullness
- Close to the head on top, frequently with a center part
  - 1730s: a bit of width at the temples
- Hair dressed at the crown of the head, either:
  - A bun
  - A braided bun
- Short ringlets
- Nape of the neck, either:
  - One or two long hanging curls
  - Short ringlets across the back of the head, from around the ear to the nape of the neck

A young French woman wears her hair drawn up to the crown of the head, where it is covered by a frilled cap. Two tendril curls lie on her forehead.

—

Watteau, Antoine. Detail from *Seated Woman Looking Down*. Red and black chalk with stumping on laid paper, with later framing line in brown ink, c. 1720-1721. NGA.

If the title is correct, then Anne's father was a British merchant and philanthropist. Her hair is straight and pulled back smoothly, probably to the back of the head. The blue veil is an artistic touch.

Richardson, Jonathan the Elder. Detail from *Lady Anne Cavendish (daughter of Elihu Yale ?)*. Oil on canvas, c. 1725. YBA.

The French queen's (age 22) hair is short and curled around the face, with a center part and slight width at the temples. Long ringlets hang from the nape of the neck over the shoulders.

Cars, Laurent after Carle Van Loo. Detail from *Marie Leszczynska of Poland, Queen of France*. Engraving and etching, 1728. NGA.

Both French ladies wear their hair pulled up to the crown. The woman on the left has curls at the crown of her head, and the hair at the sides of her face is waved. On top, she wears a lace cap accented with flowers. On the right, she has short wispy curls at her neckline and on the sides of her face. The crown arrangement is covered by a white cap.

—

Lancret, Nicolas. Details from *Dance Before a Fountain*. Oil on copper, 1724. Getty.

Marie Anne de Cupis de Camargo (left, age 20) was a famous Parisian dancer. She is wearing a stage costume, with her hair curled and worn close to the head. It may be powdered. On the right, this French spectator's hair is curled and arranged at the crown of the head, from which short ringlets hang down until the nape of the neck. A small cap with blue flowers is perched on top of the head.

A British lady's hair is worn straight and close to the head. A lace and ribbon cap covers the top and sides of her head.

Lancret, Nicolas. Details from *La Camargo Dancing*. Oil on canvas, c. 1730. NGA.

Highmore, Joseph. Detail from *Portrait of a Lady*. Oil on canvas, c. 1730/5. NGA.

Two Frenchwomen wear their hair waved and close to the head, arranged at the crown, with short tendril curls in front of the ear and at the nape of the neck. In the left image, her bun (possibly braided or twisted?) is woven with pearls. Right, her blonde or powdered hair is accented with flowers. More flowers lie on her right shoulder. No hair is clearly visible here, but this could be a narrow hanging ringlet entwined with flowers.

This Englishwoman's hair is curled and arranged with more fullness around the top and sides of the face than seen in previous images. A ruffled cap covers the back of her head and frames the face, while small tendril curls are at the nape of the neck.

Pater, Jean-Baptiste Francois. Details from *Fête Galante in a Landscape*. Oil on canvas, c. 1730-35. Rijksmuseum.

Highmore, Joseph. Detail from *Mrs. Sharpe and Her Child*. Oil on canvas, 1731. YBA.

Two genteel English ladies wear their hair close to the head and covered with ruffled caps.

—

Hamilton, Gawen. Detail from *Group Portrait, Probably of the Raikes family*. Oil on canvas, 1730-32. YBA.

The wife of the director of the Académie de France in Rome wears her hair in short, tight curls with a center parting. These curls extend across the back of her head, from ear to ear. The hair at the crown is long and straight, and styled into a braided bun.

—

Bouchardon, Edme. Detail from *Marie-Thérèse Gosset (1703-1756), wife if Nicolas Vleughels, director of the Académie de France in Rome, called Madame Vleughels*. Marble, 1732. Photo: Herve Lewandowski. Musée du Louvre, Paris, France. © RMN-Grand Palais / Art Resource, NY.

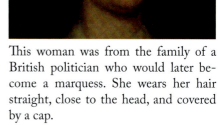

This woman was from the family of a British politician who would later become a marquess. She wears her hair straight, close to the head, and covered by a cap.

—

Philips, Charles. Detail from *The Watson-Wentworth and Finch Families*. Oil on canvas, c. 1732. YBA.

A French dancer wears her hair drawn up to the crown of the head, with small curls at the nape of the neck. A flower or bow is on the side of the head.

Two lower-class Englishwomen wear their hair tight to the head and covered by caps. On the right, the back of her hair is pulled up smoothly to the crown of the head, with short curly tendrils at the nape of the neck.

This English lady's hair is curled and arranged with width at the sides, and covered by a cap. Long ringlets hang over her shoulders.

—

Larmessin IV, Nicolas de after Nicolas Lancret. Detail from *Mlle. Salle*. Engraving and etching, 1732. NGA.

—

Hogarth, William. Detail from *A Rake's Progress: pl. 8*. Etching and engraving, 1735. NGA.

—

Dandrige, Bartholomew. Detail from *A Lady with a Book*. Oil on canvas, c. 1735. YBA.

A young English lady's hair is curled and pulled up to the crown of the head, where it is covered by a cap. Short curly tendrils are at the nape of the neck.

The hair of this French lady is waved and drawn up to the crown, where it is accented with a ribbon bow. Short tendril curls are at the sides of the face and the nape of the neck. She wears flowers in her hair.

A Frenchwoman is dressed for hunting. Her hair is curled and arranged at the crown of the head, and covered by a hat. The back of the head is arranged in short ringlets.

—

Hogarth, William. Detail from *Portrait of a Family*. Oil on canvas, c. 1735. YBA.

Larmessin, Nicolas de. Detail from *L'Adolescence*. Etching on paper, 1735. Rijksmuseum.

Lancret, Nicolas. Detail from *Picnic after the Hunt*. Oil on canvas, probably c. 1735/40. NGA.

A young American wears her blonde hair parted in the middle and close the head, with long hanging ringlets at the nape of the neck. The hair around the face appears to be combed in a different direction, or possibly cut shorter.

This French lady's hair is curled into short, disheveled ringlets. She wears a cap on top of her head. The lack of color applied to her hair suggests that it may be powdered.

Lady Smyth (age 23-4) was the wife of an English baronet. She is wearing "historical" dress. Her hair is curled and worn drawn back, with a bit of curl hanging at the nape of the neck. The jewels in her hair are probably part of the historical mood of the painting.

—

The Gansevoort Limner (possibly Pieter Vanderlyn). Detail from *Young Lady with a Fan*. Oil on canvas, 1737. NGA.

Portail, Jacques-André. Detail from *A Music Party*. Red and black chalk on off-white paper, 1738. Getty.

Attributed to Soldi, Andrea. Detail from *Sir Robert and Lady Smyth with Their Son, Hervey*. Oil on canvas, 1738-9. YBA.

Women's Styles: Year-by-Year 37

SIMPLE PULLED-BACK STYLES
Fashionable: 1740s

Primary style:
- Pulled back softly and smoothly around the face, now generally without a part
- Hair is straight or in soft curls, worn close to the head
- Back of hair:
  - Soft bun or other arrangement on crown of the head
    - Sometimes with either:
      - A few short curls at the nape of the neck
      - Short ringlets

Also worn in America:
- Simple Parted Styles (1730s) worn through the 1750s

Also worn in France, late 1740s:
- Front: "*tête de mouton*," small and close to the head
  - Frizzed
  - Narrow defined curls or rolls at temples, or all the way across the front of head, starting about 1/2 - 3" back from hairline and running perpendicular
- Back usually either:
  - Straight, pulled up smoothly to the top or crown of the head, where it is frequently arranged in rolls ("*chignon relevée*")
  - Same small curls or rolls all over ("*bichon frisé*" – yes, like the dog)
- Optional 1-2 long ringlets coming from nape of neck

This English lady's hair is waved and pulled up, arranged at the crown of the head, and covered by a cap. A few tendril curls are at the nape of the neck.

Arabella was the wife of a Scottish earl and politician. Her hair is parted in the center, arranged loosely around the head, with an arrangement at the crown of the head accessorized by a blue bow. Shorter ringlets lie across the back of the head.

Mary (age 41) was the wife of the famous painter and printmaker. Her hair is worn close to the head and arranged at the crown, with ringlets falling from the nape of her neck. It is covered with an elaborately ruffled cap.

—

Gravelot, Hubert-François. Detail from *A Game of Quadrille*. Oil on canvas, c. 1740. YBA.

—

Ramsay, Allan. Detail from *Arabella Pershall, Lady Glenorchy*. Oil on canvas, 1740. YBA.

—

Hogarth, William. Detail from *Mary Hogarth*. Oil on canvas, c. 1740. YBA.

If the title is correct, this is Margaret "Peg" Woffington, a famous London actress of Irish origins (in her 20s). Her hair is curled and arranged loosely, with shorter curls at the sides of the face. A ruffled cap ties under the chin. Long waves fall on her left shoulder. The image has been lightened to better see the hair.

—

Beare, George. Detail from *An Unknown Woman, Called Peg Woffington*. Oil on canvas, 1740-9. YBA.

This Frenchwoman's hair is pulled up to the crown of the head where it is covered by a cap. Short curls lay across the lower portion of the back of her head, with a few in front of the ear.

—

Larmessin IV, Nicolas de after Nicolas Lancret. Detail from *L'Apres-Diner*. Engraving and etching, 1741. NGA.

Madame Bonnier was a Baroness and a leader in Parisian society. Her hair is powdered light grey, curled, and styled loosely around the face. She wears a small "pompom" of flowers on top.

—

Nattier, Jean-Marc. Detail from *Portrait of Constance-Gabrielle-Magdeleine Bonnier de la Mosson as Diana*. Oil on canvas, 1742. Getty.

A well-to-do Englishwoman wears her hair curly and relatively close to the head, with short ringlets on the lower half of the back of her head. A pleated cap tops her coiffure.

A female servant wears her hair curled and close to the head, ending in a braided bun at the back of the head. Short curly tendrils are at the nape of the neck

Mrs. Pigott, an American, is dressed in a fantasy historical ensemble. Her hair is curled, parted in the center, and arranged loosely around the face. Long ringlets hang from the nape of the neck. The pink ribbons and jewels are probably part of the fantasy theme of the painting.

—

Frye, Thomas. Detail from *Mrs. Wardle*. Oil on canvas, 1742. YBA.

Surgis, Louis de Surugue de after Jean-Baptiste Joseph Pater. Detail from *Les Plaisir de l'Ete*. Etching and engraving, 1744. NGA.

Blackburn, Joseph. Detail from *Portrait of Mrs. John Pigott*. Oil on canvas, c. 1700-63. LACMA.

Women's Styles: Year-by-Year 39

The wife of a noble French government official, Magdaleine's hair is powdered dark grey and styled in tight diagonal curls from ear to ear. In back, her chignon is pulled up smoothly. She wears a pompom of blue flowers, with a bit of white lace.

An idealized French country maiden wears her hair curled in front, probably in a *tête de mouton*. Her chignon is left straight, drawn down to the nape of the neck, then braided with a blue ribbon; the braid is pinned to the crown of her head, with the curly ends loose on top.

This middle-class English wife wears her hair close to the head, with medium-length long sausage ringlets at the back of the head. Her cap is decorated with flowers.

—

Perronneau, Jean-Baptiste. Detail from *Magdaleine Pinceloup de la Grange, née de Parseval*. Oil on canvas, 1747. Getty.

Boucher, François. Detail from *The Fountain of Love*. Oil on canvas, 1748. Getty.

Scotin, Louis Gerard after William Hogarth. Detail from *Marriage a la Mode: pl. 1*. Etching and engraving, 1745. NGA.

A well-to-do English lady is dressed for riding. Under her jockey cap her hair – blonde, and possibly powdered – is curled and arranged loosely around the face, with short curls at the nape of the neck.

Two English ladies wear their hair close to the head and covered by ruffled caps. The young lady on the left has short curls at the nape of the neck, while the right-hand lady's chignon is straight and pulled up.

—

Hudson, Thomas. Detail from *Portrait of a Young Woman of the Fortescue Family of Devon*. Oil on canvas, c. 1745. YBA.

Unknown artist, 18th century, British. Details from *A Family Being Served with Tea*. Oil on canvas, c. 1745. YBA.

French Queen Marie Leczinska's hair is curled, center parted, and pulled back with a bit of width at the sides. Short curls lie on the sides of the face. Long hanging ringlets fall over both shoulders.

—

Rue de Charenton Manufactory (Paris) or Chambrette Manufactory (Lunéville). Detail from *Pair of Busts: Louis XV and Marie Leczinska*. Glazed earthenware (faience), c. 1745-55. Getty.

Under her cap, this British lady wears her hair curled and dressed loosely around the face, with short curls at the nape of the neck.

—

Knapton, George. Detail from *A Man and a Woman, Possibly of the Missing Family, of Little Park House, Wickham, Hampshire*. Oil on canvas, 1747. YBA.

Marie-Josèphe (age 18) was the wife of the heir to the French throne. Her hair is powdered light grey. It is styled in the *tête de mouton*, with rows of curls from ear to ear. She wears a small blue pom-pom and a cap or piece of lace on top.

—

Liotard, Jean-Etienne. Detail from *Portret van Marie Josèphe van Saksen (1731-67), Dauphine van Frankrijk*. Pastel on vellum, 1749. Rijksmuseum.

A young Frenchwoman's hair is straight and drawn up to the crown, where it is covered with a cap or other decoration. Ringlets lie in front of the ear, and on each side of the nape of the neck.

—

Demarteau, Gilles. Detail from *Jonge Vrouw met Bloemenmand, Ruikend aan Boeketje Bloemen*. Etching on paper, 1732-1776. Rijksmuseum.

This Englishwoman's hair is curly, with a center parting. She has short ringlets at the sides of the face and back of the head. A blue bow worn as an accent.

—

Zincke, Christian Friedrich. Detail from *A Lady of the Booth Family*. Enamel on porcelain, n.d. YBA.

Elizabeth was the wife of an English MP and an earl's daughter. She is wearing fantasy historical dress. Her hair is curled and dressed loosely around the face, with short ringlets at the nape of the neck and sides of the face. The pearls and bow in her hair are probably an element of her fantasy dress.

—

Hudson, Thomas. Detail from *Portrait of a Woman, Probably Elizabeth Aislabie, of Studley Royal, Yorkshire*. Oil on canvas, 1749. YBA.

Women's Styles: Year-by-Year

SIMPLE PULLED-UP STYLES
Fashionable: 1750s - late 1760s

France & Great Britain:
- *Tête de mouton* in front, small and close to the head, with *chignon relevée* or *bichon frisé* in back (see 1740s Simple Pulled-Back Styles)

Also worn in Great Britain & America:
- 1750s:
  - Hair is straight or slightly wavy
  - Pulled back in front without a part, or with a center part
  - Very close to the head on top and sides
  - Bun at the crown of the head, or braid turned up flat and pinned to the back of the head

- 1760s:
  - Hair is straight
  - Somewhat loose around the sides of the face and on the nape of the neck
  - Loose bun on top
  - One or two twists on the side, frequently entwined with a ribbon
  - Optional 1-2 ringlets at the nape of the neck

Also worn in America:
- Simple Parted Styles (1730s) and Simple Pulled Back Styles (1740s) worn through the 1750s

Top left & right: Brigitte was the wife of a chevalier and lieutenant-colonel. Her hair is styled in the classic *tête de mouton* style, with narrow, defined rolls across the sides and top of the face. The hair around her face is tightly curled and smoothed back until the rolls begin. The chignon is straight and pulled up smoothly from the nape of the neck, and finished in the horizontal rolls on top of the head – the *chignon relevée*.

Bottom left & right: Adélaïde (sister of Brigitte) wears the *bichon frisé* style: short, defined rolls in rows across the entire head. The hair around the face is curled and combed to the top of the head, where the rolls begin.

—

Pigalle, Jean-Baptiste. Details from *Busts of Two Sisters: Brigitte Françoise Elisabeth de Lansire and Adélaïde Julie Mirleau de Neuville*. Marble, 1750s. Getty (artworks in the public domain; top and bottom left photographs provided by the museum; top and bottom right are personal photographs by author).

A French lady wears her hair in the *tête de mouton* in front, with rows of curls from ear to ear, across the top of the head. In back, her hair is in a wide braid, pinned to the top of the head. There is a bust of Marie-Antoinette from 1770 that shows a similar back treatment.

—

Boucher, François (possibly). Detail from *Naar Rechts Ziend Dameshoofd met een Kanten Halskraagje*. Impression of a drawing in red chalk on paper, 1713-1710. Rijksmuseum.

Mrs. Hill, an Englishwoman, is an older lady with grey hair; she may also be wearing powder. Her curled hair is pulled back, with ringlets at the nape of the neck, and covered with a cap.

—

Devis, Arthur. Detail from *Mr. and Mrs. Hill*. Oil on canvas, 1750-1. YBA.

Marie-Louise O'Murphy (age 15), the daughter of an Irishman but born and raised in France, was a mistress of Louis XV. Her hair is drawn to the nape of the neck, then braided and pinned to the crown of the head. Short tendril curls are at the ears and nape of the neck. A blue ribbon is woven throughout.

—

Boucher, François. Detail from *Resting Maiden*. Oil on canvas, 1752. Alte Pinakothek (WC/Yorck).

This is probably a posthumous portrait of French countess Elizabeth Sophie Gilly de Montaud (1735-1774), which would account for a hairstyle more typical of the 1750s than the 1770s. She wears her hair in the *tête de mouton*, with wide diagonal curls across the top of her head from ear to ear. Her chignon is pulled up straight and smooth, partially arranged in curls at the crown of her head. One short ringlet hangs from the crown on the left, and one long, looped up ringlet on the right.

—

Houdon, Jean Antoine. Details from *La Comtesse de Jaucourt*. Marble, 1777. (C) RMN-Grand Palais / Art Resource, NY.

Margaret, the Scottish artist's wife, was a baronet's daughter. Her hair is straight and pulled back tight to the head. One (probably of three) braid or twist is pinned to the back of the head. Her pompom consists of a bit of gauze and a blue feather.

—

Ramsay, Allan. Detail from *Porträt der Margaret Lindsay, der Gattin des Künstlers*. Oil on canvas, c. 1755. Scottish National Gallery (WC/Yorck).

Women's Styles: Year-by-Year 43

Mary was the wife of a chief burgess in Pennsylvania. Her hair is worn in a dated style by English standards: parted in the middle, close to the head, with long hanging curls over the shoulders.

Jane's father was a New Hampshire minister. She is wearing fantasy historical dress. Her hair is a fancier version of the same dated style seen in the previous image: pulled back, slightly full around the face, with long hanging ringlets. The pearls in her hair are a nod to her fancy dress.

This young French mother wears her hair frizzed and powdered light grey, probably in the *tête de mouton* style.

West, Benjamin. Detail from *Mary Bethel Boude (Mrs. Samuel Boude)*. Oil on canvas, 1755/6. NGA.

Copley, John Singleton. Detail from *Jane Browne*. Oil on canvas, 1756. NGA.

Drouais, François-Hubert. Detail from *Family Portrait*. Oil on canvas, 1756. NGA.

This lady is from the family of a British politician and baronet. She wears her hair slightly waved, styled close to the head, and covered with a cap. The hair appears to be arranged at the back of the head.

Susannah was the widowed daughter of the English artist; she wears half-mourning. Her heavily powdered hair is frizzed and pulled back loosely around the face, possibly in the *tête de mouton*, and covered with an elaborate black lace cap.

Although this drawing is dated 1770, the hairstyle shown is much earlier. A Frenchwoman wears her hair in the *tête de mouton*, with curls in front at the sides and top, and the chignon pulled up smoothly in back. There are short tendril curls at the side of the face and behind the ears, and a ribbon pompom on top.

Devis, Arthur. Detail from *Members of the Maynard Family in the Park at Waltons*. Oil on canvas, c. 1755/62. NGA.

Hoare, William. Detail from *Susannah Hoare, Viscountess Dungarvan, later Countess of Ailesbury*. Pastel on paper, c. 1750-60. Getty.

Demarteau the Elder, Gilles after François Boucher. Detail from *Young Girl Reading "Héloise and Abélard."* Chalk-manner printed in black, blue, and red inks, 1770. NGA.

The official mistress of King Louis XV wears the *tête de mouton* hairstyle, powdered medium grey, with a pompom of blue, pink, and white flowers. The back of her hair, a braid pinned flat to the head, can be glimpsed in the mirror.

This American's hair is pulled back smoothly and worn close to the head, with short ringlets across the back of her head. The image has been lightened to better see the hair.

Boucher, François. Detail from *Portrait of the Madame de Pompadour*. Oil on canvas, 1756. bpk, Berlin / Alte Pinakothek, Bayerische Staatsgemaeldesammlungen, Munch, Germany / Art Resource, NY.

Hesselius, John. Detail from *Portrait of Elizabeth Chew Smith*. Oil on canvas, 1762. LACMA.

This (probably Scottish) lady's grey hair is clearly due to powder rather than age. Her hair is curled and pulled back loosely, probably in the *tête de mouton* style. She wears a cap and pompom.

An Englishwoman wears her hair softly pulled up. The sides are twisted, ending in a braided arrangement at the crown. Long ringlets fall over her shoulder.

A well-to-do Frenchwoman wears her hair in a powdered *tête de mouton*, with frizzy curls across the sides and top of her heard, and topped with a ruffled cap.

Ramsay, Allan. Detail from *Lady in a Pink Silk Dress*. Oil on canvas, c. 1762. YBA.

Fisher, Edward after Joshua Reynolds. Detail from *Catherine Trapaud*. Mezzotint on laid paper, 1762. YBA.

Carmontelle, Louis de. Detail from *Portret van Madame de Montainville, Gitaar Spelend*. Drawing on paper, 1758. Rijksmuseum.

Women's Styles: Year-by-Year

Mary, an English aristocrat, has her hair styled in the *tête de mouton*, with defined rolls across the sides and top of the head. Her pompom consists of a jewel and a pink ribbon, and pearls are woven into her hair.

Anne was the wife of a Rhode Island landowner. Her hair is straight and pulled back tightly, and covered with a lace-edged cap.

An Englishwoman wearing "Turkish" fancy dress has her hair styled fashionably. It is pulled back loosely, with a large twist around the side of the head that has been entwined with pearls.

—

Gainsborough, Thomas. Detail from *Mary Little, Later Lady Carr*. Oil on canvas, c. 1763. YBA.

Copley, John Singleton. Detail from *Anne Fairchild Bowler (Mrs. Metcalf Bowler)*. Oil on canvas, c. 1763. NGA.

Reynolds, Joshua. Detail from *Portrait of a Woman*. Oil on canvas, n.d. MMA. Bequest of George D. Pratt, 1935.

Marguerite was the wife and sister of important French art patrons. Her hair is powdered light grey and worn in the *tête de mouton* style, with a floral pompom on the side of her head.

Louisa was an English countess. Her blonde hair may be powdered. It is styled in the *tête de mouton*, with wide horizontal rolls from ear to ear. Note how the rolls start about 2" back from her face. Her cap is bordered with pleated lace.

A rare back view of the uniquely British style, with the hair pulled up smoothly in back and a twist on the side. She wears a blue ribbon and pearls in her hair. The background has been lightened in order to better see the hair.

—

Boucher, François. Detail from *Madame Bergeret*. Oil on canvas, possibly 1766. NGA.

Zoffany, Johann. Detail from *John, Fourteenth Lord Willoughby de Broke, and his Family*. Oil on canvas, c. 1766. Getty.

Wright, Joseph of Derby. Detail from *An Experiment on a Bird in an Air Pump*. 1768. Tate Britain (WC/Yorck).

HIGH STYLES
Fashionable: late 1760s - late 1770s

Primary style:
- Hair is straight or frizzed
- Pulled back in front without a part
- Raised high in a hot air balloon shape, close to the head at the sides
- Narrow buckles (rolls) at side of face, angled diagonally
- Chignon (back hair) either:
  - Straight, hanging down and then swooping up (like a loose, wide ponytail) and attached at top of the back of head
  - Same shape but braided in a wide braid, or twisted in a wide twist
- 1-2 long hanging curls coming from behind the ear

Secondary style:
- *Tête de mouton* in front, but higher on top, in an egg shape (see Simple Pulled-Back Styles, 1740s), worn with *chignon relevée* in back (fashionable through about 1775)

Also worn in Great Britain & America:
- High version of 1750s British style:
  - Hair is straight or wavy
  - Pulled back in front without a part
  - Raised (4-8" of extra height) in an egg shape
  - Loose around face and at nape of neck
  - A loose bun at the top of the head
  - One or two twists on the side, frequently entwined with a ribbon
  - Back hair: unclear. Either pulled up smoothly in back, or styled like the Primary Style chignon (see left)
  - Styled over a roll, wide around the face

A design from a book by Legros de Rumigny, one of the earliest celebrity hairdressers at the French court. This same year, he founded the *Académie pour la Coëffures des Dames* to teach hairdressing. The powdered style consists of numerous small rolls, built high on top.

The Art of Hairdressing in Paris, 1767 (colour litho), Legros or Le Gros, Sauveur (Jean Saveur) (1754-1834) (after) / Bibliotheque Mazarine, Paris, France / Archives Charmet / The Bridgeman Art Library.

There are few images of women of African descent living in Europe who are not wearing exoticized servant wear. This young lady, probably French, is a rare exception. She wears her hair high, wrapped in a beautiful scarf.

Detail from *Portrait of a Young Woman* (pastel on paper), Liotard, Jean-Etienne (1702-89) (previously attr. to) / Saint Louis Art Museum, Missouri, USA / The Bridgeman Art Library.

An American lady wears her hair in an up-to-the-minute style, exactly as was worn in Britain. The hair is straight and styled loosely. It is drawn up to the top of the head, where it is arranged high in a loose bun. Pearls are woven throughout. The background has been lightened in order to better see the hair.

Copley, John Singleton. Detail from *Elizabeth Green (Mrs. Ebenezer Storer II)*. Pastel on paper mounted on canvas, c. 1767. MMA. Purchase, Morris K. Jesup Fund and Lila Acheson Wallace Gift, 2008.

This fashion plate, probably English, shows a woman with her unpowdered hair dressed high (about 5" extra) on top. Both the front and back are pulled up smoothly, with a bit of looseness at the nape of the neck. Two ringlets or buckles are placed behind the ears. On top, she wears a lace cap.

—

Detail from *The Head and Shoulders of a Woman in Profile to the Right Wearing a High Wig with Lace and Ribbons*. N.d. Wellcome.

This Englishwoman's hair is raised about 4" and arranged in a loose bun at the crown of the head. Short buckles are at the side of the head, with ringlets at the nape of the neck. Her blonde hair appears to be powdered.

—

Meyer, Jeremiah. Detail from *Portrait of a Lady*. Watercolor and gouache on ivory, n.d. YBA.

Catharine was the daughter of a New Jersey farmer and painter. Her hair is straight and dressed high, about 7-8" off the forehead, and covered with a large decorative cap.

—

Attributed to Daniel Hendrickson. Detail from *Catharine Hendrickson*. Oil on canvas, c. 1770. NGA.

This Englishwoman wears her hair about 6" high, pulled up smoothly in front and arranged in a twist with pearls at the side. A long ringlet hangs over her shoulder. The loose hair at the nape of the neck is smoothed up towards the crown. Note the overall egg shape of the hair, very characteristic of British styles of this period.

—

Mortimer, John Hamilton. Detail from *An Unknown Woman*. Oil on canvas, c. 1770. YBA.

An English lady wears her hair high, with about 4" of extra height, and similarly wide. The hair is clearly styled over a roll that extends from ear to ear, across the top of the head. Her chignon is draped up with a bit of looseness at the nape of the neck.

—

Wright, Joseph of Derby. Detail from *Portrait of a Woman, Her Head Turned to the Right, Wearing an Earring*. Pastel on blue laid paper, c. 1770-2. MMA. Rogers Fund, 2007.

Mary Boyle was a prominent London literary hostess who later married an earl. Her hair is straight and styled up towards the crown, with about 6" of height. Three vertical twists of hair are at the sides. The chignon is pulled up smoothly towards the crown of the head, with small ringlets at the nape of the neck. Her cap ties under the chin.

—

Watson, James after Hugh Douglas Hamilton. Detail from *Countess of Cork and Orrery*. Mezzotint, 1771. YBA.

An English servant wears her hair straight and somewhat loose, pulled up the crown where it is arranged in a loose bun and accented by a ribbon. Short curly tendrils are at the nape of the neck.

This British fashion plate shows the same hairstyle from both front and back. The hair is straight and raised on top by about 4", with vertical buckles along the sides and behind the ear. The chignon is slightly loose at the nape of the neck and pulled up smoothly to the top of the head, where the hair is arranged in multiple flat puffs of different sizes. A string of pearls is woven through the hair, and a small feather (an "aigrette") stands up at the side.

—

Atkinson, John. Detail from *Girl Bundling Asparagus*. Oil on canvas, 1771. YBA.

—

Details from *Patterns for the Newest & Most Elegant Head Dresses: May 1771*. Print on laid paper: etching & engraving, 1771. LWL.

This English aristocrat wears her hair pulled up to the crown of the head, where it is woven in large sections; there is about 5" of extra height. She has one diagonal buckle on the side, and a wide ringlet on her neck.

The mistress of Louis XV of France wears her hair in a high *tête de mouton*, with rows of curls across the sides and top of her head. In back, her chignon is drawn up to the crown of the head and crossed with a ribbon or other ornament. Two ringlets fall on the left side, and one on the right.

A well-to-do American wears her hair in the loose style popular in Britain during the 1760s. Her slightly wavy hair is looped up on top of the head in an unstructured bun or similar arrangement. There is about 2-3" of extra height. The image has been lightened in order to better see the hair.

—

Smart, John. Detail from *Lady George Sutton*. Watercolor and graphite on laid paper, n.d. YBA.

Pajou, Augustin. Detail from *Madame du Barry, née Marie-Jeanne Bécu (1743-1793) (back view)*. Soft bisque porcelain, 1771. Photo: Martine Beck-Coppola. Cité de la Ceramique, Sevres, France. © RMN-Grand Palais / Art Resource, NY.

—

Copley, John Singleton. Detail from *Portrait of a Lady*. Oil on canvas, 1771. LACMA.

Women's Styles: Year-by-Year 49

Sophia Baddely was an English actress, singer, and courtesan. Her hair is dressed smooth and high (about 6-7" of extra height). Two buckles at the sides are almost horizontal. The hair in back is looped up loosely towards the crown, where it is covered by an elaborate cap and pearls.

This older English lady may have naturally white hair, and/or may be wearing powder. Her hair is dressed over a small (2-3") roll and drawn smoothly up towards the crown. A vertical buckle can just be glimpsed behind and above each ear. Her elaborate lace cap ties under the chin.

A young French lady wears her blonde hair pulled up on top, with the ends rolled under. Her chignon is straight and looped up very loosely to the crown of the head. Two buckles point diagonally on the sides, with a short curl behind the ear.

—

Laurie, Robert after Johan Joseph Zoffany. Detail from *Mrs. Baddely*. Mezzotint on wove paper, 1772. YBA.

Mortimer, John Hamilton. Detail from *Mrs. Lushington*. Oil on canvas, 1774. YBA.

Bonnet, Louis Marin. Detail from *Portret van een Jonge Vrouw*. Pastel, 1774-93. Rijksmuseum.

This Frenchwoman's hair is pulled up towards the crown of the head in a similar style to the previous image, but with the chignon tighter to the head and only one side buckle. She wears a high ruffled cap on top.

A French lady's hair is raised about 4" at the crown, with four diagonal buckles on the side. One curl hangs behind her ear, and her chignon is styled into a large, wide twist. She wears a cap, lace streamers and a bow.

Hannah, the earl's wife (age 16), wears her hair powdered brownish-grey. It is raised about 3", smoothly up towards the crown, where it is arranged in two or more rolls or puffs accented with pink flowers. Vertical buckles line the sides of the hair.

—

Bonnet, Louis Marin. Detail from *Portret van een Jonge Vrouw*. Pastel, 1774-93. Rijksmuseum.

Moreau le Jeune, Jean-Michel. Details from *"Have No Fear, My Good Friend."* Pen and brown ink and brush and brown wash, 1775. Getty.

Zoffany, Johan Joseph. Details from *The Gore Family with George, 3rd Earl Cowper*. Oil on canvas, c. 1775. YBA.

This middle-aged lady wears her hair powdered medium grey. It is dressed high, with a severe angle towards the crown. A long buckle points towards the crown, while another hangs down behind her ear.

—

Wheatley, Francis. Detail from *Family Group*. Oil on canvas, c. 1775/80. NGA.

Susanna, from Massachusetts, was the artist's wife. Her hair is dressed high, with at least 4-5" of extra height. It is pulled up smoothly from the front towards the crown. Naturalistic curls (an artistic choice?) are at the sides, with short ringlets hanging at the nape of the neck. She wears a gauze veil that is woven into her hair. The final painting shows that her dark hair is unpowdered.

—

Copley, John Singleton. Detail from *Sketch for the Copley Family*. Oil on canvas, 1776/7. NGA.

This English caricature provides excellent information about fashionable hairstyles. The buckles point diagonally towards the crown, which features more rolls and puffs of hair. The chignon is pulled up loosely in a fishtail braid. The hat is worn flat along the front of the hair, wrapping down on the sides; it extends up and beyond the crown.

—

Detail from *Oh heigh oh—Or a view of the back settlements*. Engraving, 1776. LoC.

A well-off Frenchwoman wears her powdered hair high on top of the head, with about 6" of extra height. Two wide buckles point diagonally on the side, and a wide ringlet falls behind the ear.

—

Duplessis, Joseph Siffred. Detail from *Madame de Saint-Maurice*. Oil on canvas, 1776. MMA. Bequest of James A. Aborn, 1968.

The wife of the French artist wears her hair artistically, but still maintains elements of fashionable styles: dressed high on top (about 4"), with the chignon looped up in loose waves. Ringlets fall from the top and sides of the head, and a braid is at the side of the chignon.

—

Detail from *Madame Pajou, nee Angelique Roumier*, 1777 (terracotta), Pajou, Augustin (1730-1809) / Private Collection / Photo © Agnew's, London / The Bridgeman Art Library.

This French lady's hair is drawn high in a coiffure that leans towards the crown. Three wide buckles are on the side back, ending in two hanging ringlets. The chignon is looped up loosely.

—

Houdon, Jean Antoine. Detail from *Madame Servat, née Marie-Adélaide Girault (back view)*. Molded plaster, 1776. Photo: Stephane Marechalle. © RMN-Grand Palais / Art Resource, NY.

Women's Styles: Year-by-Year 51

HIGH & WIDE STYLES
Fashionable: late 1770s - early 1780s

Primary style:
- Hair is straight or frizzed
- Pulled back in front without a part
- Raised very high
  - c. 1777-80: shaped like a hot air balloon, but wider at the top than pre-1777
  - c. 1780-2: shaped like a hot air balloon with the same top width, but the sides are wider as well
  - Optional dip on top of head
  - Optional bump above forehead
- Wide buckles at side of face, placed horizontally or diagonally
- Wide, short curls hanging down behind ears ("*chien couchant*" – literally "sleeping dog"), sometimes with a straight portion at the top (root) end
- Chignon (back hair) either:
  - Straight, hanging down and then swooping up (like a loose ponytail) and attached at the top of the back of head
  - Same shape, but braided in a wide braid, or twisted in a wide twist, and attached at the back of the head

Secondary style:
- Hair is frizzed
- Cut into long layers at top and sides of head
- Shape is somewhat high, but even more so is wide and rounded
- Wide buckles at side of face, placed horizontally or diagonally
- Wide, short curls hanging down at side back of head ("*chien couchant*")
- Back hair either:
  - Straight, hanging down and then swooping up (like a loose ponytail) and attached at back of head
  - Same shape, but braided in a wide braid, or twisted in a wide twist, and attached at back of head
- Left hanging, straight or in ringlets

Two members of an English merchant and banking family wear high hairstyles. On the left, her unpowdered hair is worn high, with the line of her hat showing the silhouette of her hair. The back of her hat no doubt extends beyond her hair. She has a wide ringlet behind her ear. The lady on the right has high powdered hair covered almost completely by her elaborate gauze cap. She too has wide ringlets behind the ear.

—

Wheatley, Francis. Details from *The Oliver and Ward Families*. Oil on canvas, c. 1778. YBA.

Mary, the daughter of an English physician, is wearing "Turkish" draperies. Her hair is powdered medium grey, frizzed and rounded. One short ringlet is behind each ear, and at least two long hanging ringlets are at the nape of the neck. This lower, wider style can be seen in more of Gainsborough's paintings from this era, and presages the bushy styles of the 1780s.

—

Gainsborough, Thomas. Detail from *Mary Heberden*. Oil on canvas, c. 1777. YBA.

Left: "Chignon in Chevalier's Cross surmounted by a *fichu* Bonnet bordered with pearls." The chignon is looped up loosely, with a bow halfway up its length that separates the chignon both vertically and horizontally, creating a cross effect. An elaborate bonnet ("*fichu*," or neckerchief, probably refers to the sheer material or its triangular shape) is on top.

Right: "Chignon knotted in three parts, surmounted by a *fichu* Bonnet." Two wide rolls are placed horizontally at the sides, with a wide ringlet hanging behind the ear. The chignon is looped up loosely in two separate sections that are split by a higher loop. The whole coiffure is topped by another elaborate bonnet.

—

Esnauts et Rapilly, French, 18th century. Details from *Gallerie des Modes et Costumes Français. 6e. Cahier de Modes Françaises pour les Coeffures despuis 1776. F.31 "Nouvelle Coëffure dite la Frégate la Junon..."* French, 1778. Hand-colored engraving on laid paper. Museum of Fine Arts, Boston. The Elizabeth Day McCormick Collection, 44.1290. Photograph © 2014 Museum of Fine Arts, Boston.

This English countess wears her hair straight, smoothed up, and very high, (about 10"), widening up from the temples. On top, her hair is arranged in loops. A braid is placed asymmetrically across the front. One very wide ringlet hangs behind the ear.

—

Gainsborough, Thomas. Detail from *Portrait of Anne, Countess of Chesterfield*. Oil on canvas, 1777-8. Getty.

Left: "La Cleopatre." This French fashion plate shows the hair pulled back smoothly from the forehead, with about 4-5" of extra height. The hair is then twisted into large buckles across the top and sides of the hair, with wide ringlets on both sides of the neck. The chignon is looped up loosely. On top, she wears a gauze *bonnet* with a hanging tail.

Right: "The *pouf* [bonnet] from the right side." The lady's hair is drawn smoothly up to the crown. Two long buckles are laid in a row, pointing diagonally, with another at the same angle on the neck.

—

Details from *18th Century Print showing Headdress [Gallerie des Modes]*. Engraving, hand tinted, gouache, 18th century [1778]. LACMA.

Women's Styles: Year-by-Year

Above: this French coiffure is styled high, with a large bump over the forehead. Three wide buckles are laid horizontally on the side of the head, with ringlets hanging on either side of the neck. The chignon may be braided, and hangs low on the neck before looping up. A yellow ribbon is intertwined through the coiffure.

Below: the hair is a similar shape. Two buckles are laid on the sides, with a ringlet on each side of the neck. Feathers, roses, and a ribbon ornament the coiffure.

—

Janinet, Jean-François. Details from *Modeles de Coiffures*. Color crayon manner etching, n.d. NGA.

Both ladies' hair is dressed incredibly high and wide – perhaps an exaggeration, perhaps not! This is one of the few existing images showing hair at this extreme height and width. The hair is straight, with extra height equal to about two times the length of their face. Both coiffures have a bump over the forehead, and dips in the center top. On the left, the "*Pouf à l'Asiatique*" is indicated by pearls, tassels, and stripes. Three buckles are arranged in a line along the sides, with a wide ringlet on each side of the neck. On the right, the "*Coeffure à la Flore*" features garlands of flowers wound around the entire hairstyle, with a gauze bonnet and feathers on top. Two wide ringlets hang horizontally on each side of the neck.

—

Various Artists. Details from *Galerie des Modes et Costumes Francais... (volume I)*. Bound volume with 198 hand-colored and black and white etchings and engravings, published 1778/1780 [1778]. NGA.

This is probably Rosalie Duthe (age 39), a famous French courtesan. Her hair is drawn up from the forehead with an extra 3-4" of height at the crown, where it is arranged loosely and circled with a ribbon. Two horizontal buckles are at the sides. One short, wide ringlet hangs behind the ear, and longer ringlets fall over the shoulders. The chignon appears to be looped up loosely.

—

Janinet, Jean-François. Detail from *Mademoiselle du T...* Etching and engraving printed in colors, 1779. LACMA.

A French lady dresses in front of a mirror. In her reflection, we see the front of her hairstyle: it is unpowdered, straight, and dressed very high and wide, with four very wide buckles on the sides. In the foreground, we can see the back of her hair: the chignon is left straight and looped up loosely, with a very large roll at the crown of the head. A ribbon is tied around the hair, with a bow in back.

—

Schall, Jean Frédéric. Detail from *Morgentoilet*. Oil on panel, 1780-1820. Rijksmuseum.

Although much of this American's hair is hidden by her elaborate cap, we can assume that the shape underneath follows similar lines. Her hair has been powdered medium-grey and pulled up smoothly from the forehead, with at least 4-5" of extra height.

—

American 18th Century. Detail from *Lady Wearing a Large White Cap*. Oil on canvas, c. 1780. NGA.

"Hedgehog [see pg. 28] accompanied by seven side buckles topped by a feather and belted by a rolled ribbon." The hair is brushed straight up and spiky on top, while the chignon is twisted.

—

Publisher: Esnauts et Rapilly, French, 18th century. Detail from *Gallerie des Modes et Costumes Français, 29e. Cahier de Costumes Français, 7e Suite des coeffures à la mode en 1780. ee.169 "Pouf d un nouveau gout..."* French, 1780. Hand-colored engraving on laid paper 41.9 x 26.7 cm (16 1/2 x 10 1/2 in.). Museum of Fine Arts, Boston. The Elizabeth Day McCormick Collection, 44.1459. Photograph © 2014 Museum of Fine Arts, Boston.

Elizabeth was the wife of a British MP. She is shown in "Turkish" fancy dress. Her hair is drawn loosely up to the crown, with about 8" of extra height. A wide twist lies along the visible side, and another presumably on the other. Wide ringlets fall behind the ears.

—

Reynolds, Sir Joshua. Detail from *Lady Elizabeth Compton*. Oil on canvas, 1780-2. NGA.

The daughters of the British Earl Waldegrave (ages 20, 19, and 18). All wear very similar hairstyles powdered light grey and pulled up smoothly in front, about 3-5" above the forehead. The shape is vaguely squared off at the corners, with a slight indentation on top in which sits a loose, looped bun. The ladies on the left and center have horizontal buckles, a similarly-sized ringlet behind the ear, and the chignon draped up loosely. The lady on the right has two horizontal rolls at the side, two ringlets behind the ear, and her chignon is tied with a ribbon.

—

Reynolds, Joshua. Detail from *The Ladies Waldegrave*. Oil on canvas, 1770-80. National Gallery of Scotland (WC/Yorck).

Women's Styles: Year-by-Year 55

The French countess (age 17) was a lady-in-waiting to Marie Antoinette. She wears her hair waved and pulled towards the crown. In back, her chignon is looped up loosely to the crown, then falls in three or four ringlets. Multiple ringlets hang on her shoulders, with their tops straight. A ribbon crosses the top of the coiffure.

—

Houdon, Jean-Antoine. Details from *Bust of Anne-Marie-Louise Thomas de Domangeville de Serilly, Comtesse de Pange*. Marble, 1780. Art Institute of Chicago (artwork in the public domain; photographs provided by Flickr user kimberlykv, CC BY 2.0).

This French fashion plate shows a lady with frizzed, bushy hair that is (comparatively) low on top and wider on the sides. One buckle lays diagonally on the side, and a ringlet hangs behind each ear. The chignon is draped up loosely, and hangs in ringlets from the back of the head.

—

Designed by: Pierre-Thomas LeClerc, French, about 1740–after 1799. Engraved by: Pélissier, French. Publisher: Esnauts et Rapilly, French, 18th century. Detail from *Gallerie des Modes et Costumes Français. 34e Cahier de Costumes Français, 8e Suite de Coeffures à la mode en 1780. 201 "Coeffure à l'Enfant..."* French, 1780. Hand-colored engraving on laid paper 36.8 x 25.4 cm (14 1/2 x 10 in.). Museum of Fine Arts, Boston. The Elizabeth Day McCormick Collection, 44.1500. Photograph © 2014 Museum of Fine Arts, Boston.

The hair is straight and dressed very high (about 9-10"), leaning back at the crown (perhaps the *hérisson*?). A twist or series of poufs decorates the top, coming down in a V shape at the center front. Three buckles are on the sides, and a ringlet behind the ear. The chignon is looped up loosely.

—

Lewis, Anna Frankland. Detail from *Collection of English Original Watercolor Drawings*. Watercolor on paper, 1774-1807. LACMA.

A British fashion plate shows two high coiffures topped with caps. Both have ringlets behind the ears that are straight for a few inches before curling. On the right, multiple horizontal buckles are placed at the sides. The left-hand lady wears her hair very curly, in almost horizontal rows. The chignons appear to be braided.

—

Detail from *Twelve Fashionable Head-Dresses for Women*. Etching, 1781. Wellcome.

This Frenchwoman's hair has been frizzed and drawn up to the crown, with about 3-4" of extra height. One short ringlet hangs behind each ear, with longer, looser curls falling from the nape of the neck. The chignon is looped up loosely, bound at the back of the head (where the chignon indents) and then attached a few inches higher, near the crown of the head.

—

Attiret, Claude. Detail from *Portrait of a Woman*. Marble, 1781. Musée du Louvre, Paris, France. © RMN-Grand Palais / Art Resource, NY.

BUSHY STYLES
Fashionable: 1780s

- Hair is frizzed or curled
- Top and side hair:
  - Cut into long layers, or pulled back to look as though it is
  - Raised into a big, rounded shape, with more width than height
- Optional wide buckles at side back of head
- Wide, short curls hanging down at side back of head ("*chien couchant*")
- Chignon (back hair) either:
  - Straight, hanging down and then swooping up (like a loose ponytail) and attached at back of head
  - Same shape but braided in a wide braid, or twisted in a wide twist, and attached at back of head
  - Left hanging, straight or in ringlets

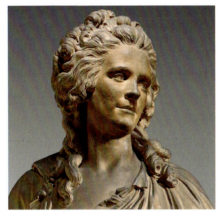

The wife of the French sculptor wears her hair waved and dressed in a rounded halo, wider than tall. The ends of the hair end in ringlets. Long ringlets fall from the chignon.

—

Roland, Philippe-Laurent. Detail from *Thérèse-Françoise Potain Roland, Wife of the Sculptor*. Terracotta, c. 1782/3. NGA.

This British lady is wearing "Turkish" dress, with a veil that suggests a turban. Her hair is powdered light grey, frizzed, and dressed in a rounded shape. Multiple ringlets fall from the ear to the neck, with a long ringlet falling over her right shoulder.

—

Day, Thomas. *Portrait of a Lady*. Gouache and watercolor on ivory, 1783. YBA.

Arabella was the wife of an Irish politician. Her blonde hair appears to be lightly powdered; it is frizzed and rounded. The chignon is long and straight, shaped into curls at the ends.

—

Romney, George. Detail from *Lady Arabella Ward*. Oil on canvas, 1783-8. NGA.

The French queen lost much of her hair after the birth of the dauphin in 1781 (when the original version of this portrait was painted). According to the memoirs of her *coiffeur* Léonard, at that time he created for her the *coiffure à l'enfant*, with short sides and long, curly chignon — but there are images of this hairstyle that predate 1781. Marie-Antoinette's hair is powdered light grey. It is frizzed and worn bushy on the sides of the face, with one buckle on the outside edge at ear level. Long ringlets fall from the chignon.

—

After Elisabeth-Louise Vigée Le Brun. Detail from *Marie-Antoinette*. Oil on canvas, after 1783. NGA.

Women's Styles: Year-by-Year

A well-to-do American lady wears her heavily powdered hair in a frizzy, bushy, squared-off halo around her head. The hair is styled in curls at the ends, with a slight V shape on top of the head. A long straight piece, ending in a curl, lies on her shoulder, with more ringlets hanging behind.

—

Brown, Mather. Detail from *Lady with a Dog*. Oil on canvas, 1786. MMA. Purchase, The Bertram F. and Susie Brummer Foundation Inc. Gift, 1964.

Françoise was a leading French salon hostess. Her hair is in short waves in front. The back of her hair, seen in a mirror, has the chignon hanging straight from the crown down past the shoulders, with slight waves on the ends. Two short ringlets lay on her shoulder, and a ribbon is tied around her head.

—

After Houdon, Jean-Antoine. *Bust of the Comtesse of Sabran*. C. 1785. Musée d'Art et d'Histoire de Provence (artwork in the public domain; personal photograph by author).

A British fashion plate shows the hair cut short and frizzed on the top and sides of the face. Two horizontal buckles are placed at the sides of the head. One wide ringlet falls behind the ear. The chignon is twisted and looped up loosely, with another buckle or ringlet placed inside of (or next to?) the loop.

—

Delegal, James. Detail from *The Head and Shoulders of a Woman Looking to her Right and Wearing Curled Hair-Pieces Attached to her Natural Hair*. Engraving, n.d. Wellcome.

Harriet, the sister of the Duchess of Devonshire, was about 24 in the original portrait. Her hair is frizzed and rounded. Short ringlets are at the bottom of the frizzed portion, with longer ringlets falling over the shoulder and in back.

—

Grozer, Joseph after Sir Joshua Reynolds. Detail from *Viscountess Duncannon*. Mezzotint and etching, c. 1785. YBA.

This Frenchwoman's hair is frizzed and pulled back. Small buckles ornament the ends of her coiffure, with larger rolls at the side back and on the shoulders. Her chignon is straight and tied into a low cadogan knot (see page 67).

Designed by: Claude-Louis Desrais, French, 1746–1816. Publisher: Esnauts et Rapilly, French, 18th century. Detail from *Gallerie des Modes et Costumes Français. 12e Cahier des coeffures les plus à la mode en 1785. Sans nos. (280bis) "Chapeau au gout du Siecle…"* French, 1785. Hand-colored engraving on laid paper. 31.4 x 24.1 cm (12 3/8 x 9 1/2 in.). Museum of Fine Arts, Boston. The Elizabeth Day McCormick Collection, 44.1601. Photograph © 2014 Museum of Fine Arts, Boston.

This caricature satirizes fashionable Londoners mingling in a theater lobby. This lady's hair is mostly obscured by her hat, but we can see that her chignon is very long (past her waist) at the center back, tapering shorter towards the shoulders, and worn mostly straight.

—

Rowlandson, Thomas. Detail from *Box Lobby Loungers*. Pencil, pen, and black & grey ink and watercolor, 1785. Getty.

Victoire-Pauline (age 21) was a French aristocrat. Her hair is powdered brownish-grey. It is short and frizzy around the face, wider than tall. Longer curls hang from the chignon. She wears a sheer pleated hat on top.

Elizabeth Linley was an English actress and wife of a famous playwright. Her hair is curled and rounded on top and sides, widest around the temples, and ending in ringlets. Long curls fall over her right shoulder.

This American's hair is in a somewhat dated style: frizzed and pulled up from the crown, taller than wide. Long ringlets fall from the nape of the neck. The coiffure is accented with flowers and pearls.

—

Vigée Le Brun, Elisabeth Louise. Detail from *The Vicomtesse de Vaudreuil*. Oil on panel, 1785. Getty.

—

Gainsborough, Thomas. Detail from *Mrs. Richard Brinsley Sheridan*. Oil on canvas, 1785-7. NGA.

—

The Sherman Limner. Detail from *Portrait of a Lady in Red*. Oil on canvas, c. 1785/90. NGA.

An Englishwoman's hair is powdered light grey. It is frizzed and rounded on top and sides, widest around the temples. Two short rolls are placed along the bottom edge of the rounded hair. A long curl, straight and then curling, falls over each shoulder.

This Frenchwoman's hair is curled and cut shorter on top and back, and styled into a rounded shape. Ringlets fall over the shoulders. Her chignon is left straight and looped up loosely to the crown, from where a few trailing ringlets fall.

On the far left, a fashionable Frenchwoman wears her chignon long, straight, and with ringlets at the ends. A kind of barrette clamps the chignon midway down the back. In 1786 the *Cabinet des Modes* reported, "As chignons are worn very long, & it is impossible that all the hair is equally long... we suggest a kind of ligament of bronzed iron, which is tied around the chignon, in the middle, & which holds the hair firmly."

—

Alleyne, Francis. Detail from *Margot Wheatley*. Oil on canvas, 1786. YBA.

—

Janinet, Jean-François after Nicolas Lavreince. Detail from *La Comparaison*. Etching and wash manner, printed in blue, red, carmine, yellow, and black inks, 1786. NGA.

—

Lecour, Louis. Detail from *The Palais Royal Garden Walk*. Print, 1787. Rijksmuseum.

Marie-Louise Poulletier de Perigny was the wife of a wealthy Montpellier government official. Her hair is unpowdered and worn short and curly on top and sides. Long curls come from the chignon and drape over her shoulders. The myrtle leaf wreath is a classical symbol.

—

Fabre, François-Xavier. Detail from *Portrait of Madame Joubert*. Oil on canvas, 1787. Getty.

Maria was an English painter, composer, musician, and hostess. Her hair is powdered light grey and cut short on top and sides, longest around the temples. It is dressed in tight curls, with longer ringlets over the shoulders.

—

Green, Valentine after Maria Cosway. Detail from *Maria Cecilia Louisa Cosway*. Color mezzotint, 1787. NGA.

This lady's hair appears to be powdered light grey. It is cut short on the top and sides and styled into frizzy curls. One ringlet falls behind her ear. The chignon is long and straight with a slight curl at the bottom, ending near her waist. Note how the chignon begins at the crown of the head.

—

Debucourt, Philibert-Louis. Detail from *Les Bouquets, ou la Fete de la Grand'Maman*. Color aquatint and etching, 1788. NGA.

The French marquise wears her hair very wide, in bushy curls around her face, with ringlets on the neck. Her hair is only powdered right around her face.

—

Barbier Le Jeune, Jean-Louis Le. Detail from *Madame de Villeneuve-Flayosc*. Oil on canvas, 1789. Ackland Art Museum, The University of North Carolina at Chapel Hill (artwork in the public domain; photograph provided with permission by the museum).

Marie Catherine de Lamoignon de Basville was a French marquise and the wife of a politician and diplomat. Her hair is cut shorter on top and sides, widest around the ears. Long curls fall from the back. The braid wrapped around her turban-esque veil is a nod to the Turkish theme to the painting.

—

Vigée Le Brun, Elisabeth-Louise. Detail from *Madame d'Aguesseau de Fresnes*. Oil on wood, 1789. NGA.

This English lady's hair is cut shorter on top and sides and styled into curls, with longer ringlets falling from the underside and back.

—

Downman, John. Detail from *Portrait of a Lady, Facing Left*. Black and red chalk with watercolor and stumping on wove paper, n.d. YBA.

Frances Wilton, an Englishwoman, was the wife of a judge. Her hair is cut short on top and sides, widest around the cheekbones, and curled. The chignon is long and curly.

Clarissa, from Connecticut, was the daughter of a Revolutionary War officer. Her hair is cut short on top and sides and styled wide into large puffy curls. The chignon is slightly waved and long, ending in ringlets.

The French countess wears her hair waved and bushy on top and sides, with a bump above her forehead. Large ringlets hang on the upper and lower sides. In back, the chignon is draped up to the top back of the head, where it is looped and hangs in ringlets. A ribbon is tied across the top in front.

—

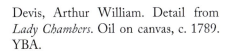

Devis, Arthur William. Detail from *Lady Chambers*. Oil on canvas, c. 1789. YBA.

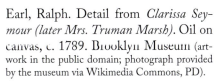

Earl, Ralph. Detail from *Clarissa Seymour (later Mrs. Truman Marsh)*. Oil on canvas, c. 1789. Brooklyn Museum (artwork in the public domain; photograph provided by the museum via Wikimedia Commons, PD).

Monot, Martin-Claude. Details from *Marie d'Aguesseau Comtesse Louis-Philippe de Ségur (1756-1828)*. Marble, c. 1783. Photo: Gerard Blot. Chateaux de Versailles et de Trianon, Versailles, France. © RMN-Grand Palais / Art Resource, NY.

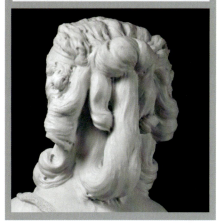

A French lady wears her hair cut shorter and curled around the head. The chignon begins above the crown, and falls in long ringlets that spill over her shoulders. More ringlets fall on the upper portion of her chignon, which seems to tuck under.

—

Pajou, Augustin. Details from *Madame de Wailly, née Adélaïde-Flore Belleville (1765–1838)*. Marble, 1789. MMA. Fletcher Fund, 1956.

SIMPLE SHORT & LONG STYLES
Fashionable: 1790s

Primary style:
- Hair is frizzed or curled
- Side and top hair:
  - Loose, short, and curly around sides and top of head (much smaller than previously)
  - Shorter than back hair
  - Sides wider than top
- Chignon (back hair) either:
  - Straight, hanging down and then swooping up (like a loose ponytail) and attached at the top of the back of head
  - Same shape but braided in a wide braid
  - Left hanging, straight or in ringlets

Secondary style ("crop"):
Seen only on the extremely fashion-forward in the very late 1790s, primarily in France
- Hair is straight, wavy, frizzed, or curly
- Cut short and choppy all over head

This French lady's powdered hair is cut short on top and sides, and frizzed in nearly horizontal rows of curls. The chignon is left long and straight, with ringlets on the sides. A large bow is placed on the crown.

Debucourt, Philibert-Louis. Detail from *La Promenade Publique*. Etching and wash manner, printed in blue, carmine, dark pink, yellow, and black inks, 1792. NGA.

An Englishwoman wears her hair powdered light grey, cut short on top and sides where it is frizzed, with the chignon in longer curls.

Nasmyth, Alexander. Detail from *Eleanor and Margaret Ross*. Oil on canvas, 1785-90. YBA.

This British lady's hair is cut shorter on top and sides, and longer in back. It is styled into naturalistic curls.

Devis, Arthur William. Detail from *Mr. and Mrs. Fraser*. Oil on canvas, 1785-90. YBA.

Stéphanie Félicité du Crest de Saint-Aubin, a French countess, was a writer, harper, and educator. Her hair is powdered medium grey. It is cut short on top and sides and frizzed. Longer curls fall from the back.

Elizabeth was married to a Connecticut army captain. Her hair is cut short on top and sides, widest at the cheeks, and frizzed. One long, narrow ringlet falls on the shoulder. Her chignon appears to be long and straight.

An English lady wears her hair cut shorter around the face, longer at the sides, and waist-length in back. It is styled into naturalistic curls.

Labille-Guiard, Adelaide. Detail from *Portrait of Madame de Genlis*. Oil on canvas laid down on board, 1790. LACMA.

The Denison Limner (probably Joseph Steward). Detail from *Mrs. Elizabeth Noyes Denison*. Oil on canvas, c. 1790. NGA.

Morland, George. Detail from *The Squire's Door*. Oil on canvas, c. 1790. YBA.

This Frenchwoman's hair is styled in tight curls all over. The top and sides have been cut short, while the back hangs long. A wide scarf is tied around the head.

This English lady wears her hair cut short on top and sides. It is styled into waves that end in ringlets, curlier and shorter at the lower sides. The chignon falls in long ringlets. A blue bow is tied across the top.

Catherine was the daughter of a Scottish landowner. Her hair is cut short on top and sides, and styled into distinct ringlets. Pearls are looped around the coiffure, with a green bow at the crown.

Detail from *Bust of a Young Woman, in the Louis XVI Style* by Joseph-Charles Marin (1759-1834) c.1790 (terracotta) / Private Collection / © Partridge Fine Arts, London, UK / The Bridgeman Art Library.

Downman, John. Detail from *Portrait of a Woman with a Blue Sash*. Black chalk and watercolor, 1791. NGA.

Stuart, Gilbert. Detail from *Catherine Yates Pollock (Mrs. George Pollock)*. Oil on canvas, 1793/4. NGA.

Women's Styles: Year-by-Year 63

The eldest child, and only daughter, of Louis XVI and Marie-Antoinette wears her hair in short, bushy curls on the sides and top. The curls around the face are less structured. One buckle hangs on the side, as well as a ringlet behind the ear. The chignon hangs in more ringlets. A classically-inspired diadem wraps across the top of her head.

Gault, Jacques Joseph de. Detail from *Marie-Thérèse-Charlotte (1778–1851), Daughter of Louis XVI*. Ivory, 1795. MMA. Bequest of Millie Bruhl Fredrick, 1962.

Englishwoman Miss Lysons's hair is cut short on the top and sides, with more length at the sides. It styled into choppy, wavy pieces. The chignon hangs straight, possibly looped up.

—

Lawrence, Sir Thomas. Detail from *Portrait of Miss Lysons*. Graphite with black and red chalk on paper, 1795. YBA.

This British lady's hair is powdered blondish grey. It is cut short on top and sides, with more width on the sides of the face. The hair is frizzed, with slightly longer curls along the underside. The chignon is straight.

—

Wheatley, Francis. Detail from *Mrs. Stevens*. Oil on canvas, c. 1795. YBA.

This American's hair is cut short on top and sides. It is worn frizzy, but with only a (comparatively) small amount of volume. Two longer pieces end in curls on either side of her neck.

An American woman's powdered coiffure is worn in short curls at the top and sides of the head, with longer ringlets falling from the chignon. A blue ribbon is entwined in her curls.

The hair of this English lady is cut short on the top and sides, where it is styled into tight curls. The chignon hangs in long ringlets. A wide scarf is tied around the head.

—

Jennys, William. Detail from *Mrs. Asa Benjamin*. Oil on canvas, 1795. NGA.

—

Stuart, Gilbert. Detail from *Mrs. Joseph Anthony Jr. (Henrietta Hillegas)*. Oil on canvas, c. 1795-98. MMA. Rogers Fund, 1905.

—

Downman, John. Detail from *Portrait of Lady Marjorie Jenkins*. Black chalk with watercolor and stumping on paper, 1798. YBA.

A French fashion plate shows a classically-inspired coiffure, with short tendril curls in front. The back must be longer in order to create the larger shape. A wide scarf is tied around the head, and a small braid is wound on the sides. The looped braid or ornament on top seems serpent-like, and is perhaps a reference to Medusa.

—

Detail from *Untitled Fashion Plate* [Probably France]. Engraving on paper, late 18th century. LACMA.

This lady's ash grey hair may be powdered. It is cut short around the face and long in back, with more length on the sides than seen in previous images. The hair around the face is styled in curls, as are the ends of the chignon. A white scarf is tied around the head.

—

Plimer, Andrew. Detail from *Portrait of a Lady*. Watercolor and gouache on ivory, n.d. YBA.

Two British ladies both wear their hair powdered medium grey. On the left, the younger wears her hair long, with shorter curls around the face. The chignon is twisted up and pinned to the back of the head. A white scarf is tied around the head, knotted on top. The elder lady wears a high, ruffled cap.

—

Raeburn, Sir Henry. Detail from *John Johnstone, Betty Johnstone, and Miss Wedderburn*. Oil on canvas, c. 1790-95. NGA.

An extremely fashion-forward Frenchwoman wears her hair cropped in short layers all over. The hair is straight, with slight waves on the ends. A (possibly false) braid lies across the forehead.

—

David, Jacques-Louis (circle of). Detail from *Portrait of a Young Woman in White*. Oil on canvas, c. 1798. NGA.

Two ladies from a British fashion plate; both may be wearing the crop in short curls, or may have arranged their hair on top or back of the head so as to mimic the crop.

—

Detail from *Fashion Plate (Full Dress for Decr. 1798) [Lady's Monthly Museum or Polite Repository of Amusement and Instruction]*. Hand-colored etching on paper, 1798. LACMA.

Men's Styles: Year-by-Year

There were over 200 named wigs that were worn at one time or another over the course of the eighteenth century. Most of these would begin as fashionable wear, but then continue to be worn as a sign of a man's age, profession, or rank long after they had gone out of vogue. Some details would change over time – for example, the full-bottomed wig became the square wig, while a Ramillies wig worn in the 1730s with messy side curls would feature structured buckles in the 1770s. Thus, even if a man is wearing an "out-of-date" wig style, fashion trends still applied.

I have first provided a visual guide to the most popular wigs worn over the century. Then, I present images charting the changes in men's hairstyles, grouped into arbitrary eras that share common stylistic elements.

In order to contextualize the images, I have given basic biographical information when available. All ages listed are approximate.

MEN: GENERAL TRENDS

Wigs

Worn by nearly all men until the 1770s.
Exceptions:
- American colonies/United States: lower class men less likely to wear a wig
- Great Britain: brief trend for natural hair in the 1760s

In the 1780s, the lower classes, as well as fashionable or forward-thinking middle/upper class men, were less likely to wear a wig. In the 1790s, it was mostly (but not only) older and/or conservative men who wore wigs.

Powdering

A study of art (paintings, drawings, etc.) across the eighteenth century yields the following trends:

France & Great Britain:
- 1700s-1710s: popular, but not ubiquitous
- 1720s-1770s: nearly ubiquitous
- 1780s-1790s: more likely to be worn by older and/or conservative men

American colonies/United States:
- 1700s-1720s: unusual
- 1730s-1770s: popular, but not ubiquitous
- 1780s: nearly ubiquitous
- 1790s: more likely to be worn by older and/or conservative men

POPULAR WIG STYLES

Bag wig (*perruque en bourse*): with the queue enclosed in a rectangular silk fabric bag, usually black. The top end of the bag was closed with a drawstring, hidden behind a decorative bow (or, less frequently, a rosette) of the same fabric. Worn from c. 1709 for informal wear, c. 1730 for formal wear. Although very fashionable, the bag also protected the clothing from powder and pomatum, and kept the queue tidy.

—

Bénard, Robert after J.R. Lucotte. Details from *A Variety of Wigs*. Engraving, 1762. Wellcome.

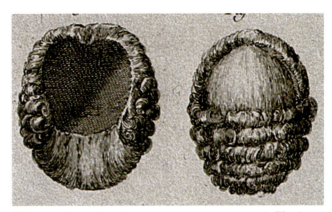

Bob wig (*bonnet*): without queue or hanging curls. The hairline around the face, and the bottom portion of the back hair, was curled. The short bob ended at the top of the neck, the long bob at the bottom of the neck. Worn from c. 1684. Particularly associated with tradesmen. Informal.

—

Bénard, Robert after J.R. Lucotte. Detail from *A Variety of Wigs*. Engraving, 1762. Wellcome.

Full-bottom/ed wig (aka "in-folio"; *perruque à large fond, à longue suite, Binette*): Very long, with curls hanging over the shoulders. Associated with professional men and the aristocracy. Fashionable from the 1670s until c. 1730 for formal occasions.

—

Drevet, Pierre after Hyacinthe Rigaud. Detail from *Louis-Alexandre de Bourdon, comte de Toulouse*. Engraving, 1714. NGA.

Cadogan (aka "catogan" or "club wig"): curls across the top and sides, with the hair left straight in back, looped up multiple times and then secured with a small piece of hair wrapped around the middle of the looped portion. Named for the Earl of Cadogan. Worn from the 1760s; particularly popular with the English Macaronis (fops).

—

Bénard, Robert after J.R. Lucotte. Detail from *A Variety of Wigs*. Engraving, 1762. Wellcome.

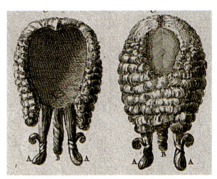

Knotted wig (aka "campaign wig"; *perruque à noueds*): short rolls all over, with two pieces knotted on themselves hanging in back and a short ringlet in between. Particularly associated with travelers, sportsmen, and soldiers. Fashionable from the late seventeenth century until c. 1750.

—

Bénard, Robert after J.R. Lucotte. Detail from *A Variety of Wigs*. Engraving, 1762. Wellcome.

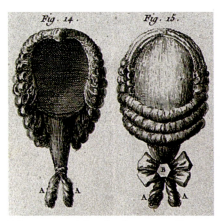

Major wig (aka "military wig"; *perruque à Brigadiere*): with short curls on the sides, long curls across the lower back, and queue tied with a bow and ending in two ringlets. Worn from the 1750s to the 1770s. Particularly associated with military men.

—

Bénard, Robert after J.R. Lucotte. Detail from *A Variety of Wigs*. Engraving, 1762. Wellcome.

Natural wig (*perruque naturelle*): with short curls along the sides, the back left straight and untied, ending in a horizontal roll. Sometimes with small ringlets along the sides of the queue.

—

Bénard, Robert after J.R. Lucotte. Detail from *A Variety of Wigs*. Engraving, 1762. Wellcome.

Physical wig: a later version of the bob wig. Front smoothed back, bushy around the sides and back. Particularly associated with doctors and those in the "learned professions." Fashionable from the 1750s.

—

Doughty, William after Sir Joshua Reynolds. Detail from *Samuel Johnson*. Mezzotint, 1779. NGA.

Ramillies wigs: with a long braided queue, tied with a large bow at the top and small bow at the bottom; the queue could be doubled on itself. Starting c. 1780, the braid was often turned up and secured on the back of the head. Named after a battle of 1706. Particularly associated with military men.

Chéreau, Jacques (publisher). Detail from *Redingote/Dame en Habit d'Hyver en Manchon/Veste et Parrement d'Etofe d'Or*. Engraving with etching on laid paper, 1720s (?). NGA.

Scratch wig: A short, natural looking wig, either worn smooth or disheveled. Particularly associated with tradesmen and the lower classes.

—

Zoffany, Johan Joseph. Detail from *Patrick Heatly*. Oil on canvas, 1783-7. YBA.

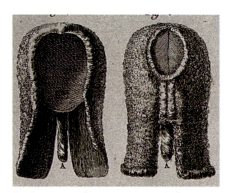

Square wig (*perruque quarrée*): remnant of the full-bottomed wig, with the wig extending past the shoulders in two flaps and a center ringlet. Worn by lawyers and judges (still worn in England to this day).

—

Bénard, Robert after J.R. Lucotte. Detail from *A Variety of Wigs*. Engraving, 1762. Wellcome.

FULL-BOTTOMED STYLES
Fashionable: 1700s-1710s

- Long – to the middle of the back
- Very curly, except for a straighter portion on the back of the head
- Full on top with center part and two distinct, peaked halves
- Long hair usually left hanging, but can be knotted or in a bag

The Marquis, a French politician, wears a long full-bottomed wig, with a high top and deep part. The hair is styled into distinct ringlets.

—

Drevet, Pierre after Pierre Gobert. Detail from *Marquis de la Vrilliere*. Engraving, 1701. NGA.

The Scottish marquess (age 38) wears a very similar style to the previous image, but with slightly less height on top and fuller curls. The dark color suggests that this wig was unpowdered.

—

Smith, John after Sir Godfrey Kneller. Detail from *William Johnston, Marquess of Annandale*. Mezzotint with engraving on laid paper, 1702. NGA.

A French musician wears a curly full-bottomed wig with a high top and center parting. The length has been combed straight and tied in a large knot, in which the hair is looped up on itself, with a short ringlet coming from the center of the knot.

—

Picart, Bernard. Detail from *Manier Waarop Heren Muziek Maken*. Etching on paper, 1704. Rijksmuseum.

This French drawing shows multiple views of the full-bottomed wig, worn with and without cocked hats (the eighteenth-century term for what we now call a "tricorn"). All feature bushy long curls. The wig on the bottom left has a very high top with a clear center parting. On the bottom right, the top is lower, with long layers starting around the shoulders (and shorter pieces around the face). The hair is straighter on the back of the head.

—

Picart, Bernard. Detail from *Zes Mannenhoofden met Pruiken en Hoeden*. Etching on paper, 1704. Rijksmuseum.

Men's Styles: Year-by-Year 69

This British physician wears an unpowdered full-bottom wig. The curls of the wig are puffy and indistinct. There is a bit of height to the top hair with a center part. The ends of the wig appear to be cut shorter in front than in back.

A lascivious Frenchman wears the full-bottomed wig, high on top, in bushy curls. The hair is shorter in front.

George II of England wears a curly full-bottomed wig with a high top and center part. His wig is white and/or heavily powdered.

Kneller, Sir Godfrey. Detail from *Sir Theodore Colladon*. Oil on canvas, c. 1705. YBA.

Picart, Bernard. Detail from *Man Betaalt een Vrouw*. Etching on paper, 1705. Rijksmuseum.

Arlaud, Benoît. Detail from *George II (1683-1760), Koning van Engeland*. Miniature on cardboard, 1706. Rijksmuseum.

Berkeley was the younger son of an earl who was also a British Member of Parliament (MP). His full-bottomed wig appears to be made with white hair. It has the same center part seen in previous images, but less height on top.

Three English aristocrats wear a variety of full-bottomed wigs. Only the duke (right, age 59) appears to be unpowdered. Both he and the gentleman at the front left have knots tied at the ends of their wigs. All of the wigs are made of bushy curls, with center parts and high tops.

An elegant Frenchman wears a full-bottomed wig in bushy curls. The hair on top is high. The long hair in back has been tied into a silk fabric bag, tied or accented with a bow.

Zincke, Christian Friedrich. Detail from *Hon. George Berkeley*. Enamel on copper, 1706-46. YBA.

Unknown artist, 18th century, British. Detail from *Elihu Yale, the 2nd Duke of Devonshire, Lord James Cavendish, Mr. Tunstal, and a Page*. Oil on canvas, c. 1708. YBA.

Gacon. Detail from *Elegant Gezelschap Speelt het Kaartspel Jeu de l'Hombre*. Etching on paper, 1709. Rijksmuseum.

BOB STYLES
Fashionable: 1720s-1730s

- Toupet (top and sides) either:
  - Bushy with center part and two distinct halves (although not as tall as previous era)
  - Brushed back on top
    - About 2-4" of short cropped hair around the face
    - Sometimes there is a small peak at the center of the forehead
- Bushy around ears and back of the head
- Length between top of chin (short bob) or top of shoulders (long bob)

An American wears a modest hairstyle: long, in soft waves, with a center part. He could be wearing a wig, or this could be his natural hair.

—

The Schuyler Limner (possibly Nehemiah Partridge). Detail from *Mr. Willson*. Oil on canvas, 1720. NGA.

A short bob, with a tight, frizzy curl, distinct center part, and overall squared-off silhouette. The hair is white and/or powdered.

—

Possibly British 18th Century. Detail from *Portrait of a Gentleman*. Oil on canvas, c. 1720/1740. NGA.

This French aristocrat's full-bottomed wig is powdered and tied loosely with a black bow. Note the slight widow's peak hairline.

—

Oudry, Jean-Baptiste. Detail from *Henri Camille, Chevalier de Beringhen*. Oil on canvas, 1722. NGA.

A Frenchman wears a long, full-bottomed wig. The curls are cut shorter and worn high on top. There is a distinct center part, which continues down the back of the head.

—

Coustou, Guillaume the Elder. Detail from *Samuel Bernard*. Marble, c. 1727. MMA. Purchase, Josephine Bay Paul and C. Michael Paul Foundation Inc. Gift and Charles Ulrick and Josephine Bay Foundation Inc. Gift, 1966.

  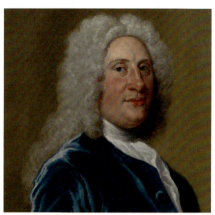

Morris (age 55) was the governor of New Jersey. His powdered full-bottom wig is combed back on the forehead and then parted, with the ends combed straight and tied in knots. Note how his wig is placed further back from his own (widow's peak) shaved hairline.

Watson, John. Detail from *Governor Lewis Morris*. Oil on canvas, c. 1726. Brooklyn Museum (artwork in the public domain; photograph provided by the museum via Wikimedia Commons, PD).

The British army commander (stationed in the American colonies, later Lieutenant-Governor of Nova Scotia; age 45) wears a powdered full-bottomed wig. It is very bushy on the sides, parted in the center, and tied with a bow at the nape of the neck.

Smibert, John. Detail from *Portrait of Major General Paul Mascarene*. Oil on canvas, 1729. LACMA.

This Englishman wears a long, center-parted, powdered full-bottomed wig.

Highmore, Joseph. Detail from *An Unknown Man*. Oil on canvas, 1730-5. YBA.

One of the foremost British painters of his period, Richardson (age 68) wears a powdered (note the powder on his shoulders), white knotted wig under a cocked hat.

This English gentleman wears a powdered long bob wig. The hair on top is brushed back with a small peak at the center of the forehead, rather than the center parting seen previously. The ends of the hair are cut slightly shorter in front, and longer in back.

The French king wears a Ramillies wig, with the queue braided and tied with bow at the nape of the neck. The hair on top and sides is short and curly.

After Richardson, Jonathan the Elder. Detail from *Portrait of the Artist*. Oil on canvas, 1733 or after. YBA.

Highmore, Joseph. Detail from *An Unknown Man in Black*. Oil on canvas, 1735. YBA.

Daullé, Jean after Hyacinthe Rigaud. Detail from *Louis XV*. Engraving, 1737. NGA.

QUEUE STYLES
Fashionable: 1730s-1740s

- Toupet (top and sides):
  - Short and curly
  - 2-4" section around front hairline cropped short
  - Top either:
    - Smoothed back
    - Parted in the middle (less frequent)
- Rest of hair pulled back into a queue – tied with bow, in bag, braided, ringlets, etc.

Smyth (age 29-30) was an English baronet. He wears what is probably a queue wig, short and brushed back on top and curly on the sides. It is white and/or heavily powdered.

—

Attributed to Soldi, Andrea. Detail from *Sir Robert and Lady Smyth with Their Son, Hervey*. Oil on canvas, 1738-9. YBA.

Ligonier was a British military commander in the colonies. His knotted wig is curly, center-parted, and slightly high on top. Unusually, powder is only applied to the top, front portion of the wig, which thus appears grey on top and brown at the ends.

—

Detail from *Sir John Ligonier, c.1738* (oil on canvas), Mercier, Philippe (1689-1760) / The French Hospital, Rochester, Kent, UK / The Bridgeman Art Library.

The French artist and playwright (age 40) wears a heavily powdered, light grey, full-bottomed wig. It is parted on top and styled into bushy curls. The ends are straight and tied into one (or more) knots.

—

Coypel, Charles-Antoine. Detail from *Self-Portrait*. Pastel, 1734. Getty.

Both Frenchmen are dressed for riding. The man on the left wears a wrapped version of the Ramillies wig, with a ribbon wrapped around the length of his long braid and a bow at the top. On the right, he wears his powdered wig with queue in a bag. Both options offer practical protection for the queue during physical activity.

—

Lancret, Nicolas. Detail from *Picnic after the Hunt*. Oil on canvas, probably c. 1735/40. NGA.

Men's Styles: Year-by-Year 73

A French gentleman wears a bagwig. The hair is long on top and brushed back to the nape of the neck, where it is tied in the bag and accented with a wide bow. The hair on the sides of the head is styled in short, tousled curls.

Dodd (age 22) was an English politician. His dark blonde, powdered wig is parted on top and styled into unstructured curls on the sides. There is probably a queue hidden in back.

This Englishman's wig is cut short and curly on the sides, with a slight peak at the top of the forehead. The queue is long, with curly ends, and is tied with a bow at the nape of the neck.

—

Le Bas, Jacques-Philippe after Charles Eisen. Detail from *La Comete*. Engraving and etching, n.d. NGA.

Vanderbank, John. Detail from *John Dodd, of Swallowfield, Berkshire*. Oil on canvas, 1739. YBA.

Verschaffelt, Peter Anton von. Detail from *An Englishman*. Carrara marble, 1740. MMA. Purchase, C. Michael Paul Gift, 1978.

The marquess (age 21) wears his blonde hair cut short and curly around the face. The queue is similarly curly and tied with a black ribbon. This is the father of the duke who would marry the famous Georgiana, Duchess of Devonshire.

The wig worn by this French gentleman is cut short on top, with a wider, curlier side section. The queue is long and straight, ending in ringlets, and tied with a bow.

—

Hogarth, William. Detail from *William Cavendish, Marquess of Hartington, Later 4th Duke of Devonshire*. Oil on canvas, 1741. YBA.

Lemoyne, Jean-Baptiste the Younger. Details from *Bust of a Man*. Pale gray terracotta, covered with a buff colored wash Pedestal, breccia violetta marble, c. 1745-50. MMA. Purchase, Charles Ulrick and Josephine Bay Foundation Inc. Gift, 1975.

A British naval officer wears an unpowdered queue wig, with a small peak at the top and unstructured curls at the sides. There is the hint of a curly queue on his right shoulder.

This Englishman wears a light grey, powdered long bob wig with a center part. The hair is center parted and curly on top. The crown is smooth and straight, with bushy curls from the temples to the neck. There is an obvious wigline around his face.

An aristocratic French government official wears a short bob wig that is powdered light grey. The hair is cut short on top, with longer rows of horizontal curls at the temples.

Wollaston, John. Detail from *Unidentified British Navy Officer*. Oil on canvas, c. 1745. NGA.

Beare, George. Detail from *An Unknown Man*. Oil on canvas, 1746. YBA.

Perronneau, Jean-Baptiste. Detail from *Charles-François Pincloup de la Grange*. Oil on canvas, 1747. Getty.

De Villiers was a high-ranking French politician. He wears a powdered full-bottomed wig, with center parting and rows of horizontal curls. Note the obvious wig line around his face, and the powder on his shoulder.

The French army leader (age 52) wears a powdered Ramillies wig that was so typical of military men. The hair is cropped on the top and sides, with one horizontal buckle at each ear. In back, the long queue is braided and then wrapped with a black ribbon. A ribbon bow is tied at the top of the queue.

Prince Frederick of Wales, the heir to the British throne, wears a long queue wig. It is cut short on top and sides. The hair atop the forehead and on the crown of the head is straight and brushed back, while the sides and queue are very curly. The queue is tied with a bow.

Aved, Jacques-André-Joseph. Detail from *Portrait of Marc de Villiers*. Oil on canvas, 1747. Getty.

Liotard, Jean-Etienne. Detail from *Portret van Graaf Herman Maurits van Saksen (1696-1750), Maarschalk van Frankrijk*. Pastel on parchment, 1748. Rijksmuseum.

Detail from *Frederick Louis (1707-51), Prins van Wales*. Battersea enamel on copper, 1745-1755. Rijksmuseum.

BUCKLE/QUEUE STYLES
Fashionable: 1740s-1770s

- Toupet (top and sides):
  - Smoothed back
  - Cropped shorter
    - 1740s: about 2-4" section around front hairline, sometimes with a small peak on top
    - 1760s: from front hairline to the top of the head
  - Defined buckles (rolls) on sides
- Rest of hair pulled back into a queue – tied with bow, in bag, braided, ringlets, etc.

Pigott, an American, wears an unpowdered queue wig (note the ribbon on his left shoulder). It is brushed back on top with two structured buckles (rolls) low on the sides of the face.

—

Blackburn, Joseph. Detail from *Portrait of Captain John Pigott*. Oil on canvas, c. 1700-63. LACMA.

Quin was an Irish politician and landowner. His wig is brushed back in front with a small peak, with two buckles low at the sides of the face, and a probable queue hidden in back.

—

Slaughter, Stephen. Detail from *Windham Quin of Adare, Co. Limerick, Ireland*. Oil on canvas, c. 1745. YBA.

A nouveau riche character from the famous English novel wears a bagwig. The hair around his face is cut short and worn curly, while the rest is long and straight. The black silk bag is accented with a bow.

—

Highmore, Joseph. Detail from *The Harlowe Family*, from Samuel Richardson's "Clarissa." Oil on canvas, 1745-7. YBA.

The heir to the French throne (age 20) wears a bagwig with a large black bow. The hair is heavily powdered to a light grey color. On top, his hair is cropped short and stands up slightly. Four buckles are placed on each side.

—

Liotard, Jean-Etienne. Detail from *Portrait of Louis, Dauphin of France (1729–1765)*. Pastel on paper, c. 1749. Rijksmuseum.

The French artist (age 46-56) wears a light grey, heavily powdered bag wig. The hair on top of his forehead is cut short and worn standing, with a bit of curl at the ends. On the sides, rows of curls almost (but not quite) form buckles.

—

La Tour, Maurice Quentin de. Detail from *Self-portrait*. Pastel on paper, from 1750 until 1760. Musée de Picardie (WC/Yorck).

A young well-to-do British gentlemen on the grand tour of Europe wears a bag wig. A narrow section of hair around his forehead is cut short and brushed back, while the sides are rolled into three structured buckles. The rest of his hair is straight and brushed into the queue. Notice that a bit of his own, darker, hair can be glimpsed along the side back neck hairline.

—

Read, Katharine. Detail from *British Gentlemen in Rome*. Oil on canvas, c. 1750. YBA.

This American wears a short bob wig with small peak at the center top. The hair is straight on top until the temples, after which it is curled into distinct ringlets.

—

Wollaston, John. Detail from *John Stevens (?)*. Oil on canvas, c. 1749-1752. NGA.

A wealthy British banker and art patron, Henry Hoare (age 45-55) wears a queue wig. It is cut short and curled on top and sides, with a long straight queue tied with a black ribbon bow. The wig is heavily powdered, appearing light grey.

—

Hoare, William. Detail from *Henry Hoare, "The Magnificent," of Stourhead*. Pastel on paper, c. 1750-60. Getty.

Conyngham was a young Irish aristocrat on the Grand Tour. His unpowdered wig is brushed back on top, with slightly longer curls beginning at the ears. A queue can be glimpsed on his right shoulder.

—

Mengs, Anton Raphael. Detail from *Portrait of William Burton Conyngham*. Pastel on paper, laid on canvas, c. 1754-5. Getty.

This French gentleman wears his light grey, powdered wig in a queue tied with a black ribbon at the nape of the neck. The top hair is short with a hint of curl. Two structured buckles are at the ear, with the lower buckle larger than the higher.

—

Drouais, François-Hubert. Detail from *Family Portrait*. Oil on canvas, 1756. NGA.

A British army officer wears what is most likely a powdered queue wig. The hair is frizzed, with a small peak combed back at the forehead. The rest of the hair is brushed down into one buckle at each ear.

This English dance instructor wears a powdered, light grey, short bob wig. The hair is cut short and straight on top, then falls into horizontal buckles from the temples down. Note the obvious wig line around the face.

Probably Ignatius Sancho (30), a British composer, actor, and writer. Most images of Black men living in Europe depict servants wearing either close cropped hair, or exoticized turbans. The few images of free men usually depict them wearing fashionable wigs. In this case, Sancho wears an unpowdered bag wig, with curls at the sides of the face.

—

—

Detail from *Portrait of an African*, c.1757-60 (oil on canvas), Ramsay, Allan (1713-84) (attr. to) / Royal Albert Memorial Museum, Exeter, Devon, UK / The Bridgeman Art Library.

Blackburn, Joseph. Detail from *A Military Officer*. Oil on canvas, 1756. NGA.

Gainsborough, Thomas. Detail from *A Man Called Mr. Wood, the Dancing Master*. Oil on canvas, c. 1757. YBA.

  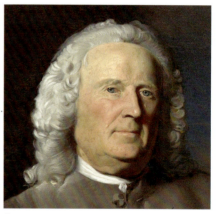

The British king (age 74-77) wears his full-bottomed wig cut short and curly on top, where it is smoothed back from the forehead. The rest is styled into tight curls. Note the obvious wig line across the forehead.

An English gentleman wears an unpowdered wig. It is cut short on top of the forehead, with a slight widow's peak, and brushed back. There is one buckle at each ear.

Sargent was a Massachusetts merchant, magistrate, and militia colonel. His white, powdered long bob is short and standing on top, with ringlets falling to just below the shoulders. Note the powder on the shoulders, and also on the skin around the hairline.

—

—

—

Detail from *Bust of George II*. White porcelain, c. 1757-60. LACMA.

Hudson, Thomas. Detail from *The Thistlethwayte Family*. Oil on canvas, c. 1758. YBA.

Copley, John Singleton. Detail from *Epes Sargent*. Oil on canvas, c. 1760. NGA.

The young English king wears a powdered white or grey queue wig. The hair around the hairline is cut short, from the top of the head to behind the ears. Two horizontal buckles are at the ears. The queue is long and straight, tied with a black ribbon at the nape of the neck.

—

Hurter, Johann Heinrich von (attributed to). Detail from *George III (1738-1820), Koning van Engeland*. Enamel on copper, 1760-99. Rijksmuseum.

An English baron (age 28) wears a powdered white queue wig. His hair is cut short on top, and rolled into a V shape on top of the head. Multiple horizontal buckles (three in the bottom row, two on top) are at the ears. His queue is tied with a black bow.

—

Zoffany, Johann. Detail from *John, Fourteenth Lord Willoughby de Broke, and his Family*. Oil on canvas, c. 1766. Getty.

A British aristocrat on the Grand Tour, John (age 19) stands in front of a mirror, allowing us to see both the front and back of his powdered grey queue wig. The front and sides are cut short all the way around to the back side of his face. This hair is frizzed, with one horizontal buckle over each ear. His smooth queue starts at the top or crown of the head, and is tied into a bag.

—

Liotard, Jean-Etienne. Details from *Portrait of John, Lord Mountstuart, later 4th Earl and 1st Marquess of Bute*. Pastel on parchment, 1763. Getty.

Whitfield (age 56), a founder of Methodism, was probably the most famous preacher in Britain and America during this period. He wears a physical wig with its characteristic silhouette: a 2-3" section around the front hairline is cut short and rolled under; the crown of the head is straight until the ears; and there is a large bushy section from the ears to the chin, which extends all of the way around the head.

—

Staffordshire pottery. Details from *Bust of the Reverend George Whitfield: with Ruddy Cheeks, Prominent Mole, Black Robes and Clerical Collar*. Staffordshire pearlware bust, c. 1770. YBA.

HIGH BUCKLE/QUEUE STYLES
Fashionable: 1770s

- Toupet (top and sides):
  - Smoothed back on top with some height (between 1-4")
  - Cropped short from hairline back to the top or crown of the head
  - Defined buckles (rolls) at ears
- Rest of hair pulled back into a queue – tied with bow, in bag, braided, ringlets, cadogan, etc.

A Frenchman wears a queue wig with a high, V-shaped roll on top. One structured buckle is on each side, while the queue is left curly and long and tied with a black ribbon. The hair is powdered a creamy grey.

—

French 18th Century. Detail from *Portrait of a Young Man*. Oil on canvas, possibly c. 1770. NGA.

This foppish gentleman wears a cadogan wig, with the queue looped up on itself and tied. The front hair is rolled under to create a high crescent across the top of the head. There are two buckles above each ear.

—

Caldwall, James after John Collet. Detail from *The Cotillion Dance*. Line engraving and etching on laid paper, 1771. YBA.

Verplanck (age 20) was a New York banker and politician. His powdered, grey wig is longer and brushed back on top, with one low, hanging roll at each side. What appears to be a cadogan queue is barely visible over his left shoulder. The image has been lightened in order to better see the hair.

—

Copley, John Singleton. Detail from *Portrait of Gulian Verplanck*. Oil on canvas, 1771. Metropolitan Museum of Art (WC/Yorck).

Johann Georg Wille was a notable engraver who worked in France. His bagwig features two structured rolls on the side, with the top hair frizzed, combed back, and rolled under to create about 2" of extra height on top of the head. The height is centered over the back of the top of the head.

—

Ingouf, Pierre-Charles after Pierre Alexandre Wille. Detail from *Jean George Wille*. Engraving on laid paper, 1771. NGA.

The museum's dating seems unlikely, given the height of the French marquis's toupet (top hair). His wig is powdered light grey. The front is brushed back smoothly into a high crescent shape. One buckle is placed above each ear. His queue is tied into a black silk bag, accented with a large bow.

—

Greuze, Jean-Baptiste. Detail from *Portrait of the Marquis de Saint-Paul*. Oil on canvas, c. 1760. Rijksmuseum.

The English painter (age 28-32) wears a very high, foppish wig. The hair appears to be blond and then powdered. His toupet curves up towards the crown of the head, with about 5" of extra height. Three buckles on the sides -- two below, one above -- point diagonally. His queue is long and straight and tied into a black silk bag.

—

Cosway, Richard. Detail from *Self-Portrait*. Ivory, c. 1770-75. MMA. Gift of Charlotte Guilford Muhlhofer, 1962.

Tyng (age 82) was a Massachusetts legislator and former soldier. He wears a physical wig, short and bushy around the ears and back. The top is cut short and standing, with a center part that starts about 1" back behind the front hairline. Note how the all of the hair looks frizzy, and the distinct wigline along the top of the forehead.

—

Copley, John Singleton. Detail from *Eleazer Tyng*. Oil on canvas, 1772. NGA.

This caricature provides an excellent view as to how the cadogan was rolled up on itself and tied. The queue is long and straight, looped up on top of itself, and tied around the middle with a section of hair. On top, the hair is rolled under to create an exaggerated high shape. One buckle is at the ear.

—

Detail from *The Head and Shoulders of Two Fashionable Women...* 1773. Wellcome.

The American painter (age 35) is wearing what is probably an unpowdered queue wig, with unstructured curls at the ears. There is a tiny bit of height on top.

—

West, Benjamin. Detail from *The Artist and His Son Raphael*. Oil on canvas, 1773. YBA.

This British soldier wears his Ramillies queue either twisted, or wrapped from nape to end with a ribbon, then pinned up to the back of the head. On top, he wears a cocked hat.

—

Darly, Matthew. Detail from *Hats*. Etching on laid paper, 1773. YBA.

A Frenchmen at a court ball wears the natural wig, with the queue unbound. The toupet is rolled under, with buckles or curls at the ears. The back is left long and straight from the top of the head. The ends of the long hair are cut in a U shape, with ringlets on the sides.

—

Duclos, Antoine-Jean after Augustin de Saint-Aubin. Details from *Le Bal Paré*. Etching and engraving, 1774. NGA.

This French gentleman wears a bagwig. The front, probably cropped until the crown of the head, is rolled back with about 2" of added height. Three buckles of graduated length are placed at the ear, the smallest on top.

—

Ducreux, Joseph. Detail from *Head of a Gentleman [recto]*. Red, black, and white chalks with stumping on brown paper, 1770/80. NGA.

Stubbs (age 51), an English painter, may wear his own hair (hence the receding hairline), or he may be wearing a half-wig with the front of his own hair worked in. His hair may be naturally white, and/or he may be wearing powder. His queue is tied in a black silk bag, and he has one buckle at each ear.

—

Craft, William H. Detail from *George Stubbs*. Enamel on copper, 1775. YBA.

Nares was a composer and musician (age 60) at the British court. His queue wig has an obvious line around the face. The toupet appears to be straight and brushed back. Three rows of buckles lay below, at, and above each ear. Each row is made up of two buckles, each row wider and longer than the one above it. His queue is tied with a black bow, just visible over his left shoulder.

—

Hoppner, John. Detail from *James Nares*. Graphite, black and red chalk on laid paper, c. 1775. NGA.

The earl (left, age 37) wears his powdered wig high on top. The toupet extends to the top of the head and is rolled under with about 3" of extra height. His queue is in a bow (or bag). Note the powder along his hairline. On the right, Charles Gore, the earl's father-in-law, may be wearing his natural hair, or may be wearing a half-wig. His powdered hair appears grey. It is receding in front, but is still cut short on top, with the back in a queue.

—

Zoffany, Johan Joseph. Details from *The Gore Family with George, 3rd Earl Cowper*. Oil on canvas, c. 1775. YBA.

Franklin (age 69-73) was an important American author, politician, scientist, and inventor. He wears a physical wig with an extra ringlet at the very bottom, which is tied with a ribbon.

—

Wedgwood & Bentley. Detail from *Portrait Plaque Depicting Benjamin Franklin*. Stoneware, black basalt, c. 1775 9. LACMA.

This Englishman wears a grey powdered with an obvious wigline around the face. The front is cut short and rolled under, with two horizontal buckles at the ears.

—

Hone, Nathaniel. Detail from *Benjamin Cole*. Oil on canvas, 1776. YBA.

The French king (age 23) wears a white powdered queue wig, with the front cut short and brushed back. Note the widow's peak at the center front. Two buckles of increasing size are at the ears, and the queue is tied with a wide bow.

—

Duplessis, Joseph Siffrède (workshop of). Detail from *Portrait of Louis XVI, King of France*. Oil on canvas, 1777. Rijksmuseum.

This man is from an English merchant and banking family. He is depicted in a powdered cadogan wig. The front hair is cropped short and brushed back. There is one buckle above the ear. The back queue is looped up on itself and tied into the cadogan knot. Note the powder on the back of his collar.

—

Wheatley, Francis. Detail from *The Oliver and Ward Families*. Oil on canvas, c. 1778. YBA.

The Baron de Breteuil was a prominent French politician. His queue wig provides an excellent example of the V-shaped roll sometimes seen in this era, where the top is cut short and rolled under. Two horizontal buckles are at the ear, and a wide bow ties the queue.

—

Pajou, Augustin. Detail from *Louis Auguste Le Tonnelier de Breteuil, 1730-1807, Bust*. N.D. Kharbine-Tapabor / The Art Archive at Art Resource, NY.

A fashionable American wears a heavily powdered wig. The hair on top is drawn back, probably to the crown of the head. Two buckles lay horizontally on the sides. His queue is long and straight, and is tied low on the back. The ends could be left hanging, or this could be a low cadogan. His wig is heavily powdered (note the powder on the back of his collar).

—

Stuart, Gilbert. Detail from *Man in a Green Coat*. Oil on canvas, c. 1779-85. MMA. Bequest of Mary Stillman Harkness, 1950.

BUSHY STYLES
Fashionable: 1780s - mid-1790s

- Toupet (top and sides):
  - Frizzed
  - Cropped short from hairline to crown of head
  - Either:
    - Brushed back
    - Rolled under
  - Sides either:
    - In buckles
- Longer than top hair, and frizzed
- Rest of hair pulled back into a queue – tied with bow, in bag, braided, ringlets, cadogan, etc.

If the title of this English fashion plate is correct (it could be a description written by the museum), this man wears a half-wig, with his own hair cut short in front and styled into buckles at the ear. His (presumably false) queue appears to be untied.

—

Delegal, James. Detail from *Head and Shoulders of a Man in Profile to the Left Wearing Long Hair-Pieces Attached to the Back of his Natural Hair*. Engraving, n.d. Wellcome.

The French artist (age 30) depicts himself in a wig with high top and two rolls on the sides. His wig appears to be powdered.

—

Hoin, Claude. Detail from *Self-Portrait*. Red and black chalks, and pastel with stumping on gray-brown laid paper, c. 1780. NGA.

Delaunay was a famous French goldsmith. His bagwig features a high top, brushed back to the crown of the head and then rolled under. Three buckles are on the sides: the lowest, at the ear, is the longest.

—

Huot, François after Augustin de Saint-Aubin. Detail from *Nicolas Delaunay*. Etching and engraving, 1780. NGA.

The heir to the British throne wears a frizzled, powdered wig. The top is short and brushed back. The sides are bushier than previously, with two buckles at the ears. The lower buckle is longer and wider than the higher.

—

Dupont, Gainsborough. Detail from *George IV as Prince of Wales*. Oil on canvas, 1781. NGA.

Jean-Baptiste Cardon was a French composer. His bagwig is cropped on top and brushed back past the crown of the head. It appears that there are two buckles at the sides of the head, with a flat section between them.

The famous English painter wears a powdered (note the powder on his collar) wig in a dark grey color. The hair is frizzy and cropped short on top. There are at least two buckles above the ears, and probably a queue hidden in back.

Cochin II, Charles-Nicolas. Detail from *J.B. Cardon*. Black chalk, 1782. NGA.

Stuart, Gilbert. Detail from *Sir Joshua Reynolds*. Oil on canvas, 1784. NGA.

The French sculptor shows himself wearing a queue wig. The hair is cut short on top, and slightly longer at the sides, where it ends in a horizontal buckle at each ear. The queue is long and wavy, tied at the nape of the neck with a ribbon.

Roland, Philippe Laurent. Detail from *Self Portrait*. Marble, c. 1785. MMA. Purchase, The Annenberg Foundation Gift, in honor of Mrs. Charles Wrightsman, 1998.

The duke (age 60) was a high-ranking French royal. His wig is cropped short on top and brushed back. Two rows of shorter buckles are at the ears, the lower row larger than the higher. A bow peeks out from the right side of the neck, indicating a queue.

Smallwood was a Maryland military officer and governor. His powdered hair or wig is cut short on top and brushed back. There are no buckles at the sides, although the overall silhouette is slightly wider at the ears. His queue is tied low with a black bow.

Sèvres Manufactory/ Josse-François-Joseph LeRiche. Detail from *Portrait Bust of Monseigneur le duc d'Orléans*. Hard-paste biscuit porcelain, c. 1785. Getty.

Pine, Robert Edge. Detail from *General William Smallwood*. Oil on canvas, 1785/8. NGA.

Men's Styles: Year-by-Year

Biré (age 58) was a high ranking French government official. He may be wearing his own hair (hence the receding hairline), or may have worked his own hair into the front of his wig or half-wig. The top of his hair is cropped and brushed back to the crown of the head. He has one buckle at each ear. The queue is long and straight, tied with a ribbon and left hanging.

—

Houdon, Jean-Antoine. Details from *Bust of Marie-Sébastien-Charles-François Fontaine de Biré*. Marble, 1785. Getty (artwork in the public domain; top image provided courtesy of the museum, bottom is a personal photograph by author).

Dr. Wright (age 55-59) was an English physician and the brother of the artist. He wears a powdered, light grey physical wig with an obvious wig line around the face. The hair is cropped short on top and around the temples, and worn longer and bushier from the ears down.

—

Wright, Joseph of Derby. Detail from *Dr. Richard Wright*. Oil on canvas, 1785-9. YBA.

Cagliostro (age 43) was a famous occultist, originally Italian but who lived in France. His hair (or possibly a half wig, with his natural hair combed into the front) has one long buckle above the ears. His own hairline is receding, particularly on top. His queue is tied with a large bow.

—

Houdon, Jean-Antoine. Detail from *Giuseppe Balsamo, Comte di Cagliostro*. Marble, 1786. NGA (artwork in the public domain, photograph provided courtesy Flickr user snowgray).

A British gentleman wears a powdered wig (or perhaps his own hair). The top is cut short and brushed back, while the sides are longer and bushy. Note the powder on his collar. The queue is long and straight.

—

Devis, Arthur William. Detail from *Mr. and Mrs. Fraser*. Oil on canvas, 1785-90. YBA.

The commander-in-chief of the revolutionary American forces was soon to be the first President of the United States. He was known for not wearing a wig. Here his natural hair is cropped short and brushed back on top. The hair below the temples is longer than the top hair, and echoes the silhouette of a buckled wig (without the buckles). There is probably a queue in back.

—

Houdon, Jean-Antoine. Detail from *Portrait of George Washington*. Marble, c. 1786. LACMA.

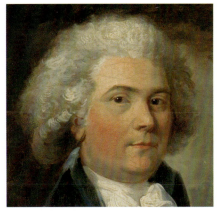  

This Englishman wears a very frizzy powdered wig (or his own hair). Note the powder along the hairline and on the collar. The top and sides are bushy, with a great deal of width at the sides, ending in one low buckle. There is probably a queue in back.

—

Unknown artist, 18th century, British. Detail from *Walter Smith*. Oil on canvas, 1787. YBA.

This man's hair or wig appears to be lightly powdered into a matte blonde color. It is cut short on top and brushed back. The sides are bushy, with one buckle. His sideburns are longer than previously seen.

—

Romney, George. Detail from *Portrait of Richard Palmer*. Oil on canvas, 1787. LACMA.

Joubert was an government official and patron of the arts in Montpellier, France. In his wedding portrait, he wears his wig or hair cropped short and curly on top and sides, with curly horizontal buckles at the ears. The hair is powdered to a blondish grey.

—

Fabre, François-Xavier. Detail from *Portrait of Laurent-Nicolas de Joubert*. Oil on canvas, 1787. Getty.

The British prime minister (age 28-30) wears his wig or hair cut short and choppy, with the hair standing up at the top and sides. The sides are frizzy, ending in a buckle at the bottom of the ear. The hair is a creamy grey color.

—

Studio of Thomas Gainsborough. Detail from *William Pitt*. Oil on canvas, 1787-9. YBA.

Boardman was a Connecticut senator and property owner. His powdered hair or wig is cropped short on top. The sides are slightly longer. The queue is long and tied low on the back, in what appears to be a cadogan knot.

—

Earl, Ralph. Detail from *Elijah Boardman*. Oil on canvas, 1789. MMA. Bequest of Susan W. Tyler, 1979.

This English gentleman wears what could be his own hair. It is powdered, cropped short and curly on top and at the sides, and tied up in a cadogan at the back.

—

Morland, George. Detail from *The Anglers' Repast*. Oil on canvas, 1789. YBA.

"NATURAL" STYLES
Fashionable: 1790s

Several distinct styles:
- Cropped short on top, slightly longer and choppy around ears and back of head *
- Layered, short on top and longer underneath; length to chin or top of shoulders *
- Overall short, but longer layers on top; tousled and brushed forward
- Short all over

* Could be worn with or without a long queue

A lower class Englishman wears his natural hair unpowdered and cropped short. The hair is brushed forward, creating a short fringe on the forehead.

—

Wheatley, Francis. Detail from *The Mistletoe Bough*. Oil on canvas, c. 1790. YBA.

Anderson was a military officer stationed in India, although this portrait was painted after his return to Britain. His powdered hair or wig is cropped short on top, and is very bushy at the sides. A queue is likely hidden in back.

—

Raeburn, Sir Henry. Detail from *David Anderson*. Oil on canvas, 1790. NGA.

A French patriot wears a short knotted wig. The horizontal rows of curls are separated into two sections in back, with a definite parting in between.

—

Morret, Jean-Baptiste after Jacques-François-Joseph Swebach-Desfontaines. Details from *Caffée des Patriotes – A Patriot's Coffee House*. Etching and wash manner, printed in blue, red, yellow, and black inks, 1792. NGA.

The American captain wears his hair cropped very short on top. The sides are slightly longer, and curl over his ears in suggestion of a buckle. His long queue is tied with a black ribbon at the base of the neck.

—

The Denison Limner (Probably Joseph Steward). Detail from *Captain Elisha Denison*. Oil on canvas, c. 1790. NGA.

This French gentleman wears a queue wig (note the wig line around the face, particularly at the temples). The top is waved and brushed back. There is one buckle at the ears. His wavy queue can be seen on his left shoulder.

Pajou, Augustin. Detail from *Portrait of a Man*. Plaster on painted wood socle and plinth, 1791. LACMA.

A foppish Frenchman wears a very frizzy and bushy wig, without any visible buckles. His Ramillies queue is bound with a ribbon, which is tied into a bow at the top.

Debucourt, Philibert-Louis. Detail from *La Promenade Publique*. Etching and wash manner, printed in blue, carmine, dark pink, yellow, and black inks, 1792. NGA.

Bailly (in his 60s) was an astronomer, mathematician, and future mayor of Paris. His natural wig is cut short on top, with three side buckles curving up towards the back of his head, and a fourth lower behind the ear. His queue is long and straight and left unbound.

Claessens, Lambertus Antonius after Boizot. Detail from *Portret van de Astronoom Jean Sylvain Bailly*. Engraving, 1792. Rijksmuseum.

Mirabeau (age 42), a French count, was a prominent politician in the early years of the French Revolution. This image is from the year after his death. His powdered wig or hair is cropped short and stands bushily across the top and sides, ending with one buckle at the ears. There is probably a queue in back.

Alix, Pierre Michel. Detail from *Portret van Honoré Gabriel Mirabeau*. Aquatint, printed in color, on paper, 1792. YBA.

A British naval officer wears his hair or wig cropped short on top and brushed back, longer at the sides, with possibly a queue in back. The hair is powdered to a medium grey (note the powder along his hairline).

Lawrence, Sir Thomas. Detail from *Admiral John Markham*. Oil on canvas, c. 1793. YBA.

Gregory was appointed High Sheriff of Nottinghamshire in 1793. His white hair or wig is straight and bushy on top and sides, with one buckle at each ear. The queue is tied with a black bow. He is wearing so much powder that it has rubbed onto his collar, shoulder, and the interior of his hat -- something he is very purposefully showing off.

Russell, John. Detail from *Portrait of George de Ligne Gregory*. Pastel on paper, laid on canvas, 1793. Getty.

Men's Styles: Year-by-Year 89

Yates was a New York merchant. His powdered hair or wig is cropped short on top and brushed back, long and shaggy at the sides, probably with a queue in back. Note the powder along his hairline.

The leader of the Jacobins in Lyons, France wears what is likely his natural hair, cropped very short on top, and longer and wavy at the sides. His queue is straight and tied just below the nape of the neck.

Louis-Michel le Peletier was a French marquis and politician. His powdered wig (note the powder on his shoulder) is cut short on top, and left long and bushy at the sides.

—

Stuart, Gilbert. Detail from *Lawrence Reid Yates*. Oil on canvas, 1793/4. NGA.

Jayet, Clément. Detail from *Joseph Chalier (1747-1793)*. Terracotta, 1793-4. Rijksmuseum.

Alix, Pierre-Michel after Jean-François Garnerey. Detail from *Michel Lepelletier*. Etching and wash manner, printed in blue, red, yellow, and black inks, 1794. NGA.

Van Rensselaer was a wealthy landowner and soon to be Lieutenant Governor of New York. His powdered hair or wig is cropped short on top and brushed back, longer at the sides, with the bow from his queue just visible over his left shoulder. Note the powder on his collar.

Anthony was a prosperous Philadelphia merchant. He wears what is likely his own hair, unpowdered and naturally greying. His hair is cropped short on top and falls naturally, with a slightly longer length, left curly, at the sides. There may be a queue hidden in back.

Symmons was an English poet and priest. His powdered hair or wig is cropped short on top, brushed back, and longer at the sides; there may be a queue hidden in back. Note the powder on his collar.

—

Stuart, Gilbert. Detail from *Stephen Van Rensselaer III*. Oil on canvas, 1793/5. NGA.

Stuart, Gilbert. Detail from *Captain Joseph Anthony*. Oil on canvas, 1794. NGA.

Beechey, William. Detail from *Reverend Dr. Charles Symmons*. Oil on canvas, 1794. YBA.

The first American president wears his hair cropped short on top, longer at the sides, with the bow from his queue visible on his right shoulder. Note the powder along his hairline and on the back side of his collar.

This Frenchman's powdered hair is worn short and standing on top and sides, with a section of slightly wavier hair just above each horizontal buckle. His queue is tied with a black ribbon. Powder is visible on the back of his collar.

Rose was a Liverpool merchant. He wears what appears to be an unpowdered wig, cropped short on top and allowed to fall naturally, with a very small buckle at the ears. There may be a queue in back.

Stuart, Gilbert. Detail from *George Washington (Vaughan portrait)*. Oil on canvas, 1795. NGA.

Vincent, François André. Detail from *Portrait of a Man*. Oil on canvas, c. 1795. Rijksmuseum.

Marshall, Benjamin. Detail from *Joshua Rose of Liverpool*. Oil on paper laid to canvas, c. 1795. YBA.

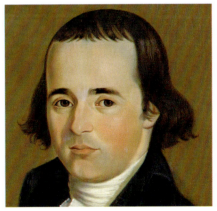

Benjamin was an organist and civic leader in Connecticut. His unpowdered hair or wig is cropped short on top and falls naturally, with much more length on the sides.

Lysons (age 36) was a British engraver and antiquary. What is likely his own hair is cropped short all over, and probably powdered given his age.

A European man wears what will become the fashion of the early 1800s: short, tousled hair that is brushed forward into the face.

Jennys, William. Detail from *Asa Benjamin*. Oil on canvas, 1795. NGA.

Lawrence, Sir Thomas. Detail from *Samuel Lysons*. Oil on canvas, 1799. YBA.

Detail from *Portrait of a Young Man in Profile*. Pastel on laid paper, c. 1800. NGA.

Part II: Techniques

Introduction

Remember that hairstyling, modern or historical, is a learned art and craft. Try not to become frustrated if your initial efforts are less perfect than you had hoped. You *will* get better with practice!

It is always a good idea to practice any hairstyle ahead of time. Do not wait until the day of the event or production to try the hairstyle. Your first attempt will teach you a lot, and later tries are guaranteed to be an improvement. You will also get a clearer idea about how much time you need to block out for hairstyling. Remember that simply setting a whole head of hair into rollers can take *at least* thirty minutes.

When it comes to wig styling, you have the advantage of being able to create the style beforehand. Keep in mind that your first try may leave something to be desired. Often, it is my second attempt that becomes the final version. This is true even today, no matter how many wigs I have created.

There are numerous techniques that are applicable when creating eighteenth-century hairstyles, whether you are using natural hair, integrating false hair, or styling a wig. This book cannot possibly teach you everything there is to know about hair and wig styling; instead, I have chosen those techniques that I believe are most useful for eighteenth-century styles. For those interested in learning even more about hairstyling and wig-making/styling, see the sources on page 294. If the instructions refer to any techniques with which you are not familiar (for example, the various methods of curling, teasing, or braiding), consult a standard hairstyling book or one of the ever-growing video tutorials available for free on YouTube (www.youtube.com).

Techniques & Historical Authenticity

The techniques demonstrated in this book rely on modern products and tools, but they have their basis in history. Eighteenth-century people wore wigs and false hairpieces, made of both human and non-human hair. They used curling irons, curlers, and heat to curl hair. They used pomade and pins to hold styles. Whole industries existed to take what was natural – the hair growing out of one's head – and change it (and, frequently, falsify it). Thus, **nearly all of the techniques and approaches demonstrated in this book can be traced back to historical precedent**. If you would like to learn more about historically accurate eighteenth-century techniques for styling hair and wigs, consult the sources beginning on page 294.

Wig or Your Own Hair?

There are equal advantages and disadvantages to wearing natural hair, false hair, or a wig. The choice you make is up to you, and I recommend experimenting with different options to decide what works best for your needs.

Wearing Your Own Hair

PRO: Looks most natural to modern eyes

PRO: Many find it most comfortable

PRO: Depending on era, gender, geography, and class, it may be the *most* historically accurate option

CON: Requires a good deal of preparation and styling on the day of wear

CON: Can be damaging to your hair

CON: Some eighteenth-century styles require specific cuts

CON: Some eighteenth-century styles are very difficult to create using your own natural hair

CON: Depending on era, gender, geography, and class, it may be the *least* historically accurate option

Wearing a Wig

PRO: Can style a wig ahead of time

PRO: Can re-wear a styled wig numerous times

PRO: Cutting a wig is low commitment

PRO: Can create effects difficult to do with only your own hair

PRO: Depending on era, gender, geography, and class, it may be the *most* historically accurate option

CON: Can look unnatural to modern eyes

CON: Can be uncomfortable

CON: Depending on era, gender, geography, and class, it may be the *least* historically accurate option

Integrating False Hair into Your Own Hair

PRO: Can preserve a natural look for modern eyes

PRO: Can augment the amount of hair you naturally have

PRO: Can style hairpieces ahead of time

PRO: Can re-wear a styled hairpiece numerous times

PRO: Can create effects difficult to do with only your own hair

PRO: Depending on era, gender, geography, and class, it may be the *most* historically accurate option

CON: Requires a good deal of preparation and styling on the day of wear

CON: Can be damaging to your own hair

CON: Depending on era, gender, geography, and class, it may be the *least* historically accurate option

Supplies

STYLING PRODUCTS

There are a number of different styling products you can use for hairstyling: gel, mousse, pomade, hairspray, and more. When it comes to historical hairdressing, you generally need two products:

Mousse, **gel**, or **setting lotion**: apply a small amount throughout the hair before styling to create texture.

Hairspray: extra firm hold, **aerosol** hairspray is a must for both hair and wig styling! There are a number of relatively new hairsprays that give an incredibly firm, lacquered hold, which is exactly what you will need. Two brands in the United States that make this kind of hairspray are Got2Be and Bed Head. Although less strong, Aquanet and Suave have also served me well.

In the eighteenth century, hairstyling was accomplished with pomade. You can certainly do the same today, but I recommend hairspray instead. Although it has different properties, hairspray works so well to set hair that I believe it is worth the trade off.

BOBBY PINS

Bobby pins come in many different colors.

Along with strong hairspray, **bobby pins are what will hold your style together.** You can never have too many on hand – I generally try to have one package of 60 on hand for a hairstyle, and two packages of 60 (120 total) for a wig.

I have had the best experiences with standard sized/shaped bobby pins, but I know others who love the jumbo size pins, the U-shaped hair pins, or the new spiral pins. You should use what works well for you, but if you are not sure where to start, a couple of packages of standard bobby pins should do the trick.

Whenever possible, hide bobby pins inside of the hair. Work them into *and* underneath hair so that they show as little as possible. If they have to show, consider covering them with another piece of hair, a ribbon, or other hair accessory. Either way, use bobby pins in a color that coordinates with your hair color: white, silver, gold, blonde, bronze, light or dark brown, or black. In my experience, the matte blonde-colored pins are less obvious than the shiny gold pins.

The key technique that will stabilize your hairstyles is to make **Xes with your bobby pins**. Crossing the pins allows them to grab on to each other, and will work wonders for securing your hair.

Xed bobby pins for stability.

Working with Human Hair

In this section, I will be discussing styling techniques for the hair that grows out of your (or someone else's) own head. For brevity, I will speak as though you are styling your own hair, although all of these same techniques apply equally if you are styling a model or actor's hair.

Most people find it easier to create the complex styles worn in the eighteenth century if their hair is unwashed on the day of styling. Squeaky clean hair has less "grab" and is more difficult to style.

CURLING

There are numerous methods of curling human hair, including curling irons, rag curls, pin curls, hot rollers, foam curlers, and more. You may have been curling your hair for years, but it is worthwhile to experiment to see which methods give you the best curls for different styles. Everyone's hair reacts differently to different methods of curling, but in general, a **wet set** (a curl that is set while the hair is wet, and then allowed to dry) **will create the strongest curl,** while a **heat set** (a curl that is set while the hair is dry, using heat to hold the curl) **will not last as long**.

Remember that curlers come in different sizes. I recommend using smaller sizes (3/8" to 1" diameter) for creating curly texture before styling. Ringlets are best created with wider irons (3/4" to 1.5", depending on desired width). For volume without curl, use a very wide curling iron (2").

Heat-Set Curling Options

- **Curling iron**: usually the quickest to lose its curl, and so only recommended for styles that need slight volume or wave, but not real curl.
- **Hot rollers**: creates a relatively strong curl, particularly if the curler is allowed to fully cool before removal, and the hair is then re-curled and pinned to the head to allow further cooling. Works well for styles that need all but the strongest, tightest curl, and for creating ringlets that will hold for many hours.
- **Papillote curls**: essentially, pincurls set with a flat iron. For instructions, see the "Papillote Curls" video listed on page 294.

Wet-Set Curling Options

- **Pincurls**: creates a strong, tight curl that will last for many hours. See the *Vintage Hairstyling* book (page 294) for excellent, detailed instructions.
- **Rag curls**: creates a strong, tight curl that will last for many hours.
- **Foam rollers**: creates a strong, tight curl that will last for many hours.

Working with False Hair & Wigs

Both false hair add-ons and full wigs are available in human and synthetic hair. My experience with human hair is that it does not seem to last much longer than synthetic, so I suggest avoiding the cost. I also like that I can permanently change the texture of synthetic hair.

Human hair should be treated like the hair on your own head. **Synthetic hair,** on the other hand, is made of plastic, and so **should not be treated with heat** unless you are doing something very specific that you know will work. There are a few techniques discussed below that carefully use heat to change synthetic hair. Beyond these, I recommend avoiding heat altogether.

Note that wig companies are now selling "heat safe" synthetic hair, which falls somewhere between the properties of synthetic and human hair. I have successfully used the heat methods discussed in the following pages to curl heat-safe synthetic wigs. Nonetheless, I strongly recommend testing any "heat safe" synthetic hair before you fully commit to styling the wig or hairpiece.

PURCHASING FALSE HAIR & RATS

False hair and wigs can be purchased both online and in brick-and-mortar beauty and wig stores. For suggested stores, see the resources on page 290.

In general, **any long wig without bangs will work well** as a base for eighteenth-century styles. Try to find a wig with a center part (or without a strong part), as side parts can be slightly more difficult to hide. Often (but not always) the most effective wigs are long all the way around, but long layers can be accommodated (and sometimes even help, depending on the style). Avoid wigs with short layers, unless your final style calls for shorter hair on top.

You can buy wigs that are straight, wavy, or curly. However, you can also change this texture yourself (see page 103-5). It is far easier and more effective to wave or curl a straight wig, than to straighten a wavy or curly wig.

Different Types of Wigs

Hard Front

A "hard front" wig is not a term you will hear very often when you are buying wigs online or in person, but it is used in the theater to distinguish from a "lace front" (see the next page). A hard front wig is one where the **front hairline consists of the same rows of wefts that are used to cover the rest of the wig**. Usually, a few wefts of hair are sewn to the underside of the cap along the front hairline, then pulled up and around the hairline to mask the edge. It is the style of wig that looks most artificial.

An example of a hard front wig.

Lace Front

A "lace front" wig is an attempt to copy a natural hairline. The top portion of the wig, including the hairline, will consist of a **netted base with individual hairs tied** ("ventilated") **onto it**. The lace extends forward of the wig's hairline, and is intended to be glued to your forehead and then covered with makeup. In my experience, this works well for theater (where the wig-wearer will be viewed from a distance) or photography (where retouching can hide any flaws). For up-close viewing, I recommend **cutting the lace away** at the edge of the wig hairline. Also, be aware that the lace mesh itself can come in different colors, which is not always easy to tell when looking at a picture of a wig online. A dark mesh can be very obvious on light skin, and vice versa.

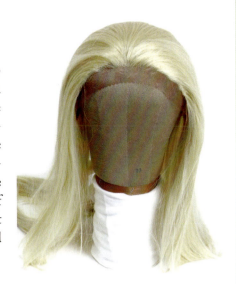

An example of a lace front wig.

Colors

False hair (human and synthetic) comes in a range of **coded colors**. Most companies use a number that is relatively consistent across brands (for example, 1 represents "jet black," no matter which brand you purchase), although you will sometimes find some slight color variation amongst brands. Many wigs and hair pieces will have only one color code. Those with multiple color codes represent mixes of colors (for example, 27/613 is light auburn [27] streaked with pale blonde [613]). These color codes will sometimes include letters; the most common are F (frosted, mostly one color with a small mix of another) and H or HL (highlights). Be aware that some mixes of color do not look natural, such as "piano blend" (chunky, side-by-side streaks of color), "tipped color" (dark base with a lighter color on the ends of the hair), and "two tone" (top half in a lighter color, bottom half in a darker color). Always consult the manufacturer's color chart to be sure that you understand their colors and color mixes.

Knowing your color number will enable you to purchase false hair and wigs online, without fear that the false hair will not match your own. In general, if you are a 27 in one brand, you will be a 27 in another. Manufacturers make hair color charts that you can view online. However, I do not recommend this method, as computer monitors can display colors differently, and it can be difficult to compare your own hair to photos. Instead, use the **color rings made by manufacturers**. These are actual swatches of hair, coded by color number, and strung on a ring. You can either purchase one online (some wig stores will allow you to return them for a refund), or go into a brick-and-mortar wig shop and ask to consult a color ring for free. Remember to compare your hair to the color swatches in natural light – ask if you can take a hand mirror over by the window, if necessary.

Many natural hair colors are actually a mix of different colored strands. Experiment with some of the different color blends mentioned above to see if you can find one that works well with your hair color. However, if you cannot find a good match, I recommend using the solid color that best matches your hair. The visual sources of the eighteenth century probably flatter the wearers, making color matches more precise than they really were in real life. Photography from the Victorian and Edwardian eras, when women frequently wore false hair add-ons, often show visible color and texture differences between the wearer's natural and false hair (obvious even when looking at black and white or sepia photographs). One of the benefits of the eighteenth-century trend for hair powder was the ability to hide the natural hair color. This is an added incentive to wear it in our era.

A typical color ring.

Buying False Hair Add-Ons

There are numerous kinds of false hair add-ons, from loose hair to styled pieces, which you can purchase.

"Braiding" Hair

Braiding hair is a package of very long, **loose strands of hair**, intended to be braided into one's natural hair as numerous small braids. This hair can be used to create all kinds of hair pieces, but is best for long braids and buckles (rolls).

Braiding hair.

"Weaving Hair"

Weaving hair is **hair that has been woven into a long seam at the top** (a "weft"), intended to be clipped, glued, or sewn into one's natural hair as extensions, or sewn to a wig. This hair is best for filling out wigs and making buckles (rolls), or any hairpiece where you would like the hair to be firmly attached on one end (like a ponytail).

Pre-Made Hairpieces

There are many pre-made hairpieces that are useful for eighteenth-century styles. Ponytails can be used to augment wigs and natural hairstyles, braided into long braids, or rolled into buns. Jaw-clip and banana-clip styles can have the clip removed, and then seam ripped to obtain individual wefts of hair – a useful trick, as these pieces are frequently available at mainstream beauty shops.

Weaving hair.

GENERAL FALSE HAIR/WIG CARE

Combing

Whenever you comb a wig or length of false hair, treat it gently. The more hair you break off, the thinner the piece will be – and false hair does not grow back. Keep these tips in mind:

- Use a wide-toothed comb, unless you are using a technique that requires something different.
- Hold the hair near the roots with one hand, while using the other hand to comb. This will keep the tension away from the root of the hair, and decrease breakage.
- Comb the ends first, then work your way up the length of the hair in sections.

Washing

Styled wigs have a lifetime. Although you can touch up a styled wig or hairpiece with a comb and hairspray, at some point, you will probably want to wash it out and restyle it. To do so, wash the wig or hairpiece in cold or lukewarm water with a gentle shampoo. Rinse out the shampoo, then let the wig dry. Do not comb out the wig while the hair is wet – this will lead to more breakage than necessary! Once dry, use a spray conditioner (either for synthetic or human hair, as appropriate) to help detangle as you comb it out with a wide-toothed comb. If this combing process removes more curl than you would like, you can re-wet the wig/piece, scrunch it, and let it dry in order to bring back the curl.

Hairspray Build-Up

The more you wear a wig or hairpiece, the more likely you are to apply yet more hairspray. At some point, the hairspray will build up and will stop having much effect. You can spray a wig or hairspray with rubbing alcohol, which will remove some of the hairspray. Eventually, you will have to wash out the wig/hairpiece and restyle it.

Sewing

Sewing a weft of hair, with the thread traced in red for visibility.

Periodically, the styling instructions in this book will tell you to sew a hairpiece or wig. When doing so, I recommend:

- Use a **thread** in a color that matches with the hair.
- To **start and stop** a seam, take three back stitches on top of each other. Leave a tail of about 1-3" hanging. This thread will merge with the hair when you style it.
- When sewing on a blocked wig, use a **curved needle**. This will allow you to sew the wig without removing it from the block.

STYLING FALSE HAIR

In this section, I will discuss techniques for making your own weaving hair and altering the texture of synthetic hair. I will also demonstrate how to make some basic hairpieces that will be used in the finished styles later in this book.

Making Your Own Weaving Hair

Loose braiding hair comes in many more colors than weaving hair. For example, I have yet to find a source for synthetic weaving hair in any of the grey colors. If you cannot find weaving hair in the color that you need, you can make your own wefts using a sewing machine.

These instructions will make a weft with two times the thickness of the hair, which will be folded in half. Alternately, you can sew the net about 2" from the cut edge of the hair. When you fold the net in half, you will have a shorter layer and a much longer layer. Keep this shorter layer to the inside of your final style, so that it does not show.

To Make Your Own Wefts

Supplies: loose braiding hair, net fabric in coordinating color, thread in a coordinating color, scissors, sewing machine.

1 Cut a strip of netting, about 2" wide and as long as you would like the piece to be.

2 Lay the braiding hair on top of the netting (outlined here in black), with the center of the hair directly on top of the center of the width of the net.

3 Using your narrowest stitch and strongest tension, sew directly down the middle of the hair and net. Keep the braiding hair together in bulk, and feed small amounts under the presser foot as you go. Try to feed the hair evenly.

Sew another row of stitches to the left of the first row, about the width of your presser foot apart. Do the same on the other side (3 rows total).

4 Fold the hair in half, using the center stitching row to mark the fold, with the netting on the outside. Straight pin the hair-and-net in half.

5 Using a zig-zag stitch, sew the folded-over hair-and-net, aligning the stitches just inside of the outer stitching line.

6 Trim the netting just below the outermost stitching line.

Curling Synthetic Hair

Wigs and hair can be purchased with curly, wavy, or straight hair, but there are times you may wish to change the texture of the hair. There are two methods for curling synthetic hair – both involve heat, so these steps must be followed very carefully to avoid melting the hair and ruining it!

Curling Method #1: Steam

This works best for creating **light curls or waves**:

I strongly recommend wearing gloves, so that you don't accidentally give yourself a steam burn!

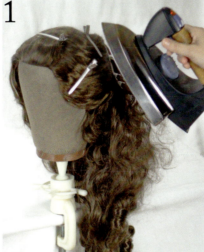

Left: the unmodified hair.

1 Set the hair in waves, pincurls, or around a roll form.

2 Steam each area of the hair for 15 seconds, using either a steamer or the steam function on an iron (if you use an iron, be VERY careful not to touch the hair with the iron, or you will have melted plastic on your iron!).

3 Remove the clips from one wave or curl to test how well the curl has set. If necessary, repeat the steaming process.

4 Allow the wig to dry.

> *Full confession: As you can see, I use my iron to steam hair, and yes, sometimes I will end up with a few strands of melted hair on my iron. I have found that if I apply the heated iron to a scrap of cloth, I can wipe off most of the melted plastic. If you wait for the iron to cool, you can also clean the iron with some household cleaner and a rag.*

Techniques 103

Curling Method #2: Boiling Water

This works best for creating **strong curls**:

I strongly recommend wearing gloves, so that you don't accidentally give yourself a steam burn!

1 Set the wig in curls using foam rollers.

2 Boil a pot of water. When the water achieves a boil, turn off the burner.

3a If you are setting the entire wig into curls, grab the wig with metal tongs and **immerse it into the water** for *literally 1-2 seconds* (in and out). Any longer and you will ruin the hair.

3b If you are setting only a portion of the wig, grasp the wig with metal tongs in such a way that you have separated the curled hair from the not-to-be-curled. Hold the wig over the sink, and **pour the hot water over the curled section**, making sure that you wet each curl.

4 Place the wig somewhere to drain (in the bathtub or sink, or on a dish dryer or towel).

5 When the hot water has cooled, remove the curlers.

6 Allow the wig to dry.

Straightening Synthetic Hair

It is possible to turn curly or wavy synthetic hair relatively straight, although it will never be as straight as if you had purchased a straight wig/hair.

To Straighten Synthetic Hair

I strongly recommend wearing gloves, so that you don't accidentally give yourself a steam burn!

1 Firmly attach the hair on one end. If you are working on a wig, attach it to a mounted wig block. If you are working with a hairpiece, find a way to attach it to a sturdy object.

Part the hair into a one inch thick section. Comb it smooth.

2 Steam each area of the hair for 15 seconds, using either a steamer or the steam function on an iron (if you use an iron, be VERY careful not to touch the hair with the iron, or you will have melted plastic on your iron!). **At the same time**, pull firmly on the ends of the hair. Repeat as necessary.

3 Allow the hair to dry.

Making Basic Hairpieces

Ponytails, Braids, Twists, and Ringlets

Braids and twists are frequently seen on the backs of women's coiffures. Ponytails are useful as men's queues, women's chignons, ringlets, or anywhere a length of hair needs adding.

  A braid can be made from either loose braiding hair or a ponytail piece. If using a ponytail piece, ask someone to hold the fixed end of the piece, or find a way to attach it to a sturdy object. Section the hair into three pieces, braiding until the end. Secure the ends with a small rubber band (which can be covered with a ribbon, or strand of hair, if it will show). A ponytail is best made from weaving hair, while a twist is best made from hair or wig hair, or a secured ponytail.

  A set of curls or ringlets can be made using a round or flat ponytail, either pre-made or made as in the following instructions. Set the hair in curls on foam rollers, and follow the instructions in the "Curling" section (pages 103-4). If you want to create shorter ringlets, you may want to cut the hair to the proper length after curling, as it can be difficult to judge just how much length you will lose in the curling process.

A set of ringlets.

To Make a Ponytail

The best way to make a ponytail is to use weaving hair, so that you have a firm end. It is too easy to pull loose braiding hair out of a rubber band.

1a For a narrow end, curl the weft of hair into a spiral. Take a needle and thread and whip-stitch this spiral together. It is easiest to do this if you stitch each layer together as you wrap the wefts.

1b For a flat, wide end, fold the weft into flat sections, as wide as you would like the top of the ponytail. Take a needle and thread and whip-stitch these flat folds together.

To Make a Braid From Loose Hair

1 The hair will come prepackaged with a rubber band around the middle of the hair. **Do not remove this rubber band**. Remove the rubber bands from the ends only.

2 Braid one end of the hair, from the middle to the end. Secure the ends with a small hairband.

3 Remove the middle-of-the-hair rubber band by carefully cutting it.

4 Braid the other side of the braid, taking care to keep the hair in the same three sections and following the pattern set by the first half. It is easiest to do this if you turn the braid over before braiding the second half. Again, secure the ends with a small hairband.

To Twist Hair

1 Separate the hair into two sections.

2 Twist both sections in the same direction (i.e. both right, or both left)

3 Twist the two around each other. Secure the end(s) with rubber bands.

Buns

A bun is best made by attaching a ponytail to the head, then wrapping that hair around a donut-shaped rat. See the Adelaide style, steps 8-9 (page 137), for a demonstration.

A braided bun is easy to make by rolling a long braid into a spiral. If you make the piece dome-shaped, it will be easier to cover your own hair. Use bobby pins to hold the bun together, and make sure the ends are hidden on the inside.

Both styles look much better if covered with a hairnet.

Left: a braided bun from the outside. Contrasting bobby pins were used for visibility. A hairnet has been looped over the bun.

Right: the underside of the braided bun. Contrasting bobby pins were used for visibility. The excess hairnet has been twisted up and pinned to the underside.

Buckles (Rolls)

There are three primary methods to make the structured rolls that are a feature of many eighteenth-century hairstyles. The key element to all of them is **tension** – you need to keep the whole width of the hair section in even tension as you roll it. The best way to ensure this is to space out the ends of the hair as wide as you will want the finished roll. This keeps the outer hair from being longer than the center (which will make it loosen as you roll up).

Left: if you start with narrower ends than your desired finished roll...

Right: ...the hair on the outer edges will loosen as you roll up.

*Left: **if you start with ends about as wide as the finished length of the roll...***

*Right: **...the tension will stay constant across the hair as you roll up, and the finished buckle will look nicer.***

Forms

You will need to choose an item to become the "form" around which you roll the hair. This will make it easier to roll the hair, and also keep the diameter of the buckle consistent. A roll form can be made from many household items – I have used broom handles, the handle of a wooden spoon, toiletry bottles, etc. The key factor is that your form have **absolutely no taper** – it must be a consistent, rounded shape all the way across. If there is *any* taper, the roll will tighten as you try to pull it off, meaning you either will not be able to remove the buckle from the form, or your buckle will get smaller as you remove the form.

PVC piping used for roll forms.

My favorite roll forms are made from PVC piping. These are easily available (you can purchase them at any hardware store), come in a number of different dimensions, cost very little, and provide you with a perfect shape around which to roll hair. You will see in the finished styles that I also use other household objects as forms, including chopsticks, pens, and lip balm containers.

Hair Thickness

On the one hand, you need enough hair to create a full buckle with no unsightly holes, and enough to go around the roll form at least twice. Usually, this means about 1/2" thickness of hair times the width of your desired final roll. You can, of course, use a larger thickness of hair – just keep in mind that the roll form will only determine the inner diameter of the buckle. If you use more hair, you will bulk up the roll on the outside.

Hair Length

Note the differences in inner and outer diameter. The inner diameter is determined by the roll form; the outer diameter is determined by how many times the hair wraps around the form.

The more times you go around the roll form, the thicker the buckle will get on the outside. If you roll up a buckle and find that it is thicker than you would like, you may wish to cut some of the length of the hair. This will mean fewer rotations around the roll form, and therefore a narrower buckle in terms of outer diameter.

Techniques 109

Buckle Method #1: Head or Wig Hair

This method is for use when you are using the hair growing from someone's head, or the hair of a wig.

Supplies: wig or head of hair, hairspray, roll form (see page 109), comb, bobby pins

1 Section the hair that you wish to turn into the buckle.

Comb the hair smooth. Spray lightly with hairspray.

2 Wrap the ends of the hair around the form, taking care to spread the hair and keep the tension even.

3 Roll the hair up.

4 Remove the form carefully. Pin the buckle to the head or wig using Xed bobby pins.

Buckle Method #2: Weaving Hair

Note that you *can* reverse this process and use the woven end of the hair as the inside of the buckle. The problem with this approach is that the loose ends of the hair will generally be of varying lengths, and you will have a large amount of flyaway hairs on the outside of your buckle.

Supplies: weaving hair, scissors, comb, hairspray, thread, needle, roll form (see page 109), bobby pins, heavy item (like a book)

1 Determine the final length of the buckle. Cut a piece of weaving hair two or three times this length, then fold it in half or thirds. Sew the ends together.

2 Comb the hair smooth. Spray lightly with hairspray.

3 Place the woven end of the hair underneath something heavy, like a book.

4 Working from the loose ends, wrap the ends of the hair around the form, taking care to spread the hair and keep the tension even.

Continued on next page

5 Roll the hair up.

6 Place Xed bobby pins on each side to keep the hair rolled.

7 Remove the form carefully. Pin the buckle to the head or wig using Xed bobby pins.

* In the 1780s-90s, women's buckles sometimes have a straight portion at the top. To make these, I recommend using weaving hair, and leaving the last few inches unrolled. Attach the buckle to the wig at the woven end. You can combine this technique with the Braiding Hair & Glue technique, as demonstrated on the Lilac style (page 219).

Buckle Method #3: Braiding Hair & Glue

This is a theatrical technique that will make perfect, permanent buckles that can be added to a wig or hairstyle (and reused).

Supplies: loose braiding hair, roll form (see page 109), clear-drying glue (I recommend Aleene's brand "Jewel-It," which you can find at most craft stores), small paintbrush, a dish or newspaper, wax paper, tape, scissors, bobby pins, comb

1 Cut a rectangle of wax paper slightly longer than your finished buckle length, and wide enough to wrap around the form, plus overlap.

2 Wrap the wax paper around the form and tape it to itself. Pour some glue into the dish or onto the newspaper.

3 Take about 1" thickness of loose braiding hair, and comb it smooth.

4 Test that you have the right amount of hair by wrapping it around the form – it needs to cover the form 2.5 times. If necessary, add or remove hair.

5 Once you're sure you have the right amount of hair, wrap about 3" around the form near one end (hair layer #1).

6 Dip your paintbrush in the glue and paint the wrapped ends lightly with glue. Do not let go of the loose hair while you do this, tension is key!

Continued on next page

Techniques 111

buckle method #3: braiding hair & glue continued

7a-b Wrap the hair back over hair layer #1, and continue the full length of the form until you reach your desired buckle length (hair layer #2), covering the glue-painted ends from steps 5-6.

8 Lightly cover all of this hair layer #2 with glue.

9a-b Wrap the hair back down the length of the form (hair layer #3), making sure to cover all of the glued hair layer #2 underneath.

10a-b To end the buckle, wrap the hair around the form one last time (not the full length, just once around the form on top of hair layer #3). Dab a bit of glue on hair layer #3 underneath. Lay the ends on top of this spot, and dab one more bit of glue on top.

11 You can trim the ends (just past where you have placed this final spot of glue) if they are too long.

12 Pin the ends of the buckle to itself/the wax paper with Xed bobby pins. Pull the hair and wax paper off of the form. *You can now use the same form to make more buckles.* Allow the glue to dry fully (usually takes about 2-3 hours).

13 Once the glue is dry, remove the bobby pins and tear out the wax paper.

14 When you attach the finished buckle to your hair or wig, keep the final spot of glue (applied in Step 10) on the side where the buckle touches the hair/wig.

Raising Hair & Wigs

Many of the women's hairstyles from the second half of the eighteenth century require height. While small amounts of height can be achieved by teasing the hair, larger shapes require some kind of internal support. There are many items that can be used as support – I have seen people make high hairstyles and wigs using wire, cotton or polyester batting-filled fabric, rolled fabric, floral foam, and even mesh shower sponges. The methods I will teach you to use are those that I have found to be effective, cheap, and comfortable: rats and wire mesh.

RATS

Rats are **pads**, generally **made of foam or netting**, that are useful understructures for hairstyles. They are sold in various colors to blend with your hair, and can be bought in either sausage or donut shapes. Both are intended for making buns and can certainly be used for that purpose, but they also work well for adding small amounts of height to your hairstyle or wig. You can cut rats to smaller shapes, or connect them into larger shapes by sewing, bobby pinning, or wiring them together.

Rats in different shapes and sizes.

You can buy hair rats from beauty supply stores, online or in person (for suggested stores, see page 290). In the Finished Styles section, the Madame du Barry, Miss Nettlethorpe, and Euridice all provide examples of basic supports for high hair made using rats. It is important to try to purchase rats in a **color close to your hair** color, so that the rats do not show through the hair.

You can also make your own rats by stuffing a hairnet with your own hair (collect it after you comb or brush it) or fake hair. Sew the hairnet closed, gathering up any excess netting into the seam.

WIRE MESH

Wire mesh is my favorite tool for supporting and shaping very high hairstyles. It is inexpensive, commonly available, and lightweight – and most important, you can securely bobby pin into the mesh anywhere that is needed. You can easily purchase wire mesh at hardware stores, online and in person, where it is also sometimes called "hardware cloth." I recommend using one of the **smaller mesh sizes** – my favorite has 1/8" squares ("Cut Soffit Screen" by Grip Rite, 27 gauge 1/8" mesh), but 1/4" squares would also work.

You may notice that my directions for using wire mesh are based on the fact that my favorite brand is 6" wide. If you are able to find a mesh you like that is wider than this measurement, feel free to adapt my instructions.

Roll of wire mesh.

When making high wig shapes out of wire mesh, you will need a few other supplies:
- **Heavy duty wire cutters**, to cut the wire mesh. Regular wire cutters will not work well. I have a pair by Master Mechanic (which unfortunately do not have a model name on them), and they cut the wire mesh as easily as scissors cut paper. If necessary, use bolt cutters.
- **Loose wire on a spool**, about 24 gauge, to "sew" the pieces of mesh together
- **Pliers,** to bend and flatten wire (optional)

Wire mesh has a tendency to catch on your hands and clothes. For that reason, I recommend:
- Wear **old clothes**, preferably something heavy like jeans
- Wear lightweight **work gloves** to protect your hands

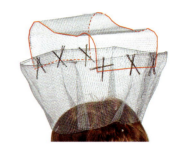

Connecting two pieces of wire mesh with Xed bobby pins.

As you connect pieces of wire mesh, I find it is easiest if I temporarily pin the two together using **bobby pins** before sewing with loose wire. This will hold the pieces stable while I sew, and also allow me to experiment with different configurations before I commit to sewing them together.

When you sew the frame to the wig, you must use a **curved needle**. This will allow you to sew the frame to the wig while it is blocked on the wig block, which will avoid reducing the size of the wig. As you sew the frame, make sure you part the wig hair and are actually connecting with the wig caul (the netted base and/or skin top to which the hair is sewn), not just the wig hair. Use regular sewing thread.

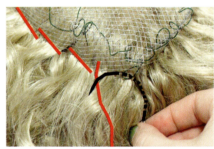

Sewing a wire mesh frame to the wig base using a curved needle.

Remember that in your finished product, no one will see the wire mesh frame. The key is to make the right shape, not to make the world's prettiest frame!

I will walk you through, step-by-step, how to make frames for high wigs from wire mesh in many of the finished style demonstrations. If and when you decide to branch out on your own – and I recommend that you do so! – here are a couple of pointers to keep in mind:
- Don't be surprised if your **first try** at making a wire mesh frame is not exactly what you pictured. I find I usually have to make a first version, then tweak it or even remake it, before I love it.
- I recommend **testing out the effect of the frame** by roughly pulling the wig hair over the frame before styling.
- Even so, **you will never *really* know the effect the frame will have until you have styled the wig hair over it**. If you style the wig and then find you would like to change the frame, remember it is not the end of the world. You can remove the bobby pins, and, if necessary, wash out the wig and start over. Have some chocolate and come back to it tomorrow!

Wig-Specific Techniques

WIG BASICS

Parts of a Wig

The important parts of a wig include:

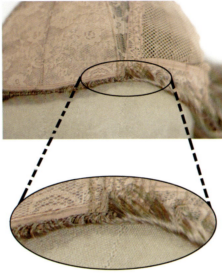

Top left: **On a hard-front wig, the wig cap frequently consists of a "skin top" (a rubber piece made to look like skin).**

Top right: **On a hard-front wig, wefts of hair are sewn to the inside of the wig cap and then brought around to the outside, to help mask the hairline.** *This wig is shown inside-out.*

Bottom left: **On a lace-front wig, the hair in front is tied, one hair at time, to netting.**

Bottom right: **On the inside, below the skin top or netting you will see rows of wefted hair sewn to pieces of elastic. When styling a wig, it is important not to do anything to reduce the ability of the elastic to stretch. For that reason, whenever sewing anything to a wig, I recommend you only do so when the wig is blocked (attached to a correctly sized canvas block) AND stretched to its full capacity (even beyond what you think will be necessary).**

Left: The section along the nape of the neckline is usually a stable piece of fabric, with yet more rows of wefted hair sewn on. The wig is shown inside out.

Right: Along the sides are generally two **elastic bands**, with hooks. You can hook these elastic bands to the various sewn slots in the stable band at the nape of the neck, in order to tighten the fit of the wig. You can also hook these elastic bands to each other, to tighten the wig even further. If you find you do not need to tighten the wig, I recommend cutting these elastic bands out. Otherwise, if unhooked, they will have a tendency to slip out from under the wig base and show.

Left: Some wigs will come with one or more wide combs sewn into the base of the wig. These are intended to help stabilize the wig, but I have found that they do not work well. Instead, I recommend that you remove them (use a seam ripper) and using the techniques discussed in "Securing A Wig" on page 125.

Blocking a Wig

"Blocking" a wig simply means **attaching it securely to a canvas head block**. These are sold in various sizes – to determine your size, simply measure around your head above your eyebrows, with the tape measure held horizontally.

It is very important to use a canvas head block, and *not* a styrofoam head. Styrofoam heads are tiny, and will be far smaller than your head. They work fine for storing wigs, but if you style a wig on a styrofoam block, you will inadvertently tighten and constrict the wig, making it too small for your head (even if you begin with a wig that fits). A canvas wig block is a bit of an investment, but a necessary and worthwhile one.

The other important supply item is a **wig clamp**. This is a base that attaches to a table, with a short pole that will fit inside of your wig block. Avoid the cheaper clamps that suction to the table, as these will not take a

Canvas head block and wig clamp.

lot of weight – look for one that screws on to the table. The wig clamp will keep your canvas head block from falling over, or even moving, while you style the wig. Careful readers may note that most of the photos in this book are not taken with a wig clamp. This is not because this advice is ignorable, but that my work space was separate from my photography space. When I worked on the wig, it was done on a clamp in my workroom.

Many wig-styling resources will tell you to use T-pins for blocking, which are pins that are folded into a wide end, to prevent you losing a pin into the canvas block. The problem is that the wide end of the pin has a small opening, and I find that I often catch the wig hair on this opening when I try to remove it. Instead, **I recommend using large sewing pins with extra large ball ends**.

No matter how well you block the wig, it can be easy to loose track of the exact orientation of the wig. To avoid unpleasant surprises, I **insert a pin into the underside of the wig cap at the exact center front**, with the ball head of the pin showing. This allows me to always know the exact center front point of my wig.

Marking the center front with a pin.

To Block a Wig

1 Align the wig on the canvas block at the front hairline.

2 Holding the front hairline in place, pull the back of the wig down, stretching the elastic.

3 Pin the wig into the block at the forehead center front, above each ear, and at both sides of the nape of the neck. Make sure you pin through a stable point on the wig's caul (the base onto which the hair is attached).

Adding Extra Hair to a Wig

Sometimes you may want to add extra hair to a wig, in order to fill out a thin or short wig, or to change the hairline.

To Add Extra Hair to a Wig

Supplies: wig, weaving hair, straight pins, curved needle, thread, scissors

1 Block the wig. Note that portions of the wig caul (the base to which the hairs are attached) are elastic. It is very important to **stretch these sections** out to their fullest extent, or you will constrict the size of the wig, before you sew the wefts of additional hair.

2 Find the edges that you wish to cover, or part the hair to where you will attach the extra hair.

3a-b Pin additional rows of weaving hair at the desired points. In this example, additional hair was added near the front hairline (but behind the wig's natural hairline), and at the nape of the neck.

4 Using a curved needle and thread, whipstitch the wefts of weaving hair to the caul of the wig. Take caution that you keep any elastic portions of the caul stretched.

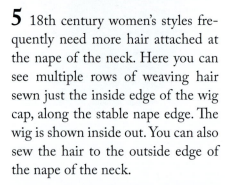

5 18th century women's styles frequently need more hair attached at the nape of the neck. Here you can see multiple rows of weaving hair sewn just the inside edge of the wig cap, along the stable nape edge. The wig is shown inside out. You can also sew the hair to the outside edge of the nape of the neck.

6 Triple check the fit by trying the wig on your head after sewing on the weaving hair, before styling, to prevent any surprises.

Changing a Hairline

Some eighteenth-century styles will have a widow's peak, a point at the top center of the hairline, which is difficult (if not impossible) to find on commercial wigs. Also, people with slightly larger heads may find that the front hairline measurements that are standard on most wigs are too small to fully cover their hair, and large size wigs are surprisingly few and far between (and expensive!). Finally, you may wish to follow the line of your natural hairline, which will usually be irregular.

Look at the base wig to see how wefts are attached to the hairline. On a hard front wig, 1-3 wefts are usually sewn underneath the wig's hairline, then wrapped up and around it, in order to mask that edge. You should copy this technique, unless you are trying to create a man's obvious wigline (eighteenth-century wigs do not appear to have used this technique).

If you are making a man's wig and you want to emulate the obvious wigline seen in the period, you can **remove some of the wefts of hair from the hairline of the wig**. Note that the hair on top of the wig tends to be sewn parallel to the hairline – this is relatively easy to remove with a seam ripper. If you need to cut the weft of hair, finish the end with fray check/block. The hair along the sides of the face is generally sewn perpendicular to the hairline. This can be harder to remove. You may wish to leave it as is, or to cut the wefts at the hairline and secure them with fray check or fray block.

To Change a Hairline

Supplies: wig, weaving hair, plastic wrap (aka cling film), tape (wig, painter's, or masking), scissors, 1/4 yard netted fabric, 1/4" seam binding or ribbon, water soluble marker, sewing machine (optional), thread, curved needle, 1/4" wide plastic boning, bone casing

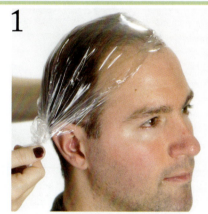

Left: The unmodified wig.

1 Take a piece of plastic wrap and cover the head, twisting the wrap at the ears.

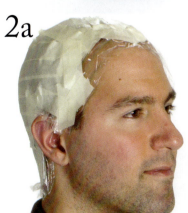

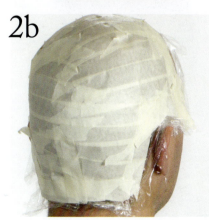

2a-b Mark the outer edge of the hairline with tape, aligning the outside edge of the tape with the edge of the hairline.

Cover the interior portion of the head with tape.

Continued on next page

Techniques 119

to change a hairline continued

3 Remove the tape/plastic combination from the head. Cut away the excess plastic. This is now your pattern.

4 Place the pattern on your wig block.

5 Mark the new hairline by applying strips of tape just outside of the pattern.

6 Remove the pattern. Now, the inside edge of the tape marks your final hairline. *If you prefer to follow the outside line, you can apply another row of tape just inside of this one, then remove the outer layer.*

7 Place the wig on the block, making sure the front hairline does not extend forward of any part of the model's hairline. The difference between the wig and the taped final hairline is what we need to cover.

8a-b Cut pieces of doubled (folded in half) netting large enough to fit these new shapes, plus at least 1" seam allowance.

Mark the final hairline shape on the netted pieces with a water soluble marker. Remove the netting pieces from the block.

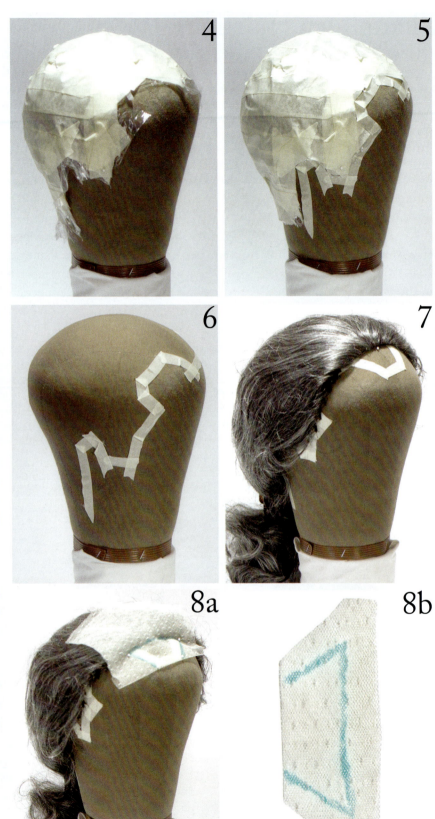

9   Fold over the netting at your marks, except for the piece that will align with the wig's hairline. Sew strips of seam binding or ribbon to the edges of the netting to stabilize them.

10 If you are planning to sew hair to the underside of the hairline, do so now: sew 1-2 rows of wefts to the underside edge of the netted piece. You can use a sewing machine to do this. Make sure that the hair on these wefts points out from the netting and away from the face.

11a-b Take the weaving hair and sew it to the top side of the netting in a zig-zag shape, filling the space. Align this hair pointing in towards the head. You can use a sewing machine to do this. Do not sew any hair to the remaining seam allowance.

to change a hairline continued

12a-b If you sewed hair to the underside in step 10, wrap the hair around the edge of the netting. Use steam to set the hair into this new direction (see page 103).

13 Pin the netting to the inside cap of the wig, aligning it so that the 1" seam allowance lays underneath the cap. Hand sew the outer edge of the seam allowance to the inside of the wig with a herringbone stitch. Sew the line where the netted piece meets the wig hairline with a straight or backstitch.

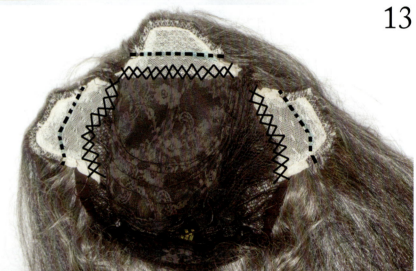

14 Cut strips of plastic boning long enough to reach from the edge of the new pieces, to about 2" inside of the original wig cap. Place the boning into bone casing, folding over the ends of the casing.

15 Hand sew the cased boning to the inside of the wig cap as shown.

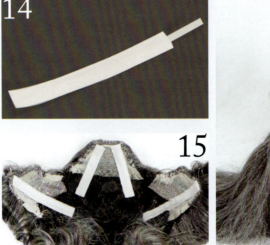

Enlarging a Wig

Most commercial wigs are made to the following measurements: 21.5" around the head, 14.25" front to back, and 13.5" from ear to ear. Many people (particularly men) may find that their head is larger than this size. Unfortunately, there are very few large size wigs available for purchase, and those that are available are very expensive.

You can enlarge a standard wig by changing the hairline (see previous section), and by expanding the room in the cap at the base of the neck as demonstrated below. I recommend sewing this on a machine for strength.

To Enlarge a Wig Cap

Supplies: elastic, thread, scissors, sewing machine

1 Cut off the elastic band meant to tighten the fit by hooking to the nape of the neck.

2 Find the elastic band at each side back of the wig. Cut this band midway through the last section, just above where the elastic meets the stable portion at the nape of the neck. Take care not to cut the hair.

3 Sew a small strip of elastic into the caul at each cut. Remember that you will need to add enough elastic to account for added size, **plus** the seam allowance that will overlap with the wig's original elastic.

Techniques 123

Making it All Look Smooth

If you are a perfectionist, you may quickly become irritated at flyaway hairs on wigs and hairpieces. One of the best ways to solve this is to use a hairnet. Hairnets can be purchased in a range of colors, and the fine ones truly are invisible on most small, firm pieces (like buns).

Most hairnets are large enough to cover the smaller styles of the 1720s-50s. Although I have been told that there is a source for extra large hairnets big enough to cover a high 1770s hairstyle, I have yet to be able to find a source. The largest hairnet that I have found is the "Bouffant Size" by Jac-o-net. You can, however, choose to cover only certain sections of a wig, or use multiple hairnets. The key is to be sure that you find a way to hide the elastic band and/or edge of the net.

Another useful technique is to use a strip of toilet paper to smooth down hairs. Spray the hair with hairspray, then draw a length of toilet paper across the hair, holding the paper taut in both hands. This sounds weird, but it works!

Wearing False Hair & Wigs

If your hair is very long, you will need to wear your own hair up, both to get it out of the way and to provide something stable to which to secure the wig. I recommend either a few small buns placed above the back of the neck, or two braids either pinned to the back of the head or simply tucked into the back of the wig. Most wigs have a bit of extra room near the nape of the neck into which your hair should fit. Experiment! You may find you need stability elsewhere. If your wig is particularly heavy, you may want to place more braids or buns on top of your head to carry the weight.

If your hair is short, you should still try to stabilize it if at all possible. This can be done through one or more small ponytails or pincurls, particularly in areas where you need stability.

Even men with short hair usually have enough hair to make the top buns.

Left: **Two small buns on top, ready for toupee clips or bobby pins.** (*The hair around the hairline is left out so that it can be combed into the wig.*)

Right: **Long hair in two buns at the nape of the neck, ready for wearing a wig.**

Securing A Wig

I recommend some combination of the following ways to secure the wig to your hair. If you do not secure the wig, you will find it slides around easily and may come off!

Toupee clip

Center front hairline: **Toupee clips** (also called "wig clips" and "comb clips") can be purchased separately and sewn into the front hairline of the wig. These come in a range of sizes; I recommend using the larger sizes. These will hold securely to even a very small bit of hair. These work best if you create small buns or pincurls at the center top of your forehead, or wherever you plan to attach the clips.

- **Sew** two into the wig cap, just behind the front hairline, with the teeth facing **down** towards your head and **forward** towards the hairline. Use the holes around the sides and top of the clip to sew through.
- **To wear**, make sure the clips are snapped open. Place the wig on your head, focusing on the front of the wig first. Slide the comb clips into your own hair, then reach underneath the wig cap and snap them closed. Finally, pull the sides and back of the wig down, covering your own hair.

If for some reason you cannot use toupee clips, then **bobby pin** at this point into your own hair. This works best if you can create small buns out of your own hair, or pin braids to your head, so as to have some secure bulk into which to pin. Use bobby pins in X shapes for security.

Toupee clips sewn into a wig cap, just behind the front hairline. (The wig is shown inside out.)

Above the ear: **Bobby pin** in Xes just above each ear.

Back neckline: **Bobby pin** in Xes at each side of the nape of the neck.

Left: The wig should be pinned and/or clipped at the center front of the forehead, in front of the ears...

Right: ... and at each side of the nape of the neck.

Techniques 125

Masking an Obvious Wigline

The best way to mask that you are wearing a wig is to work some of the front of your own hair into the wig. This practice was done in the period. My research shows that eighteenth-century women always tried to hide any false hair or wigs, while for men it was very much optional. If your own hair does not match the wig color, you can apply powder to the wig and your hair to blend (see the section on powdering, page 129).

To hide the line of the wig, it is the front hairline we need to worry about. When putting your own hair up, leave loose anywhere from a few wisps to about 1" thickness of your own hair along your hairline. Comb your hair into the front of the wig, and secure with strong aerosol hairspray. If your hair is longer than the length of the wig, finish the ends in pincurls, a roll, or some other element that will merge into your hairstyle.

Left: A 1" layer of hair pulled free, ready to work into the front hairline. The hair has been curled to match the texture of the wig.

Right: The same, but this time the hair has been left straight to match the wig.

Comb the hair into the wig, fanning it out across the front.

Left: Longer hair can be worked into the wig arrangement and bobby pinned at the ends if necessary. (The color difference here was hidden with powder.)

Right: Short hair/bangs are combed up into the wig, hairsprayed, and then bobby pinned. The bobby pins should be removed once the hairspray is dry.

126   18th Century Hair & Wig Styling

Wig Care

Wearing

The less your wig is touched, the longer it will last. Be careful when attaching hats, walking under low hanging branches, etc.!

Remember that height based on teasing will flatten under a hat. If you plan to wear a hat over a wig, I recommend using a firmer base (rat[s] and/or wire mesh).

Wearing a hat over a wig tends to create a mess, just like wearing a hat on your own hair. You may want to have specific wigs that you wear with a hat, and some for wear without.

Storage

The more carefully your wig is stored, the longer it will last. *Always* leave it on a wig block to hold its shape (styrofoam heads are fine for this purpose). Use T-pins or ball-topped straight pins to attach the wig to the head at the front hairline, in front of the ears, and nape of the neck.

Depending on the weight of the wig, you may find it wants to fall over. In that case, either lean the wig against a wall/shelf backing/etc. (so long as that will not crush that portion of the wig), or purchase a wig head stand/holder that attaches to a shelf/table/etc.

Always cover the wig to avoid it getting dusty. You can use a plastic bag, pillowcase, or even just a piece of fabric – all draped lightly over the wig.

Wig covered with a plastic bag to protect from dust.

Travel

Your wig should be safe to travel with. If you find you do not have room for the full styrofoam head in your luggage, try stuffing the "head" portion of the wig with paper, plastic bags, etc. – anything to keep the shape. Place the wig in an appropriately sized box or wig/hat box. You can buy vintage hat/wig boxes that have a built-in stand on which you can place a styrofoam head or wig block – check Etsy/Ebay.

I have saved room when traveling with a small wig by putting it, without any support, into a large, sealed plastic bag. You will need to fluff up/hairspray/revive your wig when you get to your destination, so I cannot guarantee this method!

The vintage hat box that I use as a wig case.

Ornamentation

Decorative elements were frequently added to women's coiffures, and even sometimes men's wigs, throughout the century. This book cannot possibly cover the wide range of hats, caps, and other items worn over the hair. However, there are a few ornaments that are used in the finished styles that are important to discuss.

Pompom: a few small ribbons, pearls, jewels, flowers, and/or decorative pins styled together. Named for Madame de Pompadour. Popular for women's coiffures in the 1740s to 1750s.

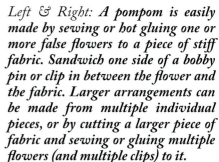

Left & Right: A pompom is easily made by sewing or hot gluing one or more false flowers to a piece of stiff fabric. Sandwich one side of a bobby pin or clip in between the flower and the fabric. Larger arrangements can be made from multiple individual pieces, or by cutting a larger piece of fabric and sewing or gluing multiple flowers (and multiple clips) to it.

Decorative models: in the late 1770s through the early 1780s, women sometimes accessorized their hairstyles with thematic arrangements that included decorative models. Appropriate items can be purchased (and altered) or made. Look for toys, Christmas ornaments, and similar items to use as-is or to paint and decorate.

Top left: A model ship was made of styrofoam, painted, and decorated with glued-on ornaments.

Top right: A small model ship, purchased inexpensively.

Bottom left: A toy birdcage.

Bottom right: The best way I have found to secure these items is to glue two pieces of millinery wire, each bent into a squared U shape, to the underside. Cover these wires by gluing a piece of fabric on top of the wires. These four wires become "legs" that can be pushed into a wire frame wig, and will hold the item very securely.

128   18th Century Hair & Wig Styling

Powdering

Powdering a hair or a wig can be difficult using modern products. I recommend beginning by buying a wig in a color that is close to the one you are trying to achieve. Without resorting to temporary color sprays, it can be difficult to dramatically change the color. If your goal is to create a powdered look without any major color change, I recommend using talcum powder or aerosol dry shampoo. If you are trying to change the color of a wig, I recommend using a temporary color spray. The trick is to find one that is not shiny.

Thus far, I have experimented with these products:

- **Bumble & Bumble - Hair Powder - White:** aerosol white dry shampoo. Worked well. Created a textured, matte white color. Moderately expensive.
- **Colonial Williamsburg - Dusting Powder** (available in Lavender, Magnolia, Rose, and Violet): loose white powder. Worked well. Created a matte light or white color, depending on color of hair underneath. Inexpensive.
- **High Beams Intense - Temporary Spray-On Haircolor - #21 Wicked White:** aerosol temporary color. Worked well. Created a matte white color. Inexpensive.
- **Jerome Russell - Team Colors - Field Line White:** aerosol temporary color. Worked well. Created a matte white color. Inexpensive.
- **Johnson's - Baby Powder - Lavender and Chamomile:** loose talcum powder. Worked well. Created a matte white color. Lavender/chamomile scent avoided the "baby powder" smell. Inexpensive.
- **Salon Grafix - Invisible Dry Spray Shampoo:** aerosol dry shampoo. Did not work well, except to remove a bit of shine. Like the product description, it really is invisible! Inexpensive.
- **Streaks 'N Tips - Temporary Color Highlight Spray - Silver:** aerosol temporary color. Did not work well. The product is indeed silver, not grey, and very shiny. Inexpensive.
- **Streaks 'N Tips - Temporary Color Highlight Spray - White:** aerosol temporary color. Did not work well. Although whiter than the silver, the product is still very shiny. Inexpensive.

To apply loose powder, you will need a powder puff or hand bellows. Powder puffs are easy to find, hand powder bellows not so much! Strange but true: I recommend using a hand powder bellows meant for using with insecticide. These are easily available and affordable, have a wide opening for inserting the powder, and create a nice, even powder application (although each spray covers a relatively small area). I purchased a "Crusader" "bulb bellows" style on Ebay for very little money.

- *To powder hair with a dry shampoo or spray color*: spray on after styling is finished.

- *To powder hair with a puff*: diffuse the powder through the hair first, **then** spray with hairspray to make the powder stick. Do not hairspray first, or the powder will go on clumpy.

- *To powder hair with a hand bellows*: spray the hair or wig with hairspray first, then diffuse the loose powder through the hair. Hairspray again after powdering.

Whichever tool you use, you will probably need to apply the powder multiple times. Remember that the goal is (usually) an all-over consistent color.

If you are planning to powder a hairpiece or wig, you should powder the piece/wig separately from your own hair. The amount of hairspray in your piece/wig will make it harder for the powder to attach; if you try to powder your piece/wig and your own hair at the same time, your own hair will grab the powder and the piece/wig will resist, leaving you with an obvious color difference between the two. Thus, you should powder your piece/wig first, then put it on, then powder your own hair.

A Few Powdering Experiments

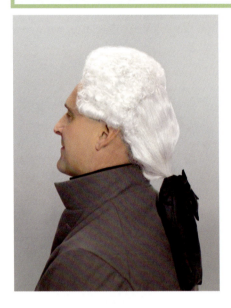

Left: **A white wig powdered lightly with Bumble & Bumble Hair Powder in White.**

Right: **Dark hair powdered heavily with Jerome Russell Team Colors in Field Line White.**

Left: **Red hair powdered lightly with Jerome Russell Team Colors in Field Line White.**

Part III: Finished Styles

Introduction

The step-by-step styles demonstrated in the following section represent many of the most popular hairstyles worn across the eighteenth century. There will, of course, be slightly less popular (or obscure) coiffures not included, and the chosen styles are likely to have had numerous possible variations. At least one style is included for every era, although there are multiple demonstrations for the second half of the century due to the popularity of that period. In some cases, the hairstyles themselves are radically different from one another. In other cases, I have used similar styles to demonstrate different techniques and approaches. Of course, the techniques that I find most successful are used most frequently.

Every hairstyle is based on one or more historical sources, the image of which I have included. A few demonstrations use one source to inspire the front, and another for the back. I have suggested variations for each of the styles. If you would like to see visual examples of these variations, consult the Year-by-Year sections of the book.

In researching this book, I have consulted most of the hair and/or wig styling manuals published in France and England in the eighteenth century. Sadly, none of them are as explicit as we might like about many key elements of hair and wig styling. Thus, I have used these sources to inform my approach to styling, but I have had to make many guesses. I have arrived at most of the shapes by closely examining images from the period and then experimenting. It is my hope that some of you will do your own experimentation and improve upon my results.

With a few exceptions, I have demonstrated the simpler women's styles on a model's natural hair, and the more complicated on wigs. However, nearly all of these demonstrations, except for the wire frame styles, could be made vice versa. I encourage you to mix and match techniques to find what works best for you.

For the demonstrations that use wire mesh frames, I have given specific measurements for these. However, head sizes and face shapes vary. I cannot guarantee that a given size of wire mesh frame will exactly suit you, practically and aesthetically. Be ready to tweak the measurements and proportions if necessary. I recommend trying things on as you work to see if you like the result. At a minimum, try on the wig after you first attach the wire mesh frame, and once you have covered the frame with hair (but before adding any decorative elements, like buckles [rolls], styling the chignon, etc.).

For ease of reference, I have given each of the hairstyles a name. However, I would like to avoid the trap of employing commonly used, but incorrect, terminology (see the discussion on pages 27-9). To that end, I have chosen to name the styles after some element of the source that inspired each – the artist or subject's name, the description of the image, or some visual element. These names are entirely my creation, and should not be considered to have been the terms used in the eighteenth century.

Basic Supplies & Instructions

I have included a supply list for each of the demonstrations. However, I have not included in these lists the basic supplies needed for any hairstyle or wig. You can assume that every style will require most (if not all) of the following:

- **Bobby pins** in a color to match your hair or wig – many! It is safest to have about 120 on hand.
- **Hairspray** – firm hold, aerosol
- Wide-toothed **comb**
- Narrow-toothed teasing **comb**
- Large **clips** for holding sections of hair while styling
- **Toupee/wig clips** (for wigs)
- Canvas **wig block** and **stand** (for wigs)
- **Needle** and **thread** in a color to match your hair/wig
- **Curved needle** for sewing on a blocked wig
- **Scissors**
- Large-headed **pins** (or T-pins)

Any supplies that will be included in the final style (e.g., bobby pins, rats, thread, etc.), as well as additional braiding or weaving hair, should be purchased in a **color** that **coordinates/matches** the model's or wig's hair color.

Similarly, I have not included specific instructions to apply hair product (gel, mousse, pomade, hairspray, etc.) in the following instructions. Instead, I recommend the following for every hairstyle or wig:

Hairstyles:
- Always **begin** hairstyles by working a small amount of **mousse, gel, setting lotion, or pomade** through the hair.
- Always **hairspray** a section of hair **before teasing**.
- Always **hairspray** a section of hair **after styling**.
- Always **hairspray** the entire hairstyle when **finished**.

Wigs:
- If you are going to use **wig clips** to attach the wig to your head, sew them to the underside before blocking or styling the wig.
- Always **block** the wig firmly before styling.
- Always **hairspray** a section of hair **before teasing**.
- Always **hairspray** a section of hair **after styling**.
- Always **hairspray** the entire wig when **finished**.

> *For ease in viewing small photographs, I have frequently highlighted small items like bobby pins in a bright color. This is only to make them more visible in the instructions. You should stick to coordinating/matching colors!*

Marie-Adélaïde
High Front Style (1700s-1710s)

134   18th Century Hair & Wig Styling

The Marie-Adélaïde, named for the fashionable dauphine of France, represents the prototypical high-front hairstyle for this period in both France and Britain. It could be appropriate for the American colonies as well. This source was chosen because of the additional decorative element of the twisted curls on the sides of the head.

This style works particularly well for models with bangs, although those without can bunch and pin the curls on top so that they appear shorter. For those with shoulder-length hair, the bun in back can be entirely false; those with longer hair could make the ringlets out of their own hair. Of course, the entire coiffure could be made as a wig, in which case I would suggest using the model's own hair for some (or all) of the top curls.

Coysevox, Antoine. Detail from *Marie-Adélaïde de Savoie, duchesse de Bourgogne, Dauphine en 1711 (1685-1712) représentée en 1710*. Marble, 1710. (C) RMN-Grand Palais / Art Resource, NY.

Supplies

Beyond the standard supplies required for all styles (listed on page 133):

- 1 pre-made set of **long ringlets**, made from a spiral ponytail according to the directions on page 106. Use weaving hair that is at least 20" long before curling. You will need 1 package of **weaving hair** for this.
- **Rolling supplies**. The hair must be rolled to start, either with foam rollers, pincurls, rag curls, or hot rollers. A curling iron is *not* appropriate. Whichever method is used, the curler should be about .75" diameter.
- 1 large **hairband** (covered rubber band)
- 1 medium donut **rat**
- 1 standard **hairnet**

1a-b Roll the entire head of hair, with the curls pointed **up** towards the top of the head, with a clear center part. Use foam rollers, pincurls, rag curls, or hot rollers.

2 Once the curls have set, part the hair on top in a triangle shape, with the point of the triangle aimed at the back of the head and the front corners above the outer half of each eye. The back point should be about 4" back from the front hairline. Clip this hair out of the way.

3 Make a parting about 1" thick along the hairline at the sides of the face and behind the ear. Clip this hair out of the way.

4 Finger comb through the back hair.

5 Pull the back hair into a loose ponytail. Do not loop the hairband too tightly, as you will need to pull more hair through it in the following steps.

6a Part the hair along the hairline into three sections vertically (one above the ear, one at the ear, one below the ear). Twist each section, rolling **up**...

6b ...then pull the twist through the hairband. Allow the ends to join the ponytail. Do this on both sides.

7 Pull the ponytail through the donut rat, pushing the rat so that it lies against the back of the head.

8 Loop the hair around the donut rat. If the hair is medium length, divide the ponytail in half and wrap first one half, then the other. If the hair is long, you may need to wrap the length around the rat multiple times.

9 Bobby pin the hair wrapped around the donut to the head, making Xes with your pins. This will keep the bun from falling away from the head, and the hair from falling out of the bun.

10 Pin the ringlets to the head underneath the bun. Make Xes with your pins.

Finished Styles 137

11 Cover the bun with a hairnet. You can twist any excess netting and tuck it under the bun, then pin it to keep it hidden.

12 Push one bobby pin through the net into the center of the bun. This will keep the net relatively invisible.

13 Unclip the top curls. With your narrow-toothed comb, tease the base of each curl, except for the curls along the very front hairline.

14 Take each distinct strand of hair and comb it out with a fine-toothed comb (be careful not to comb out the teased hair at the base).

15 Re-roll each strand around one or two fingers. Keep the curls rolled inwards towards the center part.

16 Bobby pin each curl to the head, using Xed bobby pins. Try to hide the pins along the front hairline as much as possible.

Take two curls at each farthest point along the hairline. Twist these downward, so that they lay flat against the forehead and point in towards each other. If you are working with long hair, you can roll the hair around your fingers as many times as needed, then bobby pin the curl at the top to keep the curl wrapped around itself.

Elizabeth
Simple Parted Style (1720s-1740s)

The Elizabeth was worn in many regions: in France (1720s through 1730s), usually with short curls at the nape of the neck; in England (1720s through 1740s) and the American colonies (1720s through 1750s), with either short or long neck curls.

This style works well for those with shoulder length (or longer) hair, but of course could also be made as a wig. The model's long hair, without bangs, worked perfectly, although we added false ringlets to fill out the back hair.

The Elizabeth can be easily varied through the crown arrangement (a standard bun, a looped twist, or a curl arrangement as seen on the Clarissa style would all be appropriate) and the ringlets (which can be longer or shorter, and made of tighter or looser curls).

Greenwood, John. Detail from *Elizabeth Fulford Welshman*. Oil on canvas, 1749. NGA.

Supplies

Beyond the standard supplies required for all styles (listed on page 133):

- **Rolling supplies**. This style only needs volume and not real curl, so a wide (2" diameter) curling iron was used. Alternately, wide foam rollers, pincurls, rag curls, or hot rollers could be used.
- 1 package **weaving hair,** straight or curly, at least 20" long (28" was used in this demonstration). In this case, human hair was used for the false ringlets, so they were curled with a curling iron. If you are using synthetic hair, I recommend creating the nape-of-the-neck ringlets ahead of time, and curling the ringlets using boiling water (see page 104).
- 1 small **hairband** (covered or uncovered rubber band)
- **Curling iron**, about .75" diameter

1 Take a piece of wefted hair, three times the width of the nape of the wig, and fold it into thirds. Whip stitch the thirds into one piece.

2 Roll the entire head of hair, with all of the curls pointing **away from the face** and/or **down** towards the nape of the neck. Use a curling iron, foam rollers, pincurls, rag curls, or hot rollers.

3 Section the hair into 3 sections: the back should be parted from the crown to behind the ear, and the front should be center parted on top. Clip the front sections out of the way.

4 Part a 2" horizontal section at the nape of the neck. Clip the rest of the back hair out of the way.

Divide the hair at the nape of neck horizontally, into two equal sections of about 1". Clip the upper section out of the way.

5 Pin the lower section of hair, at the nape of the neck, into 3-4 small pincurls. Pin the curls flat to the head using Xed bobby pins.

6 Pin the sewn-together weaving hair on top of the pincurls. Use Xed bobby pins.

Finished Styles 141

7 Unclip the upper 1" section of hair at the nape of the neck, and lay it on top of the weaving hair and pincurls.

8 Pull the remaining back hair into a high ponytail at the crown of the head.

9 Unclip one of the front sections. Part a 2" square of hair in the area closest to the crown of the head. Tease this section with your narrow-toothed comb.

10 Take all of the hair from this front section, both the teased and unteased sections, and loop them up loosely, creating a bend in the hair near the crown.

11 Pin that front section to the head, just above the high ponytail. Use Xed bobby pins.

12 Repeat steps 9-11 with the other section of front hair.

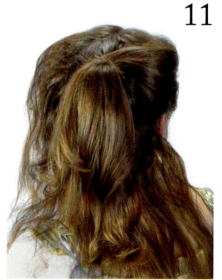

13 Take the hanging ends from the front sections, as well as the back hair ponytail, and braid them together. Tie off the end of the braid with a small hairband.

14a–c Loop the braid into a wide circle at the crown of the head, tucking the end of the braid under the loop, so that the hairband and braid end are hidden. Bobby pin the looped braid to the head, using Xed pins.

15 Using the .75" diameter curling iron, curl the hair hanging at the nape of the neck into long ringlets. In this case, because human hair was used for the additional hair, it too was curled with a curling iron. Synthetic hair should be pre-curled using the boiling water method (see page 104).

Finished Styles 143

Clarissa
Simple Pulled-Back Style (1730s - 1740s)

Clarissa is the heroine of the popular eighteenth-century English novel by Samuel Richardson. A painting of one of the characters from this novel inspired this coiffure, with its long sausage curls. It is very typical of England in the 1730s and 1740s, and probably was therefore worn in the American colonies as well. If the nape of the neck curls were shorter, it would work well for French impressions during the same era.

To vary this style, use a bun or braided bun in place of the curl arrangement at the crown. The Clarissa was generally worn with a decorative cap, which can have its own variations.

For those with shorter hair, a set of false curls could be used in back, and the curled arrangement at the crown of the head could similarly be added on separately.

Highmore, Joseph. Detail from *The Harlowe Family, from Samuel Richardson's "Clarissa."* Oil on canvas, 1745-7. YBA.

Supplies

Beyond the standard supplies required for all styles (listed on page 133):

- **Rolling supplies**. The hair must be rolled to start, either with foam rollers, pincurls, rag curls, or hot rollers. A curling iron is *not* suitable. Whichever method is used, the curler should be about .75" diameter.
- 1 large **hairband** (covered rubber band)

Finished Styles 145

1a-b Set the hair in curls. Use foam rollers, pincurls, rag curls, or hot rollers.

All the curls should point **back** and **away** from the face except:
- Set a row of curls along the nape of the neck. Use about a 1" thickness of hair, parted horizontally. Set these curls so that they roll **sideways** towards the face. You can alternate directions, or set the left side pointing left, and the right side pointing right.

Make sure to put one curl directly in front of each ear, again pointing back and away from the face.

2 Once the curls have set, unpin all of the curls except the one in front of the ear (on both sides), and the row along the nape of the neck.

3 Finger comb all of the released curls.

4 Pull all of the unpinned hair loosely into a ponytail at the crown of the head.

5 Take a 1" piece from the ponytail and comb it smooth.

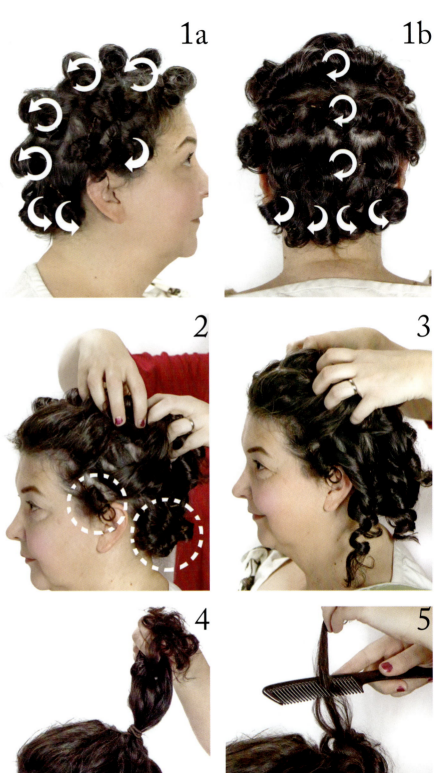

146   18th Century Hair & Wig Styling

6 Wrap this piece of hair around your finger.

7 Gently pull the roll off your finger, pulling the curl slightly so that it starts to spiral.

8a-b Bobby pin (using Xed pins) the end of each curl to the head.

Repeat steps 5-8 until all of the ponytail is curled and pinned.

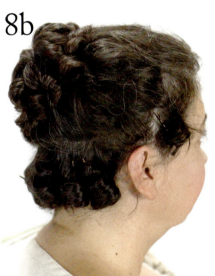
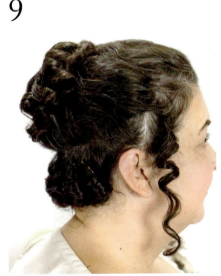

9 Unpin the curl in front of the ear.

10 Comb this curl tightly around your finger. Hairspray, wait a moment for the hairspray to set, and then gently pull it off your finger. Repeat on the other side.

11 Unpin the curls along the nape of the neck. Comb each curl around your finger, hairspray, wait a moment for the hairspray to set, then gently pull each off your finger.

Finished Styles 147

Summer
Simple Pulled-Back Style (1740s)

*T*his coiffure, copied from a French engraving called the "Pleasures of Summer," was very popular in France during the 1740s. If created with straight hair, it could be adapted into the simple English and American styles of the 1750s.

This style needs hair that is shoulder length or longer. Those with very long hair can use their own to make the braid.

Variations include using a twist instead of a braid, as well as using three twists or braids (as shown on the Madame de Pompadour style).

Surgis, Louis de Surugue de after Jean-Baptiste Joseph Pater. Detail from *Les Plaisir de l'Ete*. Etching and engraving, 1744. NGA.

Supplies

Beyond the standard supplies required for all styles (listed on page 133):

- **False braid**, long enough to reach from the nape of the neck to the top of the head, pre-made according to the directions on page 107. You will need 1 package of **braiding hair** for this.
- **Rolling supplies**. The hair must be rolled to start, either with foam rollers, pin, or rag curls, or with hot rollers. A curling iron is *not* suitable. Whichever method is used, the curler should be about .75" diameter.

1 Roll the entire head of hair, with all of the curls pointing **away** from the face and/or **down** towards the nape of the neck. Use foam rollers, pincurls, rag curls, or foam rollers.

2 Once the curls have set, finger comb lightly through all of the them.

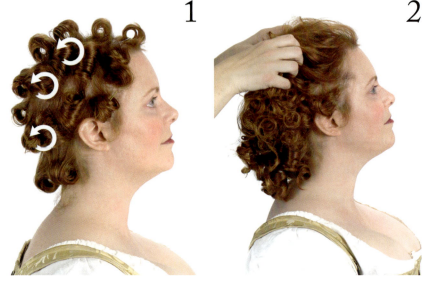

3 Gather the hair loosely at the nape of the neck.

If you are working with very long hair, start the braid or twist here.

4 Keeping the ends gathered in one hand, roll the ends under the hair.

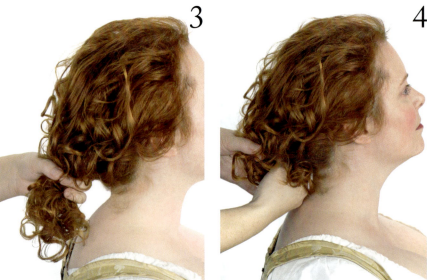

5 Bobby pin the hair at the nape of the neck, using Xed pins, to secure the rolled-under ends.

6 Take the braid and fold both ends under.

7 Pin the braid to the back of the head, with the folded under ends underneath the braid/against the head. Place one end of the braid at the crown of the head, and the other at the nape.

8 Bobby pin the braid to the head at each end, making sure to keep the folded-under ends hidden.

Madame de Pompadour
Simple Pulled-Up Style (1750s – mid-1760s)

*T*he Madame de Pompadour (the front of which was probably called the tête de mouton) was the most popular style in France during the 1750s. It was also worn in Great Britain during the same period.

This coiffure works equally well for those with or without bangs. Because the model has shoulder-length hair, loose braiding hair was used to extend the braids. Models with long hair can use their own for the entire braid, while those with shorter hair can use completely separate false braids as shown in the Summer style.

If this style were made as a wig, it would be ideal to use the model's own hair for the front curls, pulling them over the edge of the wig. If the hair is very short, or that requires too much time, incorporate very fine wisps of her hair along the hairline. Comb them back over the edge of the wig, and then pull/push the ends in between the individual rolls, using the tail of a ratting comb or other implement, and hairspray enthusiastically.

Variations include using twists instead of braids, using only one twist/braid instead of three, or pulling the chignon up smoothly as shown in the Du Barry style. Alternately, the entire head can be set in rolls in the bichon frisé style.

Pigalle, Jean-Baptiste. *Madame de Pompadour (1721-1764)*. White marble, 1748-1751.
Images copyright (C) The Metropolitan Museum of Art. Image source: Art Resource, NY.

Supplies
Beyond the standard supplies required for all styles (listed on page 133):

- A **pompom** flower arrangement, pre-made according to the directions on page 128. It should be roughly triangular (see step 21), with each side about 3". The pompom is necessary to hide the ends of the braids.
- **Rolling supplies**. The hair must be rolled to start, either with foam rollers, pincurls, rag curls, or hot rollers. A curling iron is *not* suitable. Whichever method is used, the curler should be about .75" diameter.
- 1 package **loose braiding hair**, straight
- 1 tiny **roll form**, about 1/4" diameter
- 1 narrow **roll form**, about 3/8" diameter
- 3 small **hairbands** (covered or uncovered rubber bands)

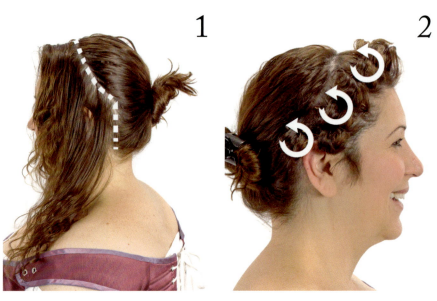

1 Part the hair along the hairline, from behind the ears and across the top of the head. The section along the hairline should be about 3" deep on top of the head, tapering to about 2" deep behind the ears. Pin the back section of hair out of the way.

2 Roll the front section of hair. Use sections about 1" wide. Place the curls perpendicular to the hairline. Roll each section **up** towards the top of the head. Use foam rollers, pincurls, rag curls, or hot rollers.

3a-b Once the curls have set, unroll them. Starting directly on top of the head, where you would place a center part, section a very narrow piece of hair.

Roll this section of hair around your **tiny** roll form, holding the roll form perpendicular to the hairline. If the model's hair is shorter in front (for example, if she has bangs), roll the longer section until you reach the shorter length, then incorporate the shorter length into the roll.

154   18th Century Hair & Wig Styling

4  **5**

4 Roll the form all the way down to the scalp.

5 Pull back on the roll form, so that the curl unwinds slightly at the hairline in front, and covers the parting slightly in back. Carefully remove the roll form.

6a  **6b**

6a-b Pin the roll to the head, using one or more Xed bobby pins. Pin into the base of the roll at the back and front.

Continue making rolls in this method across the top of the head.

7  **8**

7 When you reach the temples, continue making rolls, but switch to the **narrow** roll form.

8 Continue making rolls until all of the front hair is rolled. If any of the rolls have gaps in between them, pin a bobby pin into the sides of two rolls, catching one side of each (see the Madame du Barry style, step 31, for an example).

Finished Styles 155

9 Unclip the back hair, and part it into three equal sections beginning at the nape of the neck. Clip each section.

10 Separate the loose braiding hair into three equal sections. Each 1/3 section will be further subdivided into three sections, and then braided into each of the three natural hair sections.

11 Unclip one of the back hair sections. Braid this hair, beginning at the nape of the neck, weaving the loose hair into the braid. See the Marie-Antoinette style, steps 32-36, for a step-by-step on how to braid the false hair into the natural hair.

12 If necessary (see step 13), continue braiding past where the natural hair ends.

13 Determine where to end the braid by pulling it up to the top of the head, center, where the rolls end.

14 Loop a hairband around the braid at this point.

Repeat steps 11-14 with the two other back sections of hair.

156   18th Century Hair & Wig Styling

15  **16**

15 Pull the center braid up to the center top of the head, right where the rolls end. Bobby pin the end of the braid to this point, using Xed pins.

16 Repeat step 15 with both side braids. Bring all three braids to the center point.

17  **18**

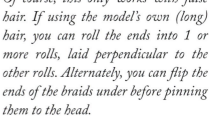
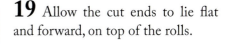

17 Secure the beginning of the braids close to the head by pinning the base of the braid to the nape of the neck, using Xed pins.

18 If the ends of the braids are longer than 1" past the rubber band, cut the ends of the hair.

Of course, this only works with false hair. If using the model's own (long) hair, you can roll the ends into 1 or more rolls, laid perpendicular to the other rolls. Alternately, you can flip the ends of the braids under before pinning them to the head.

19  **20**

19 Allow the cut ends to lie flat and forward, on top of the rolls.

20 Cover the braid ends with the pompom, pinning the pompom to the head with Xed bobby pins.

Finished Styles 157

Derby

Simple Pulled-Up Style (1760s)

*T*his hairstyle is copied from Joseph Wright of Derby's portrait of Elizabeth Bostock, who wears the British style of the late 1760s. It was also worn in the American colonies in the same period. This loose, naturalistic coiffure was nearly always shown in paintings with a string of pearls, ribbon, or scarf wound through the side twists and/or across the top of the head.

Those with very long hair can use their own for the side twists. Instead of looping false hair through the hairband, simply make a low ponytail, split it in half, then flip it under and pin. Twist each half of the ponytail, and then twist it up with the side twist. Finish the ends in the same manner.

The model's hair is a mix of many colors. This demonstration is a good example how using just one color for the false hair looks fine.

Detail from *Portrait of Elizabeth, Mrs John Bostock*, c.1769 (oil on canvas), Wright of Derby, Joseph (1734-97) / Private Collection / Photo © Christie's Images / The Bridgeman Art Library

Supplies
Beyond the standard supplies required for all styles (listed on page 133):

- **Rolling supplies**. This style only needs volume and not real curl, so a wide (2" diameter) curling iron was used. Alternately, wide foam rollers, pin curls, rag curls, or hot rollers could be used.
- 1 package of loose **braiding hair**, straight
- 1 large **hairband** (covered rubber band)

1 Roll the entire head of hair, with all of the curls pointing **away from the face** and/or **down** towards the nape of the neck. Use a curling iron, foam rollers, pincurls, rag curls, or hot rollers.

2 Part a section from above the temples to the top of the ear, as shown. Repeat on the other side. Clip these side sections out of the way.

3 Take the entire package of braiding hair, and pull it through the hairband. The rubber band should be centered halfway along the length of the hair. Do not loop the hairband around the braiding hair more than the one loop shown.

4 Comb all the hair, minus the clipped sides, straight back without a part. Make a low, loose ponytail using the hairband from step 3. Keep the braiding hair looped through the band, at the center of the length of hair, underneath the ponytail.

5 Flip the end of the natural hair ponytail under.

6 Bobby pin the flipped end under, using Xed bobby pins, making sure that the rubber band doesn't show.

160   18th Century Hair & Wig Styling

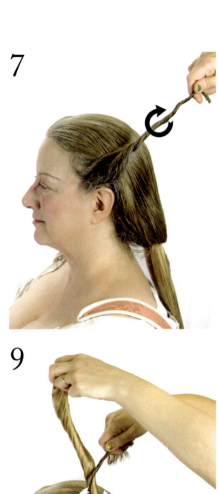
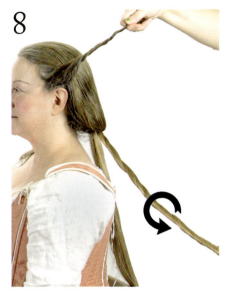

7 Unclip one of the side sections, and twist it **up** towards the top of the head.

8 While holding that twisted side section, twist the length of braiding hair that is on the same side. Twist this hair **down**.

9 Pull the twisted braiding hair loosely forward, along the side of the head. When you reach the ear, twist the twisted side section around the braiding hair length.

10 Pin the twisted hair to the top of the head, using Xed bobby pins.

Repeat steps 7-10 on the other side.

11 Take the long ends from both pieces of braiding hair and hold them together.

12 Loop this hair around two fingers, as many times as the length will allow.

Finished Styles

13 Slide the looped hair off of your fingers, pushing the ends of the hair to the inside of the loop. Center the loop directly on top of the Xed bobby pins.

14 Flatten the loop with your hand, so that hole of the loop is hidden and the loop spreads to each side. Make sure that all of the Xed bobby pins are underneath this flattened loop.

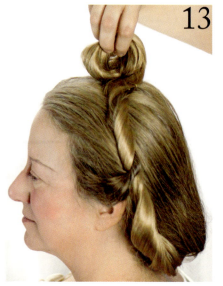
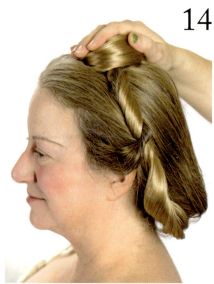

15 Bobby pin the flattened loop to the top of the head, using Xed bobby pins.

Madame du Barry
High Style (late 1760s - mid-1770s)

This coiffure is modeled after a portrait of the Comtesse du Barry, the famous mistress of Louis XV of France. It is essentially a raised version of the Madame de Pompadour. It was worn primarily in France, but also occasionally in Britain, from the late 1760s through the mid-1770s. The back treatment was inspired by the bust of Madame du Barry illustrated on page 49, minus the ribbon that crosses the chignon.

Although this demonstration is shown as a wig, it could easily be adapted for wearing with your natural hair, using the same frame made from rats. Possible variations include ringlets on only one side of the neck; in back, you could use one or three braids (or twists) as shown in the Madame de Pompadour style.

I used the "Dahlia" wig by West Bay in palest blonde (color #613). I chose a lace front so that I could change the model's hair color easily.

Drouais, François-Hubert. Detail from *Jeanne Bécu, Comtesse du Barry*. Oil on canvas, c. 1770-4. NGA.

Supplies

Beyond the standard supplies required for all styles (listed on page 133):

- 1 **wig** (22" or longer), straight, without bangs
- 1 package **weaving hair**, straight, 18" long or longer
- **Foam rollers**: about 30 small (about 3/4" diameter)
- 5 **rats** (2 large sausage, 1 large donut, 1 medium donut, 1 small donut)
- **Wire**, about 24 gauge
- **Wire cutters**
- 1 standard **hairnet**
- 1 narrow **roll form**, about 5/8" diameter

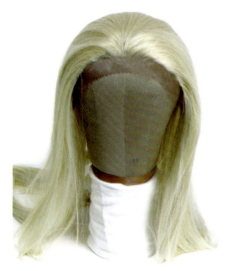

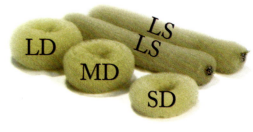

1

2

3

4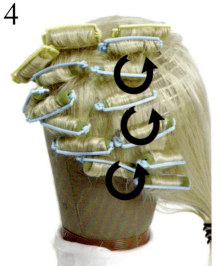

5

6

7

1 Take a piece of wefted hair, three times the width of the stable portion at the nape of the wig, and fold it into thirds. Whip stitch the thirds into one piece.

2 Whip stitch the wefted hair piece to the **inside** nape of the wig, just above the bottom edge.

3 Block the wig. Part the hair horizontally, just below the crown of the head, and vertically, behind the ears.

Clip the back hair out of the way.

4 Set the front hair in foam curlers, with the curlers horizontal to the ear. Roll the hair **up** towards the top of the head.

5 In the back section, make a vertical parting on each side, about 1" wide, from top to bottom.

6 On the left side only, part an extra 1" square section of hair, **above** (but not including) the wefted hair sewn to the nape of the neck.

7 Set these side sections on foam rollers – three on the left, two on the right – placed vertically. Roll the hair **forward** toward the face. Set all the curls by pouring boiling water over the curlers (see page 104).

Finished Styles 165

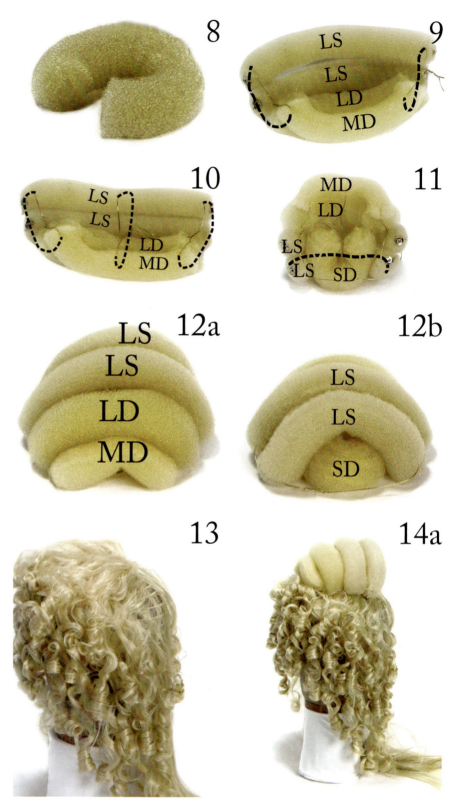

8 Cut all 3 of the donut rats so that you can use them flat.

Before beginning to work with the rats, look at steps 12a-b so that you understand the final shape.

9 Lay the two Large Sausage (LS) rats side by side, then the Large Donut (LD), then the Medium Donut (MD). Thread the ends with wire, bringing the ends of the wire together and twisting them. Do this on both sides.

10 Thread a wire through the middle of the rats, bringing the ends of the wire together and twisting them.

11 Lay the remaining Small Donut (SD) rat on the inside of your wired rats, with the center pointing at the Large Sausage rats and the two ends pointing at the Medium Donut rat. Align the outside center edge of the Small Donut flush with the edge of the outer Large Sausage rat. Thread wire through the Small Donut rat, connecting it to the four previously wired rats.

12a Your finished piece should be a dome, with the medium donut (MD) rat at the front, then large donut (LD) in the middle...

12b ...and the two Large Sausage rats in back, supported by the Small Donut rat tucked underneath. This piece will be your frame for creating height, which I will now call "the Frame."

13 Once the wig has dried, re-block it. Push all of the curls towards the front and sides of the wig, except for about 2 curls at the back of the crown (see 14b for a visual).

14a-b Place the Frame on top of the wig, aligning the outside edge of the rear Large Sausage (LS) rat flush with the back of the crown of the head, and the Medium Donut rat just behind the front hairline. Bobby pin the Frame to the wig, using Xed bobby pins at both back and front corners of the Frame.

15 Take the two curls hanging from the back of the crown and, using a fine-toothed ratting comb, tease them from root to tip. Pull this teased section up over the Frame...

16 ...tucking the ends in between the two Large Sausage rats. Bobby pin the hair to the Frame, making Xes with your pins.

17 Take a 1" section (parted horizontally) from the top of the straight back hair. Using a fine-toothed comb, comb this piece up over the teased section and the Frame.

18 Pin this section of hair to the Frame in the dip between the two large sausage rats at the back (thus about 1" in from the back edge), using bobby pins laid flat.

19 Continue bringing up sections of the straight hair over the Frame, bobby pinning the hair to the Frame on top. Be careful not to pull the back hair too tightly, which would pull the wig up from the block.

20 Stretch the hairnet over the finished back hair, hooking it on the underside of the nape of the wig and pulling it up over the Frame. The elastic of the net should keep it hooked over the nape of the wig, but if necessary, you can whipstitch this into place on the inside.

21 Take any excess in the hairnet and twist it up. Bobby pin the twist to the top of the Frame. Tuck the ends of the straight hair in between the second and third rats.

Finished Styles 167

22 Use large clips to separate the vertical back curls (from step 7) from the front hair curls.

23 Using a wide-toothed comb, comb out all of the front curls (but not the vertical side back curls).

24 Take a small section (about 1" thick) of hair to become your center roll. Make this parting directly at the center of the forehead. Comb this hair smooth with a wide-toothed comb.

25 Wrap this piece of hair around the roll form, holding the form perpendicular to the hairline and wrapping in either direction, starting at the ends.

26 Continue rolling until you reach the front the Frame. Stop here, leaving the bottom (root end) 1-2" of the hair uncurled.

27 Pull back on the roll form, allowing the curl to spiral off of the form, until you reach the very back edge of the Frame. The roll needs to end flush with the back of the Frame, covering all of the bobby pins holding the back hair into place, as well as the edge of the hairnet.

168   18th Century Hair & Wig Styling

28 Carefully remove the roll form. Pin the roll to the center back of the Frame, pinning into its base so that the roll is maintained. Make Xes with your bobby pins.

29 Continue making rolls in this same method across the entire front of the wig. They now must be rolled **up** towards the center-most roll.

30 When you reach the sides, bring the ends of the rolls diagonally up towards the crown of the head.

31 If the Frame shows between the curls, gently spread the curls and bobby pin them to each other. Open the bobby pin so that you can grab a side of each curl, and push the pin parallel to the curls (rather than into the Frame).

32 Unclip the side back curls. On the left, take the topmost of the 3 curls and attach a bobby pin halfway down its length.

33 Pin this bobby pin to the point shown by the arrow. The curl should loop down from the roots, up to the bobby pin, and then hang. Do the same on the right side.

On the left side, twist the remaining 2 ringlets together. On the right side, leave the remaining ringlet hanging.

Finished Styles 169

Miss Nettlethorpe
High Style (late 1760s - late-1770s)

$\mathcal{T}$he comparatively simple high coiffure worn by Miss Nettlethorpe is appropriate for wear early in the 1770s in Britain, France, or the American colonies. It would also work well throughout the decade for the middle classes and/or the colonies. It can be varied easily by changing the placement and number of rolls, while the chignon could be braided or twisted.

This demonstration assumes the model's hair is long enough to make an adequate chignon. If the model's hair is shorter, you can hide this using the method employed in the Euridice style, steps 29–35.

Walton, Henry. Detail from *Portrait of a Woman, Possibly Miss Nettlethorpe*. Oil on panel, c. 1770. YBA.

Supplies

Beyond the standard supplies required for all styles (listed on page 133):

- **Rolling supplies**. This style only needs volume and not real curl, so a wide (2" diameter) curling iron was used. Alternately, wide pin curls, rag curls, or hot rollers could be used.
- 6 pre-made **buckles** (rolls): 4 about 4" long, and 2 about 6" long; both made on a 1" diameter form (see pages 108–112). You will need 1 package of straight **braiding** (2 packages of 20"+ **weaving**) **hair** for this.
- 1 package **weaving hair,** straight, at least 20" long
- 3 **rats** (2 medium sausage, 1 large donut)
- **Wig block**
- **Seam ripper**
- **Wire**, about 24 gauge
- **Wire cutters**
- 1 large **hairband** (covered or uncovered rubber band)

Finished Styles 171

1 Take a piece of wefted hair, three times the width of the nape of the neck, and fold it into thirds. Whip stitch the thirds into one piece.

2 If the large donut rat has an elastic band inside of it, remove it by cutting it with a seam ripper.

3 Pin one of the sausage rats horizontally across the crown of the wig block. Lay the donut rat so that the back edge is on top of the sausage rat. Flatten the donut rat into an oval shape. Pin another sausage rat in front of the donut rat.

This creates your Frame. Sew the rats together using loose wire, then remove them from the wig block.

4 Because this style needs volume, not curl, roll the hair using a wide curling iron or large rollers. Roll all of the curls away from the face and down towards the neck.

5 After the curls have set, part the hair behind the ears and across the crown of the head. Clip the back hair out of the way.

6 Make two small buns at the back of the front section, at the crown. Use Xed bobby pins to secure these buns.

7 Pin the Frame to the head, laying the back of the Frame on top of the small buns. Bobby pin, using Xed pins, the corners of the Frame, catching the small buns.

172   18th Century Hair & Wig Styling

8 Cut a 15" length of weaving hair, fold it into thirds, and pin it to the base of the front of the Frame.

9 Tease the bottom 5" of this weaving hair.

10 Lay this teased weaving hair across the Frame, rolling the long ends under so that the weaving hair ends where the Frame attaches to the back of the head. Bobby pin the weaving hair to the base of the Frame, using Xed pins.

11 Take a 1" section of hair along the side of the Frame. Tease it.

12 Lay this teased hair across the Frame, bobby pinning it to the opposite side of the Frame.

Repeat steps 11-12 on the other side of the head.

13 Take the rest of the hair at the side of the face, comb it smooth, and lay it over the Frame. Bobby pin it to the Frame on the other side.

Finished Styles 173

14 Repeat on the other side of the face. This time, bobby pin the hair at the top of the Frame (near the back), not the sides.

15a Take the hair along the forehead, comb it smooth, and lay it across the Frame…

15b …Bobby pin this hair to the back of the Frame.

16 Unclip the back hair. Part a 1" section of hair horizontally at the nape of the neck. Pin the top portion of the back hair out of the way.

17 French braid, horizontally, the 1" section of hair at the nape of the neck.

18 Loop the braided end back on top of the French braided portion, and bobby pin the braid to the head.

19 Take the weaving hair sewn together in step 1, and bobby pin (using Xed pins) it onto the looped French braid.

20 Release the clipped back hair and comb it smooth. Trim the weaving hair attached in the previous step to the same length as the natural hair.

21 Make a low ponytail with all of the back hair, both natural and weaving. Attach the rubber band about 1-2" from the ends of the hair.

22 Loop up the back hair, flipping the end of the ponytail under.

23 Pin the ponytail to the head, pushing pins through the rubber band and into the back of the Frame.

24 Attach the six pre-rolled buckles as shown, two horizontally on the back of the head, and two diagonally on each side.

Euridice
High Style (mid- to late 1770s)

In Greek mythology, Eurydice was the wife of Orpheus, who failed to bring her back from the dead. The name (from the Gallerie des Modes) of this coiffure is probably based on a style worn by an actress in a play based on the myth. This style would be appropriate for wear across France, Britain, and the American colonies from the mid- to late-1770s. The style can be easily varied through the buckle placement and chignon treatment.

This demonstration is an excellent example of the ways that false pieces can be added to the model's own hair to create elaborate coiffures. Of course, the same style could be made as a wig, using the same connected rats as a frame, or substituting a wire mesh frame (perhaps more practical for those styling their own hair).

This demonstration also shows how you can create a longer chignon than the model's hair length. If the model's hair is long, see the Miss Nettlethorpe style, steps 20-22, for a demonstration of how to style it.

The model has hair that is much lighter at the ends. "Powder" (white colored hair spray) was used to equalize all of the different shades.

Details from *18th Century Print showing Headdress [Gallerie des Modes]*. Engraving, hand tinted, gouache, 18th century [1778]. LACMA.

Supplies

Beyond the standard supplies required for all styles (listed on page 133):

- 12 pre-made **buckles** (rolls), about 5" long, made on an 1.25" diameter form (see pages 108-112). You will need 2 packages of straight **braiding** (4 packages of 20"+ **weaving**) **hair** for this.
- 1 package **weaving hair**, straight, at least 18" long
- **Rolling supplies**. This style only needs volume and not real curl, so a wide (2" diameter) curling iron should be used. Alternately, wide pin curls, rag curls, or hot rollers could be used.
- 7 **rats** (4 medium sausage, 1 large donut, 2 small donut)
- 1 tiny **roll form**, about 1/4" diameter
- 1 small **roll form**, about 3/4" diameter
- 1 large **hairband** (covered rubber band)
- 1 ribbon bow or other **ornament**

Finished Styles 177

1 Take a piece of weaving hair, three times the width of the nape of the neck, and fold it into thirds. Whip stitch the thirds into one piece.

2 If the large donut rat has an elastic band inside of it, remove it by cutting it with a seam ripper.

3 Bobby pin the four sausage rats into the rectangular shape shown, using Xed pins.

4 Place one of the small donut rats inside the center of the large donut rat.

5 Lay the donut rats next to the long rats, as shown.

Bobby pin the rats together, stretching the donut rats so that they become oval shaped and match the length of the long rats. Use Xed bobby pins.

6 Bobby pin the other small donut rat to the front of the sausage rats, as shown. This makes the support for the high hair, which will now be called the Frame.

7 Part the hair from behind the ear, across the crown of the head. Clip the back hair out of the way.

Because the model has curly hair, we did not need to roll her hair for volume. If you are working with straight hair, you should first set your hair like the Miss Nettlethorpe style, step 4, before styling. Use a wide (2" diameter) curling iron or rollers.

8

9

8 Make two small buns on top of the head, at the very back of the front section of hair. Use Xed bobby pins to secure the buns.

9 Bobby pin the Frame to the head, pinning each back corner of the Frame to the buns. Use Xed pins. Make sure the small donut is facing front.

10

11

10 Take a 10" length of weaving hair, fold it in half, and bobby pin it across the front of the Frame using Xed pins.

11 Tease the weaving hair.

12

13

12 Pulled the teased hair over the Frame, spreading the hair to cover the Frame. Twist any excess hair into one twist at the back.

13 Flip the twisted end under. Bobby pin the twisted-under hair to the Frame.

Finished Styles 179

14 Take a 2" section, horizontally, of hair along the sides of the Frame and tease it.

15 Pull this teased hair up to the top of the Frame. Fold the excess ends under, and bobby pin the hair to the side top of the Frame.

Repeat steps 14-15 on the other side.

16 Comb the remaining side hair up across the Frame and bobby pin on top. Repeat on the other side.

17 Pin another 10" length, folded in half, of weaving hair to the front of the base of the Frame.

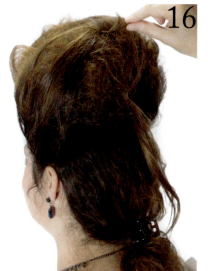

18 Comb the weaving hair across the Frame.

19 Pin the ends of the weaving hair to the back side of the Frame, about 1" down from the top, using Xed bobby pins. Let the ends hang down.

20 Take the remaining natural hair along the top of the forehead, comb it smooth, and wrap it around your **tiny** roll form.

21 Roll this hair to the eyebrows.

22 Flip the rolled hair up...

23 ...pinning it to the front of the Frame. Use Xed pins on each side.

24 Unclip the back hair. Part a 1" section of hair horizontally along the back neckline. Clip the rest of the back hair out of the way.

25 French braid this section horizontally.

26 Loop the end of braid against the back of the head, and pin it to the French braided portion using Xed bobby pins.

Finished Styles 181

27 Bobby pin the length of weaving hair sewn in step 1 to the braids.

28 Unclip the back hair. Clip the ends of the weaving hair out of the way.

29 Put the ends of the natural hair into a hairband, flipping the ends up through the final loop of the band.

30 Loop this hair up, pinning the end of the ponytail to the back of the head. The length should be determined by where you want the chignon to loop up.

31 Take the false hair pinned to the back of the neck in step 27 and put it into a very low ponytail. The length of the ponytail should be determined by how low you want the chignon to hang. Fold the ends of the false hair up through the hairband, as shown.

32 Trim any extra length of the false hair. Leave ends of at least 1-2", so that the hair doesn't fall out of the rubber band.

33 Unclip the weaving hair. Separate it into two equal sections.

34 Loop up the chignon, pinning the end in between the two sections of weaving hair.

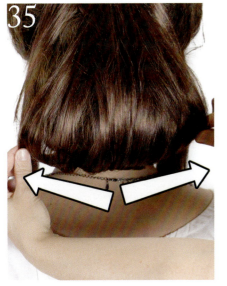

35 Fan the false hair of the chignon out, so that it fully wraps the natural hair inside.

36 Pin three buckles along the back edge of the Frame, one on top and one along each side.

37 Pin two buckles diagonally above and behind the ear. Pin a third buckle hanging behind the ear.

Do the same on the other side.

38 Pin three buckles on top of the Frame, perpendicular to the hairline. You may want to adjust the height of the roll of front hair so that it covers some of the buckle openings.

Finished Styles 183

39 In back, take one of the weaving hair sections and wrap it around the **small** roll form. Wrap the hair so that it rolls inwards, towards the ponytail end.

40 Roll the form all the way up to the head, flip it 180°, then pull it off the form.

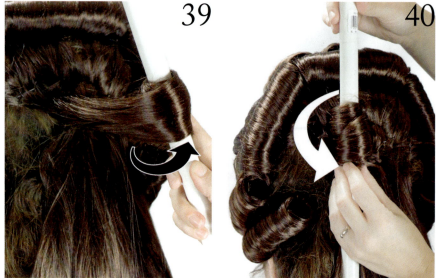

41 Pin the resulting spiral of hair to the back of the head. Do the same with the other section, reversing the roll and flip direction to create a mirror image.

42 Cover the join between the two spirals with some kind of ornament.

184   18th Century Hair & Wig Styling

Lady Betty

High Style (mid- to late-1770s)

Finished Styles 185

Reynolds, Sir Joshua. Detail from *Lady Elizabeth Delmé and Her Children*. Oil on canvas, 1777-9. NGA.

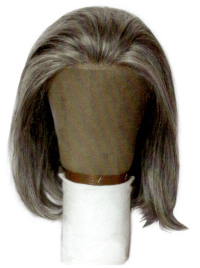

*T*his uniquely British coiffure was drawn from Reynolds's portrait of Lady Betty, as she was known to her family. It was popular from the mid- to late-1770s in Britain and the United States.

While I have located many front and side views of this hairstyle, I have yet to find any back views. Thus, this demonstration features my best guess for the back, based on the Derby style of the 1760s from which it clearly developed. Alternately, the back could have been styled with the French looped-up chignon, like the Dorothée. Images show that this coiffure nearly always had a ribbon or scarf wound through the side twists and across the top of the head.

I wanted to use a lace front in order to easily change the model's hair color, but long, lace-front, grey wigs are nearly impossible to find. Thus, I used a long bob wig ("Isabelle" by Henry Margu in light grey, #51) and augmented it with lots of weaving hair. If you are using a long wig, you can modify the instructions.

Supplies

Beyond the standard supplies required for all styles (listed on page 133):

Starting with a shorter wig and adding hair:
- 1 **wig** (at least 15" long), straight, without bangs
- 4 packages **weaving hair**, straight, at least 25" long
- **Foam rollers**: about 24 large (about 1.25" diameter), 35 medium (about 1" diameter)

Starting with a long wig:
- 1 **wig** (at least 25" long), straight, without bangs
- 1 package **weaving hair**, straight, at least 25" long
- **Foam rollers**: about 24 large (about 1.25" diameter), 6 medium (about 1" diameter)

For both:
- 1 package **wire mesh**
- 1 pair heavy duty **wire cutters**
- **Wire**, about 24 gauge
- 1 standard **hairnet**
- 1 piece of **fabric** (about 4" wide) or **ribbon** (between 1-4" wide), about 2 yards long. The fabric or ribbon is necessary to hide bobby pins and hairnet edges.
- 1 large **roll form** (about 1.25" diameter)
- 1 **small** roll form (about 3/4" diameter)

1 Review the information about creating wire mesh frames on pages 113-114. Review the information about adding extra hair to a wig on page 118.

2 Block the wig. Part the hair along the front hairline, from above one ear, across the top of the head, to above the other ear. Brush this hair forward and clip it out of the way. Clip the back hair out of the way.

Sew 6 rows of weaving hair to the hairline along the side of the neck, and 6 rows to the nape of the neck. *Do this even if you are using a long wig, although you can reduce the amount of hair at the nape to 2 rows.*

3 Set the long hair at the side of the neck in the large foam rollers. Roll the hair **away** from the face.

4 Unclip the back section of short wig hair. Set this hair in the medium foam rollers, with the hair curled **forward** towards the face. *Skip this step if you are using a long wig.*

5 Part a 1" section of hair, horizontally, from the long hair at the nape of the neck. Set this 1" section of hair into medium foam rollers, **except** for a 1" section on the far right, which will be left straight.

Remove the wig from the block. Pour boiling water over all of the hair set in foam rollers (see page 104). Allow the wig to dry.

6 Cut a piece of wire mesh, 31" by 6". Roll it into a circle, overlapping about 1", and sew through the overlap with wire to connect.

7 Make darts along the bottom edge at the side front, side, and side back. The darts should be about 3/8" wide along the edge, and extend about 2.5" up the height of the piece.

Finished Styles 187

8 Cut another piece of wire mesh, 31" by 6". Roll it into a circle, and then make about 8 small darts (spaced evenly around), so that the circle becomes a cone closed at the top. The darts should be about 1.5" wide at the top edge (they will overlap each other), and extend down the entire height of the piece.

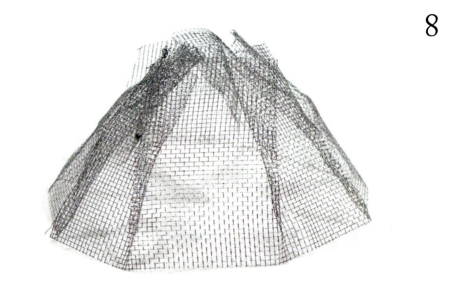

9 Align the cone with the wire mesh circle. Overlap the edges about 1". Sew the two pieces together with wire.

10 Sew (with wire) the darts down near the top of the cone. This makes the support for the high hair, which will now be called the Frame.

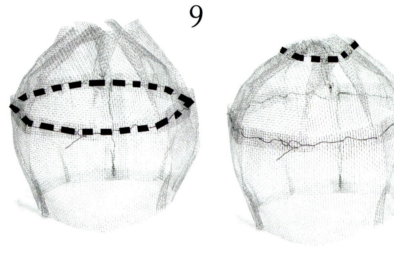

11 Block the wig. Keep the hair clipped into sections:
- The front hair, brushed forward
- The long hair added to the side neck, now curled
- The back of the short wig hair, now curled
- The hair added to the nape of the neck, minus...
- The 1" horizontal parting at the nape of the neck (curled and uncurled)

12 Push a large-headed pin through the wig, into the block, just above the wig's center front hairline. Make sure that the head of the pin is visible through the wig's hair.

Place the Frame onto the wig, pushing the bottom edge down to about eyebrow level. The bottom edge should be even all the way around the head.

Place a bobby pin in the Frame, horizontally, just above the level of the center front hairline pin.

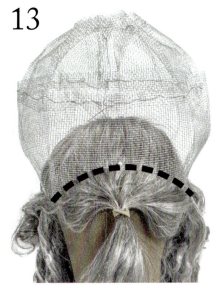

13 Remove the Frame, and cut a crescent out of the front as shown, with the highest point being where you placed the bobby pin in step 12.

Replace the Frame onto the wig and sew it on with a curved needle. Make sure the front of the Frame does not extend past the wig's hairline.

14a-b Unclip the long, curled side hair. Interweave sections of the long hair with the short, curled sections of the wig hair. Pull up a section of long hair, pull down a section of short hair, and repeat until you reach the nape of the neck.

15a-b Clip the long side hair up and out of the way. Brush the short wig hair forward and down around the **large** roll form to make a ringlet. Hairspray, wait a moment for the hairspray to set, then remove the form.

If you are using a long wig, use a 1" piece from the bottom end of the weaving hair that was added to the side of the neck. Comb this hair around the roll form, hairspray, wait a moment, and remove the form.

Repeat steps 14-15 on the other side.

16 You will still have some of the short curled hair at the center back of the wig. Twist this hair together...

Skip steps 16-18 if you are using a long wig.

Finished Styles 189

17 ... then tuck the twist under...

18 ... then bobby pin this tucked-under section to the wig, using Xed pins.

19 Keeping the front wig hair clipped, bobby pin (using Xed pins) two rows of weaving hair across the front edge of the Frame.

20 Take sections of this weaving hair, tease them, and pull them up over the Frame.

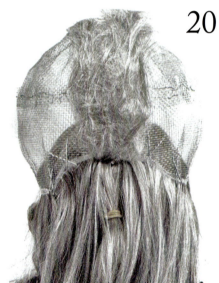

21 Bobby pin each teased section to the far side of the Frame.

22 Repeat steps 20-21 until the Frame is covered. The hair should be long enough to have covered most of the sides and back of the Frame.

Pin two more rows of weaving hair across the front of the Frame, using Xed pins.

23 Take a piece of this new weaving hair, comb it smooth, and pull it up over the Frame, covering the teased hair.

24 Bobby pin this piece of hair to the Frame at the top, just slightly towards the back. Leave the ends hanging.

25 Repeat steps 23-24 until the entire front of the Frame is covered. Bring all of the pieces of hair to the same general point on top.

26 Unclip the front section of wig hair. In pieces, comb this hair up over the Frame.

27 Bobby pin the end of each section to the top of the Frame.

28 Bobby pin (using Xed pins) two rows of weaving hair to the bottom of the Frame, along the side.

Finished Styles 191

29 Comb this hair smooth, and bring it up to the top of the Frame. Bobby pin it to the Frame, leaving the ends hanging.

30 Comb all of the hanging ends and fan them out across the back side of the Frame.

31 Bobby pin, using Xed pins, these long ends to the Frame.

This should be enough unteased hair to cover the back. If it is not, you can pin two rows of weaving hair to the base of the Frame in back and bring that up to the top of the head.

32 Unclip the long back hair section, but not the 1" section at the nape of the neck. Comb the back hair up and fan it out across the back of the wig and Frame, holding all of the ends in one hand.

33 Keeping the ends of the back hair in one hand, pull gently at the center nape of the neck to slightly loosen the hair here. Make sure to keep the sides tight, as you don't want anyone to be able to see behind this section of hair.

34a-b Bobby pin this large section of hair to the top of the Frame using Xed pins. Make sure you use enough bobby pins so that you catch all of the hair. Leave the ends hanging forward.

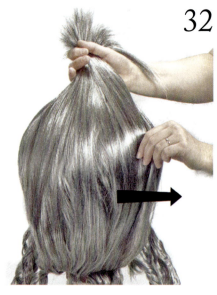
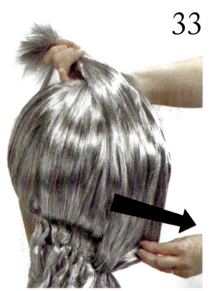

192   18th Century Hair & Wig Styling

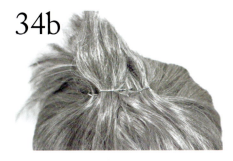

35 Unclip the long, curled side sections. Separate this hair into two equal pieces, and twist them both **forward**.

36 Twist these two sections around each other.

37a-b Bring the twisted hair up to the top of the Frame, and bobby pin them at the top (using Xed pins). You can use this twist to cover any bobby pins holding the front hair, so play with exactly where the twists lay.

Repeat steps 35-37 on the other side of the head.

38 Comb together all of the remaining ends on top of the head, and roll them forward around your roll form.

39 Carefully remove the roll form, and flatten the roll across the head, so that the ends fan out.

Finished Styles 193

40 Bobby pin this flattened roll to the top of the head.

41 Hook a hairnet around the flattened roll.

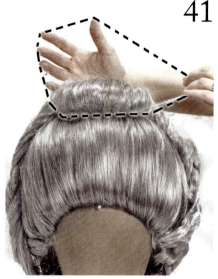

42 Pull any excess hairnet to the top of the roll, twist it, and bobby pin it to the top of the head. When you thread your scarf of ribbon through the twists, use it to cover the excess hairnet and bobby pins.

43 Unclip the 1" section of hair at the nape of the neck. Separate the piece of hair on the right that was not curled, and twist it.

44a-b Fold the twist in half, so that the hair twists around itself. Tuck the end under the pulled up back hair, and bobby pin (using Xed pins) the end to the wig.

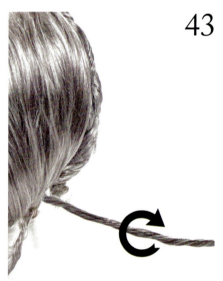

45 Comb each of the curled pieces at the nape of the neck around your **small** roll form, creating a ringlet. Hairspray, wait a moment for the hairspray to set, them remove the form.

194   18th Century Hair & Wig Styling

Dorothée
High Style (mid- to late 1770s)

Finished Styles 195

*D*orothée Dorinville, called by her stage name Mademoiselle Luzy, was a famous actress of the Parisian theater. Her coiffure is an excellent example of the elaborate French styles of the late 1770s, but would be appropriate for wear in Britain and the United States as well. Surprisingly, it is the plumes on top that really give this style its height, so it could be created using a model's own hair, provided many false hair additions were used. Any number of variations could be made with this style by changing the placement of the buckles, treatment of the chignon, number of ringlets, etc.

I used the "Showgirl" wig by Lacey Costume Wigs in dark brownish-black (color #2). Although the model has bangs, we worked her own hair into the front simply by using (a lot of) hairspray.

Detail from *Paris 3ème, Rue de Sévigné Musée Carnavalet* [Caffieri, Jacques. *Mademoiselle Luzy en Tragédienne, Actrice à la Comédie-Française*. Terracotta, 1776]. Musée Carnavalet (artwork in the public domain; photograph provided by Flickr user Medelie Vendetta, CC BY 2.0).

Supplies

Beyond the standard supplies required for all styles (listed on page 133):

- 1 **wig** (22" or longer), straight or wavy, without bangs
- 10 pre-made **buckles** (rolls), about 4" long, made on a 1" diameter form (see pages 108-112). You will need 2 packages of straight **braiding** (4 packages of 20"+ **weaving**) **hair** for this.
- 1 package **weaving hair**, at least 20" long, straight or wavy
- 1 package loose **braiding hair**, curly or kinky
- **Foam rollers**: about 4 large (about 1.25" diameter), 2 medium (about 1" diameter)
- 1 package **wire mesh**
- 1 pair heavy-duty **wire cutters**
- **Wire**, about 24 gauge
- 1 standard **hairnet**
- 1 large **roll form** (about 1.25" diameter)
- 1 medium **roll form** (about 1" diameter)
- 1 large **hairband** (covered rubber band)

1 Review the information about creating wire mesh frames on pages 113-114.

2 Whipstitch four rows of weaving hair to the bottom, stable portion of the wig's nape of the neck.

3 Block the wig. Section the hair from behind the ear, across the crown of the head, to behind the other ear. Clip the back section out of the way.

Part a 2" section, vertically, from the crown to the nape of the neck.

4 Divide the side section into three sections, vertically. Set the top two sections around two wide foam rollers. Set the bottom section around the small foam roller. Roll the hair **forward** towards the face. Do the same on the other side.

Set these six curls by pouring boiling water over the rolled hair (see page 104). Allow the wig to dry.

5 Cut a length of wire mesh, 27" by 6", and form it into a large circle. Overlap the ends by about 1". Stitch the overlapped section together with wire.

6 Make darts at the front and sides. The darts should be about 1" wide at the edge, and extend about 3" down the height of the circle.

7 Cut a rectangle of wire mesh, about 7" by 5", and round the corners to create an oval.

Finished Styles 197

8 Create darts at the corners of the oval. These darts should be about .5" along the edge, and extend about 2" in towards the center of the oval.

9 Place the oval on top of the wire mesh circle, overlapping the two by about .5". Sew the two together using loose wire. This makes the support for the high hair, which will now be called the Frame.

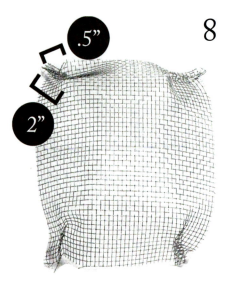

10 Once the wig has dried, re-block it. Unclip the front section and comb all the hair forward.

11 Place the Frame onto the wig. Make sure that the Frame points slightly backwards, towards the crown of the head, and does not extend past the wig's front hairline. Sew the Frame to the wig using a curved needle.

12 Starting at the side back, take about 1" thickness of hair, tease it, and pull it up and over the Frame. Use Xed bobby pins to secure the ends on top of the Frame.

13 Repeat step 12, working around the sides and front of the wig, until the entire Frame is covered.

14 Pin two rows of weaving hair across the uncovered back portion of the Frame. Use Xed bobby pins, and pin them into the base of the Frame.

15 In sections, tease the weaving hair and pull it up over the Frame, covering the back. Bobby pin the teased hair to the top of the Frame.

16 Take a small piece of the curly or kinky braiding hair and put it into the hairnet.

17 Twist the excess hairnet so that the braiding hair becomes a ball.

18 Pin the braiding-hair-in-hairnet to the center front of the Frame, just above the hairline. Shape the resulting bump into a roughly triangular shape, with the point angled down to the front hairline.

19 Take the hair at the center front of the wig, comb it smooth, and pull it up over the bump and Frame. Make this hair indent on top of the bump to emphasize the silhouette. Bring the hair as far back as it will go over the Frame, and then bobby pin the ends using Xed pins.

Finished Styles 199

20 Repeat step 19, bringing up all of the hair at the front and sides over the Frame.

21 Pin two more rows of weaving hair to the base of the Frame, across the back.

22 In pieces, bring the weaving hair up to the top of the Frame where the front and sides hair is attached, and pin it flat to the head using Xed bobby pins. Allow the ends of this back hair to lay free.

23 Form the ends of the back hair into a buckle by rolling them around the **large** roll form. Bobby pin this roll to the head, using Xed pins on each side.

24 Unclip the back hair, comb it smooth, and put it into a low ponytail. Place the hairband where you want the ponytail to attach to the head.

25 Loop the back hair up, pinning the hairband to the back of the head. Use Xed bobby pins.

200   18th Century Hair & Wig Styling

26

27

26 Take the lowest of the three pieces of hair curled in step 4, and form it into a loose ringlet by combing the hair around the **medium** roll form, **forward** towards the face, with the hair slightly spaced as shown. Hairspray enthusiastically, wait a moment for the hairspray to dry, then remove the form.

27 Take the two upper of the three pieces of hair curled in step 4, and comb them into one ringlet. This time, keep the ringlet tight by overlapping the hair. Comb the hair around the **large** roll form, hairspray, wait a moment to dry, remove the roll form.

Repeat steps 26-27 on the other side.

28

29

28 Comb the hanging ends of the back ponytail and roll them around the **large** roll form. Make a roll directly underneath the roll made in steps 23-24.

29 Bobby pin five of the pre-made rolls to the side of the head, as shown.

30

30 Repeat on the other side.

Finished Styles 201

Marine Royale

High Style (mid- to late 1770s)

*W*hen hairstyles were at their highest in the late 1770s, they were sometimes decorated with political or thematic scenes. None of these are as famous as those depicting the ships of the French *Marine Royale (Royal Navy)*: the *Coiffure* à la Belle Poule, *the Coiffure* à l'Indépendance ou le Triomphe de la Liberté, *and the one reproduced here: the* Nouvelle Coëffure dite la Frégate la Junon *(the New Coiffure called the Frigate* Junon, *commemorating the ship that captured the British HMS* Fox *in the Battle of Ushant, 1778).* From the images found in fashion plates, the models were probably not exact replicas, but rather flights of fancy. This style is appropriate for wear in France or Britain, but is possibly too over-the-top for America.

This hairstyle works well as a support for a decorative scene. See the information on page 128 for suggestions and instructions for adding decorative elements to your wig. In this case, a decorative ship model, rope of pearls, and pearl tassel were made and used.

The tallest wigs can be uncomfortable to wear depending on your tolerance. If you are new to wearing high wigs, you may wish to reduce the amount of back lean to the wig – the more the weight of the wig settles down on your head, rather than pulling back, the more comfortable it will be to wear.

I used the "Showgirl" wig by Lacey Costume Wigs in true black (color #1). The model had **very short hair**, so none of her own hair was integrated.

Esnauts et Rapilly, French, 18th century. Detail from *Gallerie des Modes et Costumes Français. 6e. Cahier de Modes Françaises pour les Coeffures despuis 1776.* F.31 *"Nouvelle Coëffure dite la Frégate la Junon..."* French, 1778. Hand-colored engraving on laid paper. Museum of Fine Arts, Boston. The Elizabeth Day McCormick Collection, 44.1290. Photograph © 2014 Museum of Fine Arts, Boston.

Supplies

Beyond the standard supplies required for all styles (listed on page 133):

- 1 **wig** (22" or longer), wavy or curly
- 8 pre-made **buckles** (rolls), about 5" long, made on a 1" diameter form (see pages 108-112). You will need 2 packages of straight **braiding** (3 packages of 20"+ **weaving**) **hair** for this.
- 4 4-6" curls made from **weaving hair**. Most packages of weaving hair come with a bang piece. I used four of these for the four curls on this style. Alternately, you could cut a small piece of weaving hair to about 4-6" length. Either way, curl it around a 1.25" foam roller with boiling water (see page 104).
- 2 packages **weaving hair**, curly
- 2 packages **weaving hair**, straight
- 2 **sausage ringlets.** I used ringlets available for purchase (14" "Triple Twist" by Sensationnel, see right). Alternately, see the Pearl style, step 36, to make your own.
- 1 package **wire mesh**
- 1 pair heavy duty **wire cutters**
- **Wire**, about 24 gauge
- 1 small **hairband** (covered or uncovered rubber band)
- 1 **ruler**, 18" or longer

Finished Styles 203

1 Review the information about creating wire mesh frames on pages 113-114.

2 Cut a piece of wire mesh, 31" by 6", and roll it into a circle, overlapping edges by about 1". Sew through the overlap with loose wire.

3 Make a dart the center front. The dart should be about .75" wide at the edge, and extend about 3" up into the wire mesh.

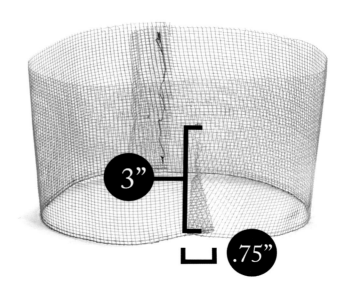

4 Make darts at the side and side back. The darts should be about .75" wide at the bottom edge, and extend the entire height of the wire mesh, tapering to 0" at the top.

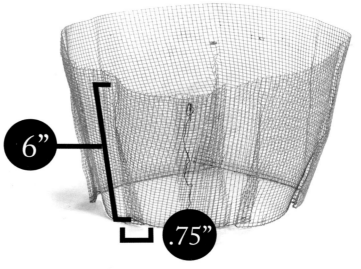

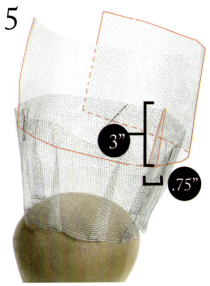

5 Pin this circle of mesh onto the wig block, and angle it slightly back.

Cut another piece of wire mesh, 24" by 6". Make a dart at the center; the dart should be .75" wide at the bottom edge, and extend about 3" up the height of the piece. Bobby pin the new piece to the bottom circle, aligning the center dart of the new piece with the center back dart of the existing circle. Overlap the two pieces about 1".

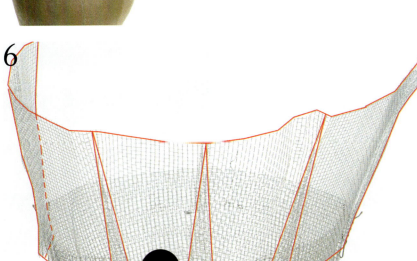

6 Make .75" darts at the same points as on the original circle (side and side back). Sew the two pieces together with wire.

7 At the top of the center back, gently fold over the top 2" of the wire mesh softly (in other words, create a curve rather than a right angle).

Finished Styles 205

8 Turn the wig block so that you are looking at the Frame from the side. Take a ruler and lay it from the top center front, to the folded over top center back. This creates a line for you to follow for the top edge.

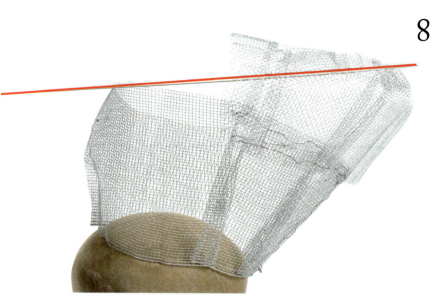

9 Fold over the wire mesh following the line created by the ruler. Keep the fold gentle and rounded. Make darts as needed on the top of the Frame.

Repeat on the other side.

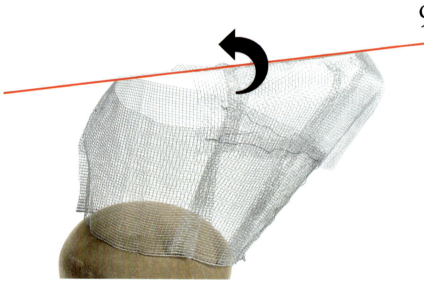

10 Cut a piece of wire mesh, 20" by 6". Align the center of this piece with the center front of the Frame, overlapping about 1". Sew the two together with wire.

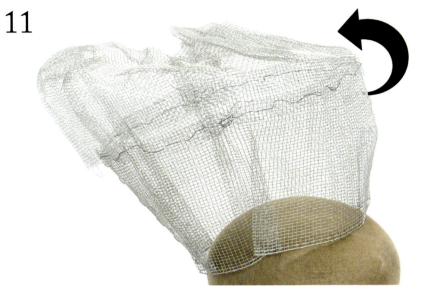

11 Fold over this new piece of wire mesh, following the line created by the ruler. Place and remove the ruler as necessary to see the line you are trying to follow. Dart the wire mesh on the top edge to shape, overlapping the darts if necessary.

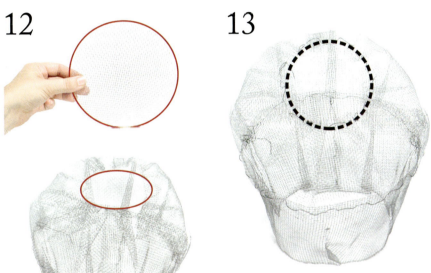

12 Cut a circle of wire mesh, large enough to cover the hole left on top of the wire mesh frame, plus about 1" overlap.

13 Place the circle of wire mesh over the hole. Sew the two together with wire. This makes the support for the high hair, which will now be called the Frame.

14 Block the wig. Part the hair from behind the ears and across the back side of the crown of the head. Clip the back section of hair out of the way.

15 Comb the front section forward.

16 Place the Frame onto the wig, making sure that the front edge does not extend past the wig's front hairline. *Check to make sure that the top back of the Frame is higher than the front. If it is not, you can cut out a crescent from the bottom front edge of the wire mesh Frame. See the Lady Betty style (step 13) for an example.*

Using a curved needle, sew the Frame to the wig.

17 Pin two rows of curly weaving hair around the entire base of the Frame.

18 In sections, tease the curly weaving hair, then pull it up and over the Frame.

19 Pin the sections of teased hair to top of the Frame, using Xed bobby pins.

20 You will probably have sections of the Frame that remain uncovered, particularly in back. Pin two more rows of weaving hair around the back half of the Frame. In sections, tease this hair and bring it up to the top of the Frame, filling in the gaps.

21 Pin two rows of straight weaving hair at the base of the Frame, from the side front, around the back, to the other side front.

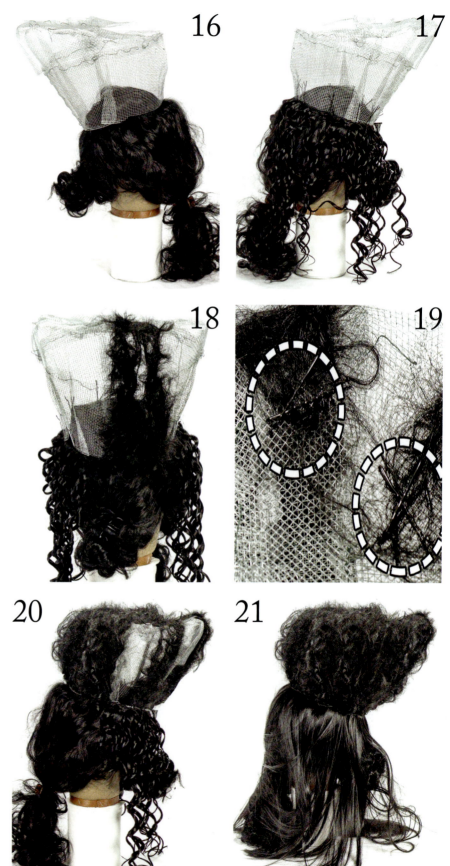

208   18th Century Hair & Wig Styling

22 In sections, bring this hair up smoothly over the Frame and the teased hair. Bobby pin the ends to the top.

23a Unclip the wig hair at the sides and front. In sections, bring this hair up smoothly over the Frame. Start with the sides, and do the front last.

23b When you bring the front pieces up, pull them towards the rear of the top edge of the Frame, then bobby pin using Xed pins. You can cover these pins with whatever ornaments you place on top of the wig.

24 Unclip the back hair. Make a horizontal parting, about 1" wide, at the nape of the neck. Clip the rest of the back hair out of the way.

25 Use the steam method shown on page 105 to straighten this section of back hair.

26 Continue straightening the back hair in 1" sections until all of the hair is straightened. Do not worry if the very ends are hard to straighten.

Finished Styles 209

27 Divide the back hair into three equal sections. Braid the back hair, starting the braid about 5" past the nape of the neck.

28 Finish the ends of the braid with a hairband, looping the ends of the hair through the last loop of the band.

29 Loop the braid up loosely, and pin the hairbanded end to the top back of the Frame.

30 Sew one of the separate ringlets to the wig, just below the Frame, so that it hangs behind the ear. Do the same on the other side.

31 Pin one of the separate buckles to the side back of the wig, on top of the Frame. Pin another just on top of the top of the ringlet. Do the same on the other side.

32a-b Take one of the short pieces of curled weaving hair, and attach it to the top edge of the side, just in front of the top buckle (see step 33 for placement). Part the hair, and tuck the woven end under the hair. Bobby pin the piece so that it curls **up** and **forward**.

33 Pin the remaining two buckles in between those pinned on in step 31. Space the buckles evenly, moving diagonally up the side back of the wig. Keep each individual buckle aligned horizontally.

Queen Charlotte
High & Wide Style (late 1770s - early 1780s)

Finished Styles 211

℘ueen Charlotte of Great Britain's high powdered hairstyle demonstrates the new width fashionable at the turn of the 1780s, while still retaining height.

Feminine coiffures seem to have standardized across Britain, France, and the new American republic in this period. Thus, this style would be appropriate for wear in any of the three.

This is another style on which I modified a bob-length wig in order to make up for the lack of availability of grey lace-front wigs. If you are using a long wig, you can modify the instructions. I used a long bob wig ("Isabelle" by Henry Margu in light grey, #51) and augmented it with lots of weaving hair. I chose a lace front to change the model's hair color easily.

This style can be varied infinitely by changing the placement of the buckles, the treatment of the chignon, and any other decorative elements.

West, Benjamin. Detail from *Queen Charlotte*. Oil on canvas, 1777. YBA.

Designed by: Claude-Louis Desrais, French, 1746–1816. Engraved by: Nicolas Dupin, French. Publisher: Esnauts et Rapilly, French, 18th century. Detail from *Gallerie des Modes et Costumes Français. 16e. Cahier des Costumes Français, 10e Suite d'Habillemens à la mode. Q.94 "Jeune Dame en robe de taffetas de couleur à volonté…"* French, 1778. Hand-colored engraving on laid paper. Museum of Fine Arts, Boston. The Elizabeth Day McCormick Collection, 44.1367. Photograph © 2014 Museum of Fine Arts, Boston.

Supplies

Beyond the standard supplies required for all styles (listed on page 133):

Starting with a shorter wig and adding hair:
- 1 **wig** (at least 15" long), straight, without bangs
- 4 packages **weaving hair**, straight, at least 20" long

Starting with a long wig:
- 1 **wig** (at least 22" long), straight, without bangs
- 1 package **weaving hair**, straight, at least 20" long

For both:
- 6 pre-made **buckles** (rolls), about 4" long, made on an 1" diameter form (see pages 108–112). You will need 1 package of straight **braiding** (2 packages of 20"+ **weaving**) **hair** for this.
- 1 package **wire mesh**
- 1 pair heavy duty **wire cutters**
- **Wire**, about 24 gauge
- 1 large **roll form** (about 1.25" diameter)
- 2 large **hairbands** (covered or uncovered rubber band)
- 1 **bow** or other ornament

212   18th Century Hair & Wig Styling

3

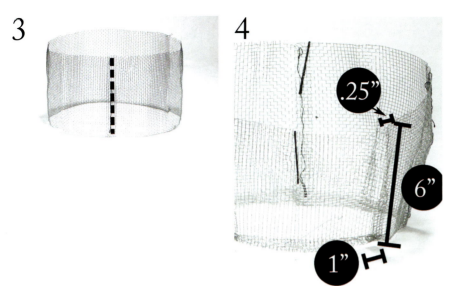

4

5

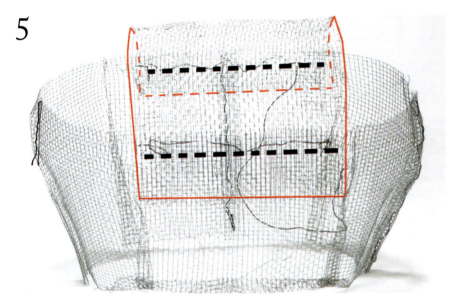

6

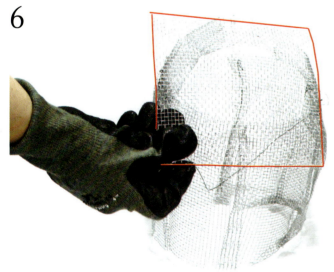

1 Review the information about creating wire mesh frames on pages 113-114.

2 Review the information about adding extra hair to a wig on page 118. This is the wig that was used as an example. Add 6 rows of weaving hair to the nape of the neck, and 4 rows across the top of the head at the parting shown.

If you are using a long wig, only add 2 rows to the nape of the neck at this point.

3 Cut a piece of wire mesh, 27" by 6", and fold it into a circle. Overlap the edges by about 1". Sew the circle together using wire.

4 Make darts at the sides and side back points. These darts should be about 1" wide along the bottom edge of the circle, tapering to .25" at the top.

5 Cut a piece of wire mesh, 11" by 6". Pin this piece so that it covers the top of the circle, from the side front darts to the side back. Overlap the ends of this piece with the circle by about 1". Sew the two together, at front and back, with wire.

6 Cut a square big enough to cover the empty corners, plus about 3" extra on all edges.

Finished Styles 213

7 Sew this piece to top and bottom. Fold the corners to fit, keeping the shape rounded (look at step 10 for the finished shape). This makes the support for the high hair, which will now be called the Frame.

8 Block the wig. Part the hair from behind the ears and across the crown. Clip the front and back sections out of the way.

9 Place the Frame on top of the wig, making sure that it leans back just slightly as shown. Place the front edge of the Frame about 1.5" back from the front hairline. Sew the Frame to the wig using a curved needle.

10 Pin two rows of weaving hair across the base of the Frame, from the side, across the back, to the other side.

11 Tease a section of this hair, then pull it up on top of/over the Frame. Bobby pin the ends of the hair to the Frame, using Xed bobby pins.

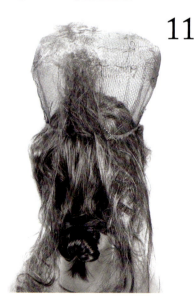

12  **13**

12 Repeat step 11 until the back half of the Frame is covered.

13 Pin two more rows of weaving hair across the same back half of the Frame.

14a  **14b**

14a-b Comb this hair smooth and, in sections, bring it up over the Frame. Fold the hair so that the ends are tucked in...

14c

14c ... Bobby pin them, using Xed pins, near the front edge of the top of the Frame.

Finished Styles 215

15 Repeat steps 14a-c until the entire back half of the Frame is covered.

16 Unclip the front section and divide it into two sections, parted horizontally. Clip the lower section (closest to the front hairline) out of the way.

If you are using a long wig, bobby pin 2 rows of weaving hair to the base of the frame. Use this hair for step 17, instead of dividing the front hair.

17 In pieces, tease the section of hair closest to the Frame and then bring it over the Frame. Bobby pin this hair, using Xed pins, to the top of the Frame. Repeat until the entire front is covered.

18a Unclip the section of hair along the front hairline. In sections, comb the hair smooth and bring it up over the Frame. Bring the hair as high as it will go (so long as it does not cross over the back edge of the top), and bobby pin it (using Xed pins) to the Frame.

18b Start at both sides and work your way inwards, so that you do the center pieces last.

18c End the center pieces just past the back edge of the top of the Frame. Fold the ends under, if necessary, as in step 14a.

216   18th Century Hair & Wig Styling

19  **20**

19 Unclip the back hair. Comb the shorter hair and tie it into a ponytail. Place the rubber band at the nape of the neck.

If you are using a long wig, skip steps 19-21.

20 Flip the ponytail end under.

21  **22**

21 Bobby pin the flipped-under end to the wig.

22 Comb out the long hair at the nape of the neck. Holding the hair in one hand, loop it up loosely and determine where you want the braid to begin.

23  **24**

23 Place a rubber band around the long hair where the braid will begin. Keep holding the long hair up while doing this, so that the tension is correct. Determine where the braid will attach to the head.

24 Braid the hair from the rubber band to where the braid will attach to the head. Secure the ends of the braid with another rubber band.

25 Bobby pin, using Xed pins, the lower rubber band to the back of the head, just below the top edge of the Frame.

26 Part the ends of the braid into two equal sections. Wrap one half around your roll form, rolling away from the center.

27 Carefully remove the roll form. Fan the roll out, then bobby pin it to the head, using Xed bobby pins in the base of each side of the loop. Repeat steps 26-27 with the other half of the braid ends.

28 To cover the rubber band at the end of the braid, fan the rolls towards each other, and insert a bobby pin into the hair so that it catches the edge of both rolls. Hide the end of the bobby pin by pushing it into the braid.

29 Cover the lower rubber band with a bow or other ornament.

Pin three of the buckles to one side of the wig as shown. Repeat on the other side.

Lilac
High & Wide Style (late 1770s - early 1780s)

Finished Styles 219

*T*his coiffure demonstrates the love of texture mixing in the last few decades of the eighteenth century. Tightly curled, frizzy hair in a triangular shape is contrasted with stick straight hair used for the buckles and chignon. Since the Gallerie des Modes did not give this style a name, "Lilac" was chosen for the flowers that decorate the fashion plate's coiffure, along with gauze, ribbon, and feathers.

This style is appropriate for Britain, France, and the United States from the late 1770s to the early 1780s.

This demonstration starts with a tightly curled, shoulder-length wig (the "Ayanna" by Wig America, in dark brownish-black, color #2), and adds straight weaving hair. Alternately, you could use a straight wig and set the top and sides into tiny curls like the Balloon style. The model's front hair was left straight, although we could have curled it first to better match the wig texture.

This is another style that can be heavy to wear. If you are new to wearing high wigs, you may wish to reduce the amount of back lean to the wig – the more the weight of the wig settles down on your head, rather than pulling back, the more comfortable it will be to wear.

Both: Designed by: Pierre-Thomas LeClerc, French, about 1740–after 1799. Publisher: Esnauts et Rapilly, French, 18th century. French, 1781. Hand-colored engraving on laid paper. Museum of Fine Arts, Boston. The Elizabeth Day McCormick Collection. Photograph © 2014 Museum of Fine Arts, Boston.

Left: Engraved by: Nicolas Dupin, French. Detail from *Gallerie des Modes et Costumes Français*. 38e Cahier des Costumes Français, 9e Suite des Coeffures à la mode en 1781. oo.222 "Coëffure d'une Dame..." 38.7 x 25.4 cm (15 1/4 x 10 in.). 44.1531.

Right: Engraved by: Pélissier, French. Detail from *Gallerie des Modes et Costumes Français*. 34e Cahier de Costumes Français, 8e Suite de Coeffures à la mode en 1780. 201 "Coëffure à l'Enfant..." French, 1780. 36.8 x 25.4 cm (14 1/2 x 10 in.).

Supplies

Beyond the standard supplies required for all styles (listed on page 133):

- 1 **wig**, shoulder length, with tight corkscrew curls
- 6 pre-made **buckles** (rolls), about 4" long, made on an 1.25" diameter form (see pages 108-112). You will need 1 package of straight **braiding** (2 packages of 20"+ **weaving**) hair for this.
- 2 pre-made **buckles** (rolls), same dimensions, but made from weaving hair with long (about 5") tops, like the example shown on page 111. You will need 1 package of **weaving hair** for this.
- 2 packages curly **weaving hair**, about 14"
- 1 package straight **braiding** hair
- 1 package **wire mesh**
- 1 pair heavy duty **wire cutters**
- **Wire**, about 24 gauge
- 2 **hairbands** (covered or uncovered rubber bands): 1 large, 1 small
- 1 large **roll form** (about 1.25" diameter)
- **Wax paper**
- **Glue**
- **Paintbrush**
- **Tape**
- 1 large **hairband**

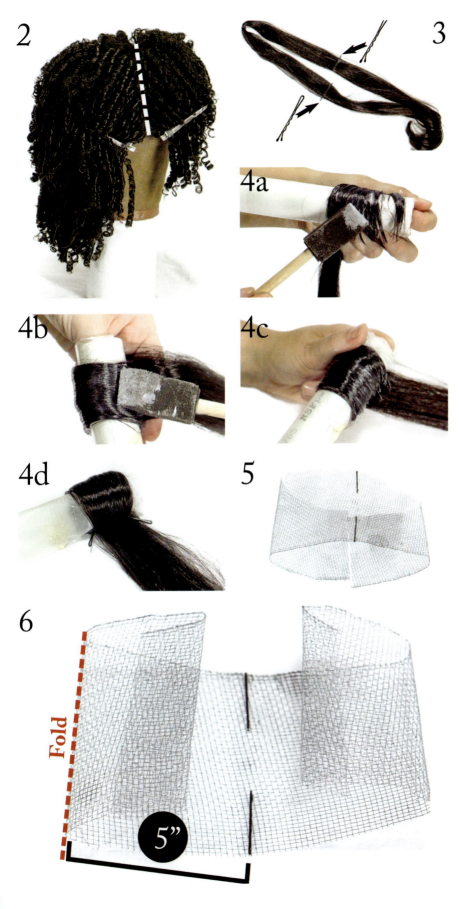

1 Review the information about creating wire mesh frames on pages 113-114. Review the information about making buckles with glue on pages 111-112.

2 Block the wig. Part the hair from behind the ears and across the top of the head. Clip the front and back sections away from each other.

3 Take a length of straight weaving hair, about 2" wide when laid flat, and tie a small rubber band around the center of its length. On each side, pin a bobby pin 7" from the center rubber band.

4a Make one buckle on each end of this piece, rolling the hair up around itself until you reach the bobby pin marker: after covering the roll form with wax paper, roll the ends of the hair around the form. Coat these ends with glue.

4b Roll the hair around the form, keeping the buckle 2" wide. Apply glue to the hair as you roll.

4c Stop gluing one rotation before you reach the bobby pin (so that the outermost layer does not show glue).

4d Pin the buckle with Xed bobby pins, one on either side, while you let the glue dry (remove the pins once the glue has dried).

5 Cut a piece of wire mesh, 21" by 6". Find the center of the 21" length and mark it, top and bottom, with bobby pins.

6 Starting at the center point, measure 5" away, lengthwise. Fold the piece here. Do this on both sides.

Finished Styles 221

7 Unfold the piece. At the line made by the fold, make a dart 1" wide on one edge, tapering to 0" at the other.

Measure 4" from the dart, moving away from the center. Fold the piece here.

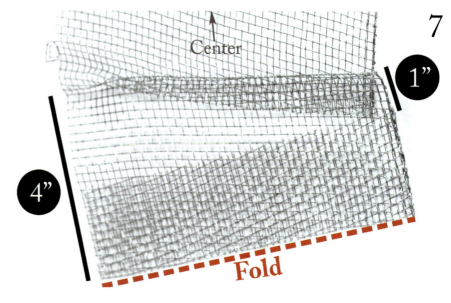

8a-b Attach the wire mesh piece to the blocked wig using large-headed pins. The wide end of the dart (marked here in red) should be the front edge.

Fold the wire mesh at the darts, so that the piece becomes U-shaped. The top should curve up, and the sides should angle in slightly.

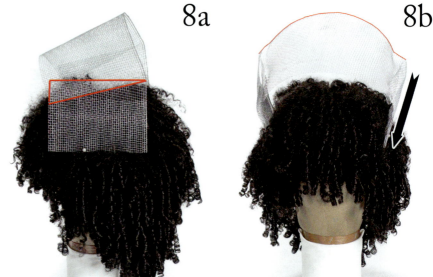

9 The bottom side edge of the wire mesh will probably stand away from the curve of the head in back. To bring the edge in to the head, clip the folded-up piece on the side edge where the frame stops following the head curve. Unfold this piece as needed to fit the curve of the head.

10 Using a curved needle, sew the finished Frame to the wig at the bottom of each side.

222   18th Century Hair & Wig Styling

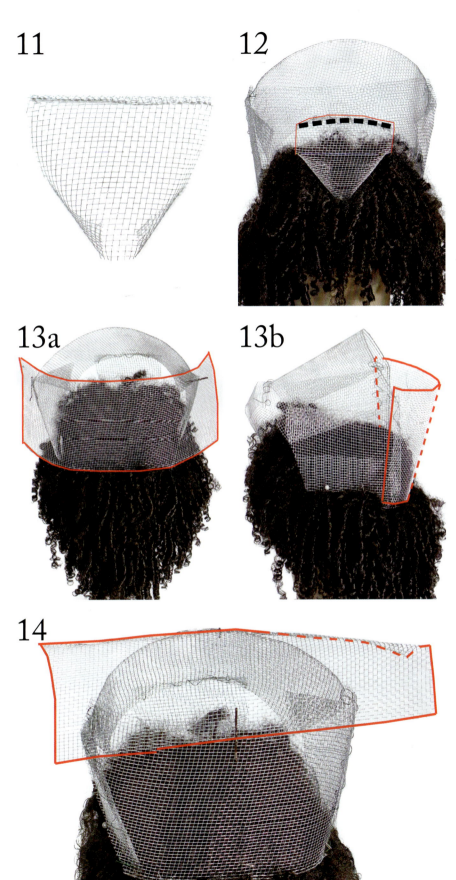

11 Cut a square of wire mesh, 5" by 5". Give one edge a soft curve about 1.5" from the edge. Fold over the corners, softly, on the other edge as shown. You have made a triangular shape.

12 Place the triangular piece so that the long folded edge is underneath the front of the Frame, with about 1.5" overlap. Match the center of the triangle and Frame. The triangle point should aim down, directly at the center of the head. Make sure that the point does not extend past the hairline. Using wire, sew the triangular piece to the Frame. Using a curved needle and thread, sew the point of the triangular piece to the wig.

13a-b Cut a piece of wire mesh, 18" by 6". Use this piece to cover the back. The wire mesh should touch the wig caul (the netted/elastic base to which the hair is sewn) along the bottom edge, and lean outwards on top. Trim the excess edges, leaving overlap, and then sew the wire mesh to the existing wire mesh piece with wire.

14 Cut a piece of wire mesh large enough to cover the empty area at the top of the back, plus overlap.

Finished Styles 223

15 Fold darts into the corners of this piece as shown. Bobby pin this to the Frame, trim the excess (leaving about a 1" overlap), and sew it to the Frame with wire. This makes the support for the high hair, which will now be called the Frame.

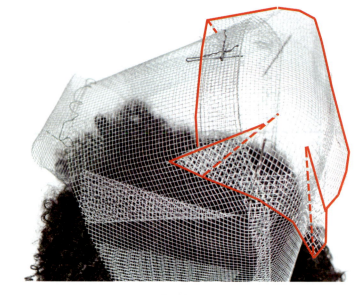

16 Take a piece of the curly weaving hair and comb it out thoroughly with a fine toothed comb, so that it becomes frizzy.

17 Pin a row of this combed-out/frizzy weaving hair along the top of the Frame, a few inches from the top edge. Make sure that the weaving hair is long enough to cover the top edge of the Frame, plus 1" or so. Use Xed bobby pins every few inches along the woven end of the hair.

18 Continue wrapping weaving hair around the back side of the Frame, near the top edge as shown.

19a-b Smooth the weaving hair up towards the top edge of the Frame and bobby pin it periodically, so that the top edge of the Frame is covered.

20a-d Continue to wrap the Frame with frizzed weaving hair, working in a spiral towards the front of the wig. Each row of weaving hair should overlap the row laid before it by 1-2". Use Xed bobby pins at the woven edge of the hair, and smooth the hair up over the previous row, bobby pinning to secure. Continue until you reach the triangular piece at the front of the Frame.

21a-b Comb out the front hair along the wig's hairline, so that it is frizzy. Smooth it up and bobby pin it to the Frame. The wig hair should overlap the previously applied weaving hair by at least 1".

Finished Styles 225

22a-b Repeat step 20 on the sides and back, with the caveat that you should only comb out/frizz about 1" thickness of hair right along the hairline. If you comb out/frizz all of the wig hair, it will probably end up too bushy.

23 Measure the wig's stable portion along the back of the neck. Cut a piece of straight weaving hair six times this length, fold it into sixths, and whip stitch it to the stable portion of the wig's nape.

24 Hold the straight weaving hair up loosely to the top back of the Frame to determine the chignon length.

25 Tie a hairband around the point where you want the chignon to end, looping the ends of the hair through the final tie of the hairband.

26 Trim the ends of the chignon so it they extend only about 1-2" past the hairband.

27  **28**

27 Pin the chignon to the Frame, using Xed bobby pins and catching the hairband and the Frame.

28 Attach two of the pre-made buckles to the sides of the wig as shown. Make sure they are visible from the front. Repeat on the other side.

29  **30**

29 Attach the two-buckle piece of weaving hair made in steps 3-4, bobby pinning the rubber banded center of the piece above the chignon end as shown. The long pieces and buckle ends can be left hanging, or the buckles can be pinned to the wig.

30 Pin two buckles, one above the other, on top of the rubber band at the center of the two-ended buckle , and the rubber-banded end of the chignon.

31

31 Pin the two pre-made buckles-with-long-tops so that they hang behind the ears, as shown.

Finished Styles 227

Marie-Antoinette
High & Wide Style (late 1770s - early 1780s)

French queen Marie-Antoinette is synonymous with the elaborately high hairstyles of the 1770s. While this is historically true, she was also among the first to champion the (comparatively) relaxed and informal styles that were introduced around the turn of the 1780s. While this bust depicts her in a very regal pose, even wearing a diadem, the lower shape and softer silhouette of her hair presage the artful "naturalism" that was to reign during the French Revolutionary period.

This style is appropriate for Britain, France, and the United States from the late 1770s to the early 1780s.

This style is primarily supported by ratting, but it also presented an opportunity to experiment with the small, triangular cushion shown on page 12. The resulting frame is not necessary to achieving the style (the same height could be created through teasing), although it would be useful to support a crown, hat, or other weighty item.

I used a long wavy wig in champagne blonde ("Cassie" by Wig America color #22), to invoke Marie-Antoinette's hair color. As the model's hair contains many different colors (which you can see in the photos of the Derby style), we integrated only a tiny bit of her own hair across the front hairline and powdered the wig front lightly to blend.

This coiffure would certainly be achievable using natural hair, provided false buckles, ringlets, and a braid were added.

Boizot, Simon Louis. Details from *Marie-Antoinette (1755-1793), Reine de France*. Marble, 1781. (C) RMN-Grand Palais / Art Resource, NY.

Supplies

Beyond the standard supplies required for all styles (listed on page 133):

- 1 **wig**, 22" or longer, straight or wavy
- 1 package **braiding hair**, straight
- 1 package **wire mesh**
- 1 pair heavy duty **wire cutters**
- **Wire**, about 24 gauge
- 1 medium **roll form** (about 1" diameter)
- **Foam rollers**: about 6 large (about 1.25" diameter), 45 medium (about 1" diameter)
- 1 small **roll form** (about 3/4" diameter)
- 1 large **hairband** (covered or uncovered rubber band)
- 1 bow, cockade, or other **ornament**

Finished Styles 229

1 Review the information about creating wire mesh frames on pages 113-114.

2 Block the wig. Part the hair from the outside edge of the nape of the neck, across the crown, to the other outside edge of the nape of the neck. Clip the back hair out of the way.

3 Part the front hair vertically, from the crown of the head to the nape of the neck.

4 Set this side portion in large foam rollers. Roll the hair **forward** towards the face.

5 Unclip the rest of the front hair. Set it into small foam rollers. Roll the hair **back** towards the crown of the head.

Set the rolled portion of the wig by pouring boiling water over it (see page 104). Remove the curlers. Allow the wig to dry.

6 Cut a piece of wire mesh, 6.5" by 6". Fold it in half. Fold back a triangle, beginning 2" from one edge, as shown. Do the same on the other side.

7 Unfold the piece. Cut off the triangular folded pieces, but round the shape slightly outward of the fold lines (marked as dashes in the image).

8 Fold this piece into waves, as shown. This will be the top of the frame.

9 Cut another piece of wire mesh, 6" by 4" (this will be the back). Align it at right angles with the straight edge of the wire mesh triangle. Sew the two together with wire, using a whipstitch effect.

230 18th Century Hair & Wig Styling

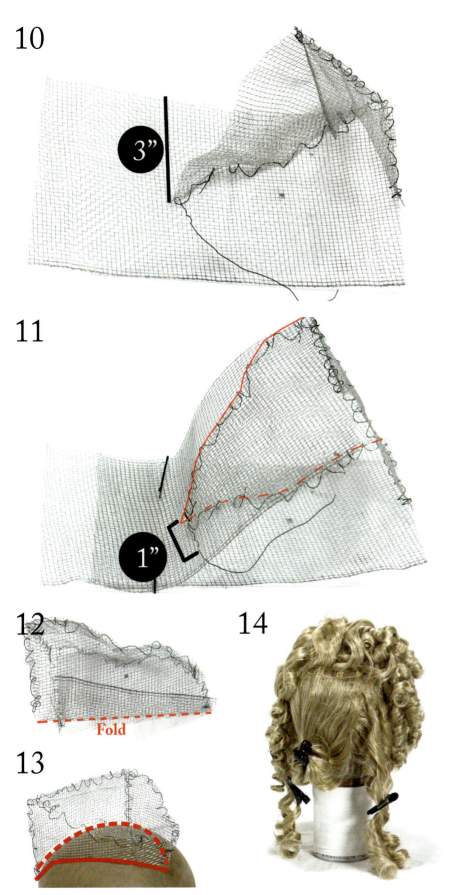

10 Lay the triangle of wire onto another, larger piece of wire (side 1). Align the back at the top right corner of side 1, on a straight line with the shorter edge. Bring the point of the top down 3" from the top edge of side 1. Sew the top and back to side 1, using a whipstitch effect.

11 Lay another large piece of wire mesh (side 2) on top of the wavy top. Align the pieces the same as in step 10, and sew them down with a whipstitch effect. This will be easiest to do if you clip the two large side pieces together at the point of the triangle.

Cut away the excess wire mesh of sides 1 and 2, above the top edge.

12 Create a 1" center front seam, parallel to the back edge, where sides 1 and 2 meet. Sew this seam together. Fold the bottom edge of side 1, from the bottom of the back to the bottom of the center front seam. Cut away the folded up piece of side 1. Repeat with side 2.

13 Place the triangle onto your wig block. Cut crescents along the lower edges of the sides and back to make it fit the shape of the head. This makes the support for the high hair, which will now be called the Frame.

14 Block the wig. Keep the back hair clipped. Clip the side back sections, which were rolled into 3 large rollers, so they stay separate from the rest of the front curls.

15 Brush the front hair forward, **except** for a 1" section of curls which should be brushed **back**.

16 Place the Frame onto the wig, making sure that the triangle point in front does not extend past the wig's front hairline. Using a curved needle, sew the Frame onto the wig.

17 Finger comb all of the front curls.

18 Using a narrow-toothed teasing comb, take a 1" section of hair at the side of the frame and tease it.

19 Bring this piece up and over the Frame, and bobby pin it to the top of the Frame.

20 Repeat steps 18-19 across the sides and front, until the Frame is covered.

232   18th Century Hair & Wig Styling

21 Take the 1" section of curls that were brushed back in step 15. Comb this section smooth.

Wrap this piece of hair around your palm, keeping the ends on the inside closest to the Frame.

22 Fan this rolled hair across the back side of the Frame, and bobby pin it to the top edge of the back piece.

23 Take a section of hair from the upper back corner of the side. Comb it smooth, then stretch it up to the top back of the Frame. Bobby pin it flat to the Frame, near the top.

24 Take that same section and cut it shorter. The goal is to have messy curls at the top back of the Frame. You will need to keep enough hair so that it can curl, but not enough that it hangs down. About 4-5" past the bobby pinned point is a good place to start, but you can always make small cuts, release the hair, and see how it lays before cutting further.

25 Part a 2" section of hair vertically, from the ear to the top of the Frame.

26 Comb that hair back towards the lower back corner of the Frame.

Finished Styles 233

27 Bobby pin this section to the Frame and wig, in a line with the bobby pin(s) placed in step 24. Leave the ends hanging.

28 Take the ends from steps 26-27 and roll them up on the **small** roll form. It is important to hold the roll form at the same angle that you will want the finished buckle to lie. Roll the hair **forward** (and outward) toward the face.

29 Continue rolling the hair around the roll form until it is directly on top of the bobby pins.

30 Carefully remove the roll form, and bobby pin (using Xed pins) the resulting buckle to the wig.

Repeat steps 23-30 on the other side.

31a-c Take sections of the remaining front hair, comb it up over the Frame, and bobby pin it near the back edge of the top. Cut this hair like you did in step 24, making sure that you leave enough hair to form curls at the top edge of the Frame.

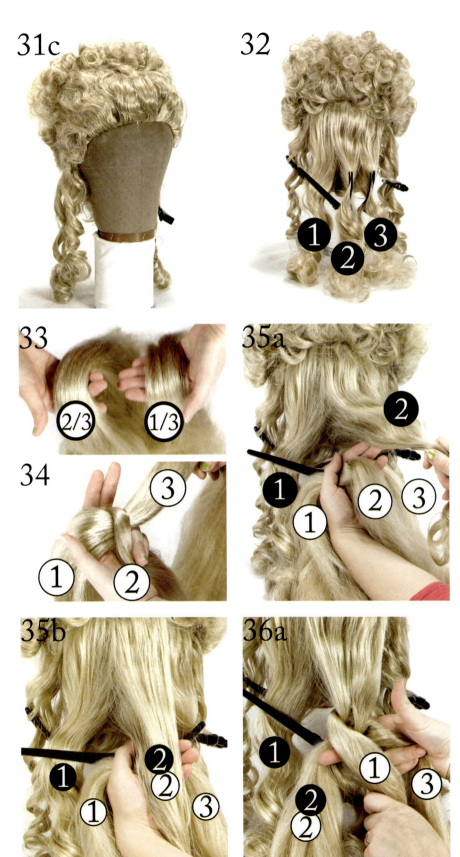

32 Unclip the main back section, keeping the side curls clipped. Comb the back section smooth, and separate it into three equal sections (labeled #1, #2, and #3).

33 Take the package of braiding hair, and divide the loose hair into two sections: one section should be 2/3 of the hair, and the other section should be 1/3.

34 Matching the centers, fold the 1/3 section around the 2/3. This should make a T, with the center consisting of both ends of the 1/3 section (#2), wrapped around the midway point of the 2/3 section (labeled #1 on the left, and #3 on the right).

35a-b Align the crossed braiding hair with the three sections of back hair. Hold the braiding hair underneath the wig hair. Combine the #2 piece of braiding hair with the #2 piece of wig hair.

36a-b Braid the wig back hair and loose braiding hair together: Cross braiding/#1 over the combined #2 sections (wig and braiding). Then, cross the wig/#1 over the #2 sections, joining braiding/#1 with wig/#1.

Do the same on the right-hand side. You now have three joined sections of hair.

Finished Styles 235

37a-b Braid this entire section until you reach the length of your chignon. Test the length by pulling the braid end up to the top back of the Frame.

38 Trim the ends of the braid to about 3" long, enough to loop over the end of the braid, as you finish the braid with a hairband.

39 Bobby pin the braid to the top back of the Frame, using Xed pins. Cover the hairband with a ribbon, cockade, flowers, or other ornament.

40 Unclip the side back curls. Comb them around the **medium** roll form, **forward** towards the face, creating one wide ringlet. Hairspray, allow the hairspray to set, then remove the roll form.

Do the same on the other side.

Pearl
High & Wide Style (late 1770s - early 1780s)

Finished Styles 237

The "Pearl" is named for the rope of pearls that are featured in so many eighteenth-century hairstyles, including this French fashion plate. The flattish top works well to support a "pouf" bonnet like the one shown here. Any number of variations can be achieved by changing the buckle placement, while the chignon could be styled as a braid or twist, among other many other options.

This style is appropriate for Britain, France, and the United States from the late 1770s to the early 1780s.

This is yet another style that can be heavy to wear. If you are new to wearing high wigs, you may wish to reduce the amount of back lean to the wig – the more the weight of the wig settles down on your head, rather than pulling back, the more comfortable it will be to wear.

I used a long, slightly wavy wig ("Ashley" by Giant) in medium auburn (color #30). Although the model has bangs, I was able to work her own hair into the front by using a lot of hairspray.

Publisher: Esnauts et Rapilly, French, 18th century. Detail from *Gallerie des Modes et Costumes Français, 29e. Cahier de Costumes Français, 7e Suite des coeffures à la mode en 1780. ee.169 "Pouf d'un nouveau gout..."* French, 1780. Hand-colored engraving on laid paper. 41.9 x 26.7 cm (16 1/2 x 10 1/2 in.). Museum of Fine Arts, Boston. The Elizabeth Day McCormick Collection, 44.1459. Photograph © 2014 Museum of Fine Arts, Boston.

Supplies

Beyond the standard supplies required for all styles (listed on page 133):

- 1 **wig**, 22" or longer, straight
- 2 pre-made **buckles** (rolls), about 4 long, made on an 1.25" diameter form (see pages 108-112). You will need 1 package of straight **braiding** (2 packages of 20"+ **weaving**) hair for this.
- 2 packages **weaving hair**, curly, at least 20" long
- 1 package **wire mesh**
- 1 pair heavy duty **wire cutters**
- **Wire**, about 24 gauge
- 1 large **roll form** (about 1.25" diameter)
- 1 large **hairband** (covered rubber band)
- 2 soup **cans** (or other similarly shaped objects), about 3" diameter, and 4" diameter
- **Foam rollers**: about 14 large (about 1.25" diameter)
- 1 bow or other **ornament**

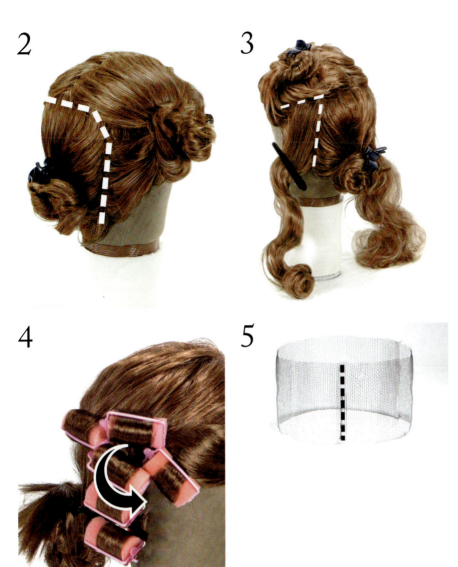

1 Review the information about creating wire mesh frames on pages 113-114.

2 Block the wig. Part the hair from the outside edge of the nape of the neck, across the crown, to the other outside edge of the nape of the neck.

Clip the back hair out of the way.

3 Part the front hair vertically, from the crown of the head to the nape of the neck. Clip the rest of the front hair out of the way.

4 Roll the side parted hair around large foam rollers Roll the hair **forward** towards the face. Do the same on both sides.

Set these rolled sections by pouring boiling water over them (see page 104). Allow the wig to dry.

5 Cut a piece of wire mesh, 37" by 6". Roll it into a circle, overlapping about 1". Sew the circle closed using wire.

6 Make darts at the following points: center front, center back, side front, side back. The darts should be about 1" wide along the bottom edge, and extend the entire height of the piece. Pin the circle to the wig, making sure that the front edge of the wire mesh circle is about 1" back from the wig's front hairline.

If necessary, tighten the darts at the bottom edge of the wire mesh circle to fit the wig block.

Finished Styles 239

7 At the center front and back, unfold the top 2" of the darts. This will create a curved shape at the front and back.

8 Cut a piece of wire mesh, 16" by 6". Fold the ends down, with one fold higher than the other. Keep the folds very curved.

9 Push this shape into the wire mesh circle, with the lower end in front. Align the center of the lower end with the center of the darted circle. Overlap the edges about 1". Use bobby pins to hold the top in place, then sew it in place with loose wire.

10 Cut a piece of wire mesh, 6" by 3". Fold it into the shape shown.

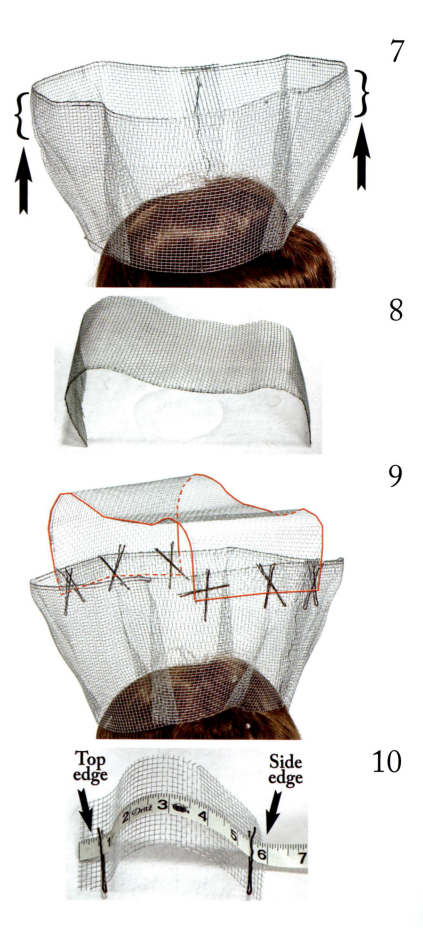

11

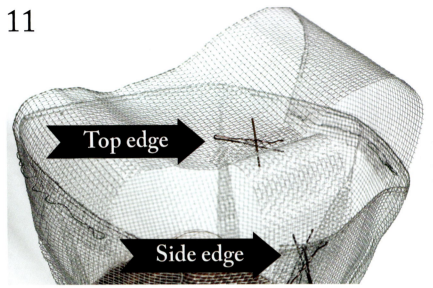

11 Align this new piece on the side of the wire mesh frame. Lay the top edge under the preexisting top piece, overlapping the two by 1". Overlap the side edge with the darted, round piece by 1". Sew the two edges together with wire.

Repeat steps 10-11 on the other side.

12

13a

13b

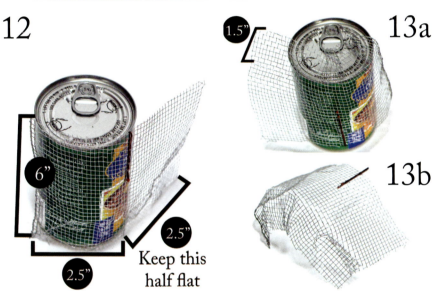

12 Cut a piece of wire mesh, 6" by 5". Mark the center of the shorter measure with a bobby pin, then bend one of the halfs around the smaller can.

13a-b Move the wire mesh up, so that it extends above the can about 1.5". Fold this edge over onto the top of the can, darting or squishing the wire mesh to fit.

14

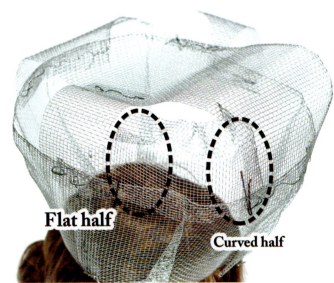

14 Align this curved piece into one of the **back** corners of the Frame. The curved side will form the back, and the flatter side will form the side. Sew them into place with wire.

There will probably still be an empty space on the top of this corner. Cut a piece of wire mesh large enough to cover this hole, plus a bit for overlap. Lay the piece on top of the hole, and sew the two pieces together.

Finished Styles 241

15 Cut another piece of wire mesh, 4.5" by 5.5". Bend this piece around the larger can, using the shorter measure as the top/bottom edge. Fold over the top 2" onto the top of the can. This piece is the **front** corner.

16 Place this new piece inside of the Frame, with the 2" folded over section at the top, covering the front corner. Sew the two together with wire.

Repeat steps 12-16 to fill the other two corners. When you make the back corner piece (steps 12-13b), you will need to make a mirror image, reversing which side is flat.

17 Make a dent in the top edge of the center front using the side of your hand. This completes the support for the high hair, which will now be called the Frame.

18 Block the wig. Clip the sections separate: front, back, and each curled side piece.

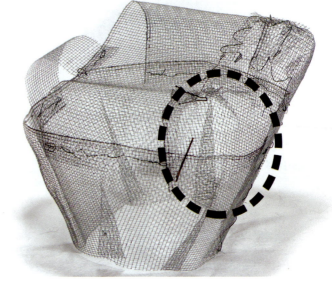

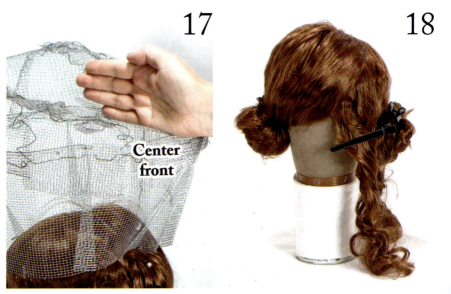

19 Place the Frame onto the wig, making sure that the front edge is behind the wig's front hairline.

Examine the top line of the Frame's silhouette. The back should be higher than the front. If it is not, align the Frame so that the top line is correct, and clip the sides to hold the piece up from the back. There will be gap between the bottom of the wire mesh frame and the back of the wig.

20 Cut a piece of wire mesh, long enough and wide enough to fill the gap. Bobby pin it to the Frame, and then whipstitch the pieces together using wire.

21 When you are happy with the shape of the Frame, sew it to the wig using a curved needle.

22 Wrap two rows of curly weaving hair around the entire base of the Frame. Bobby pin the woven edge to the base of the Frame, using Xed pins.

Finished Styles 243

23 In small sections, tease this weaving hair and bring it up to the top of the frame. Bobby pin (using Xed pins) the ends of the hair to the top of the frame.

24 Repeat step 23 until all of the weaving hair is up. The Frame is large enough that you will have gaps in the corners. Pin additional rows of curly weaving hair over these gaps...

25 ...and then tease that hair and bring it up to the top of the frame. Continue until the entire frame is covered with teased weaving hair.

Pin two rows of straight weaving hair around the base of the Frame, from one side, around the back to the other side.

26a In sections, comb the hair smooth and pull it up to the top of the frame. Loop the ends of each hair section over a pen or other similarly sized item...

26b ...so that you can fold the ends under at the center of the top of the Frame.

26c Pin the folded-under ends so that they create a line directly down center, from the center front to the center back of the wig.

27a You will have gaps at the back corners, where there is not enough straight hair to cover the teased underlayer. Pin an additional two rows of weaving hair over these corners, comb the hair smooth, and bring it up over the top of the Frame.

27b To finish the ends of the corners, do not loop the ends over the pen. Instead, twist them...

27c ...Then tuck the twisted end under, before pinning the hair to the Frame.

28 Unclip the front hair. In sections, comb this hair smooth and bring it up over the Frame. Start with the sides and work in. When you reach the center front, repeat the same twist-and-tuck maneuver to finish the ends.

29 Unclip the back hair. Comb it smooth, then put the ends into a ponytail. Loop the ends of the ponytail through the hairband, so that the ends are on top.

30 Loop the ponytail up loosely to the back of the Frame. Bobby pin (using Xed pins) the ends of the ponytail to the Frame.

31 Unclip the side curled section, pull the hair back from the hairline, and then clip it temporarily. Pin two rows of curly weaving hair along the hairline, from the ear to the nape of the neck. Using a curved needle, sew this weaving hair to the edge of the wig.

Repeat on the other side.

32a Comb the weaving hair sewn on in step 31 smooth, and then wrap the ends around your roll form. Roll the hair **down** and **in** towards the wig. Roll the hair around the form until you reach the point shown, with the hair angled towards the back of the head.

Flip the roll form horizontally, back to front...

Finished Styles 245

32b ...which will then put the buckle on the outside.

33 Carefully remove the roll form, and pin the buckle to the Frame using Xed pins on each side.

34 Pinning the buckle to the Frame will probably shorten it a bit. Spread the buckle gently.

Repeat steps 31-34 on the other side.

35 Unclip the side curled hair. Comb this hair around your roll form, wrapping the hair **forward** towards the face. Hairspray, wait a moment for the spray to set, then remove the form to create a ringlet.

Repeat on the other side.

36 Cut a 5" length of curly weaving hair. Fold it in half, and whipstitch the folded ends together.

Holding the woven end with your thumb, comb the hair around the roll form to create a ringlet. Hairspray, wait a moment, then remove the form.

37 Pin the two pre-made buckles to the back of the Frame.

38 Pin the ringlet to the top of the ponytail end, allowing it to dangle. Underneath, pin a bow or other decorative item to cover the hairband.

246   18th Century Hair & Wig Styling

Plume
Bushy Style (1780s)

Finished Styles 247

The "Plume" gets its name from the hat worn by this fashionable Frenchwoman, under which her hair is styled in the typical bushy, rounded shape of the 1780s. The chignon is no doubt long; it could be worn down, straight or in ringlets, or looped up, in a ponytail, braid, or twist.

This style is appropriate for Britain, France, and the United States in the 1780s.

This demonstration will show you how to achieve a bushy shape through teasing. This process can be relatively damaging if you try it on your own hair, in which case a safer option would be the Balloon, which relies only on frizz for volume.

I used a very long, slightly wavy wig in very dark brown ("Las Canton" by Vanessa, color #4). The model's own hair was integrated around the hairline. We curled it first before working it into the wig, so that the textures would match.

Labille-Guiard, Adélaïde. Detail from *A Fashionable Noblewoman Wearing a Plumed Hat*. Pastel on blue laid paper, c. 1789. NGA.

Supplies

Beyond the standard supplies required for all styles (listed on page 133):

- 1 **wig**, 30" or longer, straight or wavy
- 1 small **roll form** (about 3/4" diameter)
- **Foam rollers**: about 4 large (about 1.25" diameter), 30 medium (about 1" diameter)

1 Block the wig. Part the hair from the outside edge of the nape of the neck, across the crown, to the other outside edge of the nape of the neck.

2 Set the front hair into the medium rollers. Roll the hair away from the face and/or down towards the neck.

3 Part a vertical piece, 2" high by 1" wide, at the nape of the neck on each side of the back hair section.

4 Roll each of these pieces around one medium roller, rolling the hair **forward** towards the face.

Set the center portion of the back hair into the larger rollers. Divide it into four low curls, below the nape of the neck (see step 2 for a visual).

Set all the curls by pouring boiling water over the curled portions (see page 104). Allow the wig to dry.

5 Block the wig. Clip the back hair out of the way, including both the smaller and larger back curls.

6 On one side, part the curls horizontally about 1-2" above the ear. Clip the rest of the front hair out of the way. Finger comb these sectioned curls.

Finished Styles 249

7 Using a fine-toothed comb, tease the roots of this sectioned hair, creating about 3" of teased hair at the roots.

8 Part another section of the front hair, around the temples. Clip the rest of the front hair out of the way. Tease the roots of this hair, just like you did in step 7.

Repeat steps 6-8 on the other side.

9 Unclip the top portion of the front. Part a 1" horizontal piece at the back of this section. Tease the roots of this 1" piece, creating about 2" finished length of teased roots.

10 Continue ratting the top section in 1" pieces, moving forward toward the front hairline.

11 The curls at the sides are probably too long for our final shape. Grasp the hair hanging down around the neck, raise it up about 2", and trim a few inches off of the ends. Notice the finished length in the next picture.

12a-b With a wide-toothed comb, tease the ends of the hair at the sides of the wig.

12b

13

13 In back, try to preserve the look of the long straight chignon. Take any pieces of curled/teased hair that are hanging down in back, and grasp each midway down its length. Bobby pin that mid-point to the top of the chignon, so that you shorten the length.

14

15

14 Take some of the teased hair at the very bottom of the sides. With a fine-toothed comb, comb the ends smooth, leaving the 2-3" roots teased.

15 Wrap this hair around your roll form, **up** towards the top of the head.

16

17

16 Curl this piece up to the base of the teased roots. Carefully remove the roll form, and bobby pin the roll to itself to hold its shape.

17 Now we need to turn the rest of the teased front into something pretty. Take a small section of hair and comb the ends smooth with a fine-toothed comb (but do not comb out the teased roots).

18 Cut the ends so that they are only long enough to roll **once** around your roll form, measured from where the teased section ends.

19 Roll the combed ends around the roll form **up** towards the top of the head. Hairspray the curl, wait a moment for the hairspray to set, then carefully remove the roll form.

20a-b Continue combing, cutting, and rolling the ends across the sides and top of the hair.

21 With a wide tooth comb, comb the hair around the face straight up, so that none of the curls fall into the face.

22 Unclip the back. Keeping the side smaller ringlets separate, comb the center back section smooth. If the side ringlets require it, they can be reset by combing them around the roll form and hairspraying.

Georgiana
Bushy Style (1780s)

Finished Styles 253

*G*eorgiana *was* the *fashion leader in Britain during this era, so it is only fitting that she provide the model for the most elaborate of the bushy, constructed "natural" styles. Her coiffure is similar to that of the Plume, but much larger, and features sculptured curls on the ends of her hair. The chignon is no doubt long; it could be worn down, straight or in ringlets, or looped up, in a ponytail, braid, or twist.*

This style is appropriate for Britain, France, and the United States in the 1780s.

I used the "Lioness" by Wig America in color #15. As the model's own hair is slightly darker, we worked only a tiny bit of her own hair into the wig along the top of the forehead. She has a widow's peak, which made it even more important to use some of her own hair.

Dupont, Gainsborough. Detail from *Georgiana, Duchess of Devonshire*. Oil on canvas, c. 1789-96. NGA.

Supplies

Beyond the standard supplies required for all styles (listed on page 133):

- 1 **wig**, 28" or longer, curly
- 1 medium **roll form** (about 1" diameter)
- 1 tiny **roll form** (about 5/8" diameter)

1

2

3

4

5a

5b

5c

1 Block the wig. Part the hair from behind the ears and across the low end of the crown. Clip the top hair out of the way.

Note: in this example, the back section is parted somewhat low on the crown of the wig. This is because this wig has long layers, and the section from this point to the crown was too short to work for the long back ringlets. Ideally, the hair should be parted higher on the crown. There are a few images from the 1780s-90s that show this lower line for the chignon, so this example is historically accurate -- but you should not ever go any lower.

2 Section the hair into 1" pieces. Comb the bottom half of each section into a ringlet by combing it around your **small** roll form, spray with hairspray, wait a moment for the hairspray to set, then carefully remove the roll form.

3 Repeat step 2 across the entire back section of the wig. Alternate curl direction, either ringlet by ringlet, or row by row.

4 Unclip the front section. Using a fine-toothed comb, tease the roots of each piece of the entire front section. The final teased portion should be about 2" long on top, graduating to about 4" long on the sides.

5a-c Starting on the top of the head, take 1" pieces of hair, comb them smooth above the teased base, and roll them around your **small** roll form. Roll the hair **forward** towards the face, until you reach the top of the teased portion. Carefully remove the roll form. Allow the curl to "stand" on top of the teased roots.

Finished Styles 255

6a-b Continue making curls in this way, starting on top of the head and moving down the back.

7a-b For the hair around the face, continue making curls in this way, but now use your **tiny** roll form. The curls should still stand on the teased ends, but place them lower as you move towards the face. You can comb out some of the teased root if necessary to lower the curls.

8a If any of the rolls seem to need help staying curled, you can place a bobby pin into the underside of the roll.

8b Bobby pinning the roll often shortens it. After you have placed the pin, fan the roll back out.

9 When you reach the lower sides, the hair will probably be far too long to "stand" on the teased roots. Trim these sections shorter, making small, short, cautious cuts.

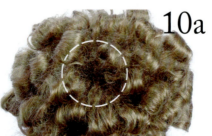

10a If you have any gaps between rolls, like in the center of the back on this picture...

10b ... you can pin two rolls together, using a bobby pin that catches the side of each roll.

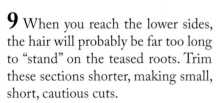

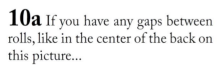

Balloon
Bushy Style (1780s)

Finished Styles 257

It is possible to achieve the large, bushy styles of the 1780s without ratting, as the Balloon will prove. The "Globe Aérostatique" (the name of the hat in this the fashion plate) was the famous hot air balloon invented by the Montgolfier brothers, which captured the French imagination in this period. It is possible that the shape of the balloon inspired the shape of hair in this decade, as references to ballooning were frequent in fashion.

This style is appropriate for Britain, France, and the United States in the 1780s. It can be easily varied by changing how the long back hair is styled.

This demonstration asks that you trim the top and side hair of the wig to the desired shape. This may seem a bit scary to those who are not professional hairdressers or wigmakers. However, if you focus on the overall silhouette and make small cuts, you should be able to complete this without problems. If you feel that you absolutely cannot cut a wig to shape, look at the Captain Robert man's wig demonstration. The same approach of leaving the top/sides hair long, pulling it back, and tucking it under appears to have also been used on women's hair. It requires less commitment, although it will be difficult to achieve as large of a shape. Similarly, this leaving-long-and-tucking-under approach is the best one to use when creating a bushy style on a model's own hair, as most models may not appreciate receiving a haircut.

I used the "Showgirl" wig by Lacey Costume Wigs in bright red (color #130). The model's own hair was curled and then worked into the front of the wig along the top of the forehead.

Designed by: Claude-Louis Desrais, French, 1746–1816. Publisher: Esnauts et Rapilly, French, 18th century. Detail from *Gallerie des Modes et Costumes Français. 12e Cahier des coeffures les plus à la mode en 1785. Sans nos. (280bis) "Chapeau au gout du Siecle..."* French, 1785. Hand-colored engraving on laid paper. 31.4 x 24.1 cm (12 3/8 x 9 1/2 in.). Museum of Fine Arts, Boston. The Elizabeth Day McCormick Collection, 44.1601. Photograph © 2014 Museum of Fine Arts, Boston.

Supplies

Beyond the standard supplies required for all styles (listed on page 133):

- 1 **wig**, 36" or longer, straight or wavy
- 2 pre-made **buckles** (rolls), about 3" long, made on an 1.25" diameter form (see pages 108-112)
- 1 large **roll form** (about 1.25" diameter)
- **Foam rollers**: about 60 frames (you will be removing the foam piece, so diameter does not matter). If you are using a straight wig, you will also need 3 large (about 1.25" diameter) curlers.
- 1 large **hairband** (covered rubber band)

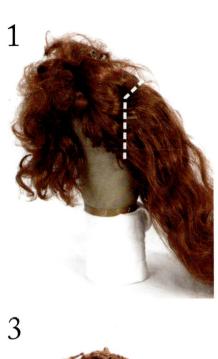
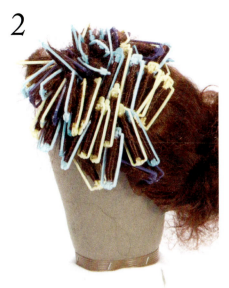

1 Block the wig. Part the hair from behind the ear, across the crown of the head, to behind the other ear. Clip the back hair out of the way.

2 Roll all of the front hair into tiny curls by wrapping small pieces around the center plastic stick of a foam roller (without the foam piece). Curl direction is not important.

If you are working with a straight wig, see step 4 for an additional note about curls.

Set these curls by pouring boiling water over the rolled hair (see page 104). Allow the wig to dry.

3 Block the wig. Clip the front hair out of the way.

4 Unclip the back hair. Make a vertical parting, about 1" wide, from the nape of the neck to behind the ear. Do this on both sides.

*Because this wig is wavy, I did not need to pre-set this side section into curls in order to achieve step 5. If you are working with a straight wig, you will need to set this section into curls by rolling them on 3 large (1.25" diameter) foam rollers. Divide the hair vertically, and set the **bottom** curl **back** away from the face, and the **middle** and **top** curls **forward** towards the face). Set these curls with boiling water.*

5 Part this side section from top to bottom into three equal sections. Take the bottom-most section and create a long ringlet by combing the bottom half around your roll form, **back** away from the face. Spray it with hairspray, wait a moment for the hairspray to set, and then carefully remove the form.

6 Turn the top and middle pieces into tighter ringlets by combing the entire length around the roll form. Roll these **forward** towards the face. Hairspray, wait a moment, then carefully remove the form.

7 Repeat steps 5-6 on the other side. The top two tighter ringlets will hold their shape better if they are clipped up in rolls, so that they are not weighed down, when the wig is not being worn.

Take the center bulk of the back hair, comb it smooth, and loop a hairband around the ends.

8 Bobby pin the ponytail to the back of the head, using Xed pins pushed through the hairband.

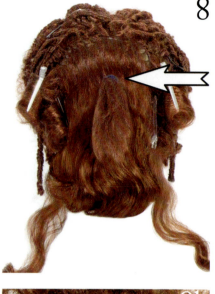

9a-b Comb out the ends of the ponytail and roll them around your roll form. Bobby pin, using Xed pins, the resulting buckle into place.

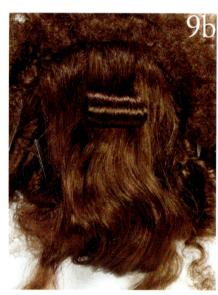

10 Place the two pre-made buckles on either side of the center. Bobby pin them into place, using Xed pins.

11 Unclip the front section. One by one, untwist each curl...

12 ...then comb it out with a fine-toothed comb.

Repeat until every single curl is untwisted and combed out.

13 Clip the front hair up temporarily so it is out of the face.

14a Turn the wig on its side, and study the silhouette on top.

We now need to shape this frizzy mass into the finished shape. **Don't panic**, *you can do this — it's all a matter of silhouette. Make tiny cuts, and keep your eye on the outside line of the shape.*

14b Trim the hair on top to create a relatively smooth, flat silhouette.

15a-b Turn the wig to face you. Trim the wig to create a rounded shape, widest at the temples. If the hair pushes into the face, as it is doing here, use Xed bobby pins, placed inside the bulk of the frizzy hair, to tighten the shape and pull the front back.

16 Repeat step 15 on the other side.

Finished Styles 261

Star
Bushy Style (mid- to late 1780s)

*T*he Star is named for the stars on Madame Chavire's diadem, and is a lovely example of a more conservative coiffure from this era. It is interesting how the hairstyle is achieved using the same techniques that were used on men's wigs.

This style is appropriate for Britain, France, and the United States in the mid- to late 1780s.

A horizontal ornament lends itself well to this coiffure -- a bit of jewelry, a ribbon, or a jeweled bandeau. In this case, a bracelet was used as it had a similar effect to the one on the bust, and it was a good length. Instructions are included for hiding the ends of a decorative band, which can be skipped if you are choosing not to ornament the hair.

I used the "Ashanti" by Wig America in 8-T124. This is an excellent example of a mixed color being a good match for the model's own hair, which was combed into the wig along the top of the forehead.

Pigalle, Jean-Baptiste. Detail from *Bust of Madame Chauvire*. [1780s.] Museum of Fine Arts, Springfield, Mass. (artwork in the public domain; photograph provided by Wikimedia Commons user Daderot, CC0 BY 1.0).

Supplies

Beyond the standard supplies required for all styles (listed on page 133):

- 1 **wig**, 28" or longer, straight or wavy
- 1 medium **roll form**, about 1" diameter
- 1 small **roll form**, about 3/4" diameter
- **Foam rollers**: 45 large or medium (1.25"-1" diameter). A mix of sizes is fine, in which case use the smaller rollers on top.
- Optional: 1 horizontal **ornament** (ribbon, necklace, bracelet, etc.)

Finished Styles 263

1 Block the wig. Part the hair from the outermost side of the nape of the neck, up to and across the crown of the head, and down to the nape of the neck on the other side. Clip the back hair out of the way.

2 Set the front hair in rollers. Set the sides of the head with the hair rolled **up** towards the top of the head. Set the hair on top of the head with the hair rolled **away** from the face.

Set all of these curls by pouring boiling water over the curled sections (see page 104). Allow the wig to dry.

3 Block the wig. Unclip the front hair, and make a horizontal parting at the temples. Do this on both sides. Clip the top hair out of the way.

4 On one side, part the side hair horizontally into three sections. The bottom section will have less hair than the middle and top (see the next few pictures) -- that's okay.

5a-b Clip the top side and middle side sections out of the way. Comb out the bottom section, and roll it around the **medium** roll form until you reach the roots. Roll the hair **up** towards the top of the head.

264   18th Century Hair & Wig Styling

6 Carefully remove the roll form. Bobby pin this buckle to the wig, using Xed pins.

7a-b Unclip the middle section. Comb this piece smooth, then wrap it around the roll form. Roll the hair **up** towards the top of the head, until you reach the roots.

8 Before removing the roll form, pull back slightly on the roll form so that the buckle spirals back slightly. Carefully remove the roll form.

9 Pin this buckle to the head, using Xed pins on either side.

10a-b Unclip the side top section. Comb it smooth, and roll it around your roll form. Roll the hair **up** towards the top of the head, until you reach the roots.

11 Before removing the roll form, pull back slightly so that the buckle spirals backwards slightly. Carefully remove the roll form, and bobby pin (using Xed pins) the buckle to the head.

Repeat steps 4-11 on the other side of the head.

12 Unclip the top hair. Using a wide-toothed comb, comb all this hair smooth.

13 If you are going to add a horizontal decoration across the top of the head, part two 1" square section at the outermost points of the front hairline.

If you are not adding a decoration, you can skip this step, and in step 14 comb all of the top hair back.

14 Comb all of the top hair back, except for the two pieces at the front hairline. Gather all of this hair up into one hand.

15a-b Loop the ends of this hair under. Play with how tightly you pull back on the hair, as this will determine how much height you have on top.

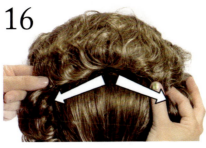

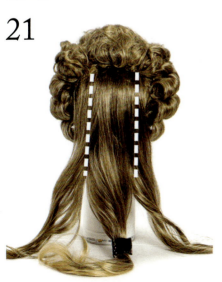

16 Fan this rolled-under section out, so that it reaches the top buckles on each side.

17 Bobby pin, using Xed pins, this rolled-under section to the wig.

If you are not using a decoration, skip to step 21.

18 Place your horizontal decoration across the top hair. Bobby pin, using Xed pins, the piece into place.

19 Take one of the pieces from the front hairline, and pull them over the outer end of the decoration, hiding the end.

20 Tuck this piece under the rolled-under section, and bobby pin it into place.

Repeat steps 19-20 on the other side.

21 Unclip the back section. Comb it smooth, and then make a 1" vertical parting on each outside edge of the back hair.

22 Take one of these 1" sections and wrap it around the **small** roll form. Apply steam to the curled section, as shown on page 103, to set the curls.

Do the same on the other side.

This will create more of a soft wavy curl rather than a true ringlet. If you would prefer a true ringlet, you will need to curl this hair on a foam roller, and set the curl by pouring boiling water over the rolled section (see page 104).

Finished Styles 267

Matilda
Simple Short & Long Style (1790s)

*T*he Matilda is very similar to the hairstyles of the 1780s, but without the volume. It is an easy style to do on your own hair, although it requires the tight curl that comes from a wet-set curl. If teased, this same style would be appropriate for the 1780s bushy coiffures.

In this case, the original coiffure was tweaked to keep the curls out of the model's face. The style could be varied by using ringlets in back, instead of/in addition to the twists.

This style is appropriate for Britain, France, and the United States in the 1790s.

American 18th Century. Detail from *Matilda Caroline Cruger*. Oil on canvas, c. 1795. NGA.

Supplies

Beyond the standard supplies required for all styles (listed on page 133):

- **Rolling supplies**. The hair must be rolled to start. This style requires very curly hair, so unless the model has very curly hair of her own, a wet set curling method (pincurls, rag curls, or foam rollers) must be used. Heat-set curls are *not* appropriate. Whichever of these methods is used, the curler should be about 3/4" diameter.
- 1 pre-made set of **long ringlets**, made from a flat ponytail the width of the nape of the neck (see page 106). In order to make very long ringlets, I made my own wefts using braiding hair (see page 102). If you are using purchased weaving hair, I suggest using the longest length you can find.
- **Curling iron**, about .75" diameter.

1 Part the hair from the nape of the neck to the crown of the head.

2 Set the front hair into curls using a wet set: foam rollers, pincurls, or rag curls. Roll the hair **back** and away from the face.

3 When the curls have fully dried, remove the curlers. Clip the back hair out of the way.

4 Finger comb all the curls.

If the model's hair is short enough, the front hair may be done! If so, steps 5-6 can be skipped.

5a-b Pinch sections of hair, about halfway down the length, and pull them up loosely. Bobby pin, using Xed pins, the hair to the head at this midway point. The goal is to create the look of shorter curls, so keep the roots loose and full, and let the ends hang.

270   18th Century Hair & Wig Styling

6a

6b

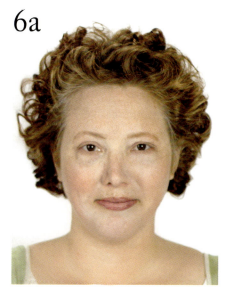
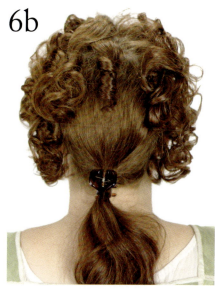

6a-b Continue pinching, lifting, and pinning until all of the curled hair forms a small halo around the head. Keep the straight hair on the back of the head visible.

7

8

7 Unclip the back hair. Make a 1" parting, horizontally, at the nape of the neck. Clip the rest of the back hair out of the way.

8 French braid this 1" section, sideways.

9

10

9 Loop the braided end back on itself, and bobby pin it (using Xed pins) to the French braided portion.

10 Pin the false ringlets onto the French braid, Xing the bobby pins.

11 Using the curling iron, curl all the natural back hair. For the top half of this hair, only curl the hair on the bottom half of its length.

12 Take each individual false ringlet and twist its entire length. Fold it in half, and twist the resulting two pieces around each other.

13 Bobby pin, using Xed pins, the ends to the tops of the false ringlets, underneath the curled natural hair.

Adela
Simple Short & Long Style (1790s)

The Adela is very similar to the Matilda, in that it is cut like the hairstyles of the 1780s, but without the volume. Short, messy curls across the top and sides of the head contrast with long ringlets in back. This style frequently has a ribbon or scarf tied around the head.

This style is appropriate for Britain, France, and the United States in the 1790s.

In this demonstration, I am going to show you the secret of the "Southern Belle" wig by Lacey (here, color #12 was used). Supposedly a mid-Victorian style, its short layers on top and long ringlets in back make it the perfect base for an easy 1780s or 1790s hairstyle. The layered top needs to be set into curls, as the waves in which it comes are not curly enough for the right look. With a lot of teasing, this wig can work for a smaller version of the bushy 1780s styles.

This is an easy style in which to change the model's hair color, as the curls hanging forward at the hairline cover both the model's own roots and the wig line.

Plimer, Andrew (attr. to). Detail from *Portrait of a Lady*. Watercolor and gouache on ivory, n.d. YBA.

Supplies

Beyond the standard supplies required for all styles (listed on page 133):

- 1 "Southern Belle" **wig** by Lacey Costume Wigs
- **Foam rollers**: 20 large (about 1.25" diameter) and 10 medium (about 1" diameter)
- 1 ribbon or scarf, at least 1.5 yards long

1 Block the wig. Part the shorter, layered hair on top -- from behind the ear, across the top back of the head, to behind the other ear -- from the longer curly hair in back.

Clip the back hair out of the way.

Set the top hair into curls using foam rollers. Graduate the sizes of your curlers, using the widest at the back, and the medium at the front. Roll the hair **back**, away from the face.

Set these curls by pouring boiling water over the rolled hair (see page 104). Allow the wig to dry.

2 Block the wig. Clip the shorter front hair curled in step 1 up and out of the way.

With a wide toothed comb, pick out each long ringlet and comb it from the roots to halfway down its length.

3 Comb the bottom half of the ringlet around two fingers. Hairspray, wait a moment for the hairspray to set, then gently remove your fingers.

Repeat on each individual long ringlet.

4 Unclip the short curled hair on top. Finger comb this hair.

5 Part a 1" horizontal section along the front hairline, and push those curls forward into the face.

6 Tie the ribbon or scarf around the head, aligning it with the horizontal part in front.

If any of the curls fall into the eyes, you can bobby pin them shorter by placing a bobby pin in the underside of the curl.

Finished Styles 275

King George
Buckle/Queue Style (1740s - 1790s)

$\mathcal{T}$he King George is modeled after a bust of the British king. It is a queue wig, and thus could be worn (in either wig or hairstyle form) from the 1740s through the 1770s across Britain, France, or the American colonies. For wear in the 1780s or 1790s, the front roll should be moved further back, so that it includes more hair from the sides and crown of the head. Alternately, this style would work for the 1730s if it were worn with curls at the sides instead of buckles.

There are any number of design variations that could be made to this style, primarily in terms of the size and number of buckles, and the styling of the queue.

Eighteenth-century visual sources occasionally show the wearer's own hair peeking out at the temples and along the sides and nape of the neck, so I suggest not worrying if the same happens to your model. You can powder the hair here to match the wig color. You may wish to trim the model's sideburns slightly, if he is agreeable.

I used the "Ashley" wig by Giant in color #56. This color of grey has a bit of brown mixed in, making it more flattering on those with warmer colorings.

Nost the Younger, John. Details from *George III*. Marble, 1764. YBA.

Supplies

Beyond the standard supplies required for all styles (listed on page 133):

- 1 **wig**, 22" or longer, straight
- 1 large **hairband** (covered rubber band)
- 1 small **roll form** (about 3/4" diameter)
- 1 **ribbon**, narrow or wide

Finished Styles 277

1a-b Block the wig. Section about 2-3" of hair along the hairline, from a center part to behind the ears. On top, part the back hair so that it comes to a slight point at the end of the center part. Clip the side front sections out of the way.

2 Comb the back hair smoothly back, and tie it with a hairband at the nape of the neck.

3 Unclip one of the sides. Part a 1" horizontal section at the bottom, around the ear. Clip this small section out of the way. Do the same on the other side.

4 Unclip the top portion of both front sections. Comb them all back from the hairline, without a part.

5 Clip the front into a temporary high ponytail, and cut the hair so that the tail is only about 5" long.

6  **7**

6 Twist the tail of the top section.

7 Fold that twisted end under…

8  … creating a roll at the hairline, and hiding the twisted end underneath the roll. Bobby pin, using Xed pins, the front roll down to the wig.

You may find that the front roll is higher than you like. The height will generally be determined by the length of the twisted tail. You can unpin the front roll, trim the tail slightly shorter, and then re-twist and tuck under again. I recommend trimming the tail in short pieces (about 1" or so) and re-twisting/tucking repeatedly until you have achieved a shape you like. This allows you to go slowly and make sure that you don't cut too much hair.

9  **10** Unclip the lower side section. Comb this smooth, and roll it around your roll form. Roll the hair **up** towards the top of the head…

10 … until you read the wig base, right above the ear. Before removing the roll form…

11 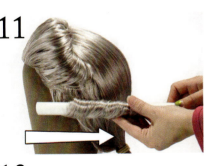 **12**

13

11 … slide it back slightly, so that the buckle spirals slightly back. Then gently remove the roll form.

12 Bobby pin, using Xed pins, the buckle to the head.

13 Gently pull the bottom portion of the front roll back and down until it meets the top of the buckle, then bobby pin to secure. See the finished model photo for reference.

Cover the hairband with a ribbon.

Finished Styles

Joseph
High Buckle/Queue Style (1770s)

*T*he "Joseph" is based on a portrait of famed British sculptor Joseph Nollekens, with the adaptation of two buckles at the sides. To complement the foppishness of the higher toupet, a cadogan knot was used for the queue. The style is appropriate for wear in both Britain and France during this period. It is probably a bit too silly for most American colonials.

This style was created using the Lacey Costume Wigs "Showgirl" wig, with the customized hairline demonstrated on pages 119-122. It can of course be made without the custom hairline.

Many elements of this wig could be varied, from the number and size of the buckles, to the height on top and width at the sides. In addition, the queue could be worn as a ponytail, in ringlets, wrapped with a ribbon in the Ramillies style, worn in a black silk bag, or any of the other styles show in the year-by-year section.

This demonstration was made using a wig customized to the model's hairline, shown on pages 119-122. I started with a Lacey "Showgirl" wig (color #44, an iron grey), which is long and wavy, and added straight weaving hair at the center front hairline and temples. Adding all of this extra hair in front meant that there was a lot of hair to put into the buckles. To mitigate this, I used a very narrow roll form. If you are not adding hair to the wig in front, I suggest using a wider roll form, like in the King George style.

Rigaud, John Francis. Detail from *Joseph Nollekens with His Bust of Laurence Sterne*. Oil on canvas, 1772. YBA.

Supplies

Beyond the standard supplies required for all styles (listed on page 133):

- 1 **wig**, 26" or longer, straight or wavy
- 1 large **hairband** (covered rubber band)
- 1 standard **hairnet** (optional)
- 1 tiny **roll form** (about 1/4" diameter)

1 Block the wig. Part the hair from the top of the head, down to behind the ears. Clip the front sections out of the way.

2 Comb the back hair out and tie it into a low ponytail, about 1" below the nape of the neck.

3 To make the cadogan, section a 1" thick piece of hair from the under side of the ponytail.

4 Take the rest of the ponytail, comb it smooth, and then loop it up.

5 Continue looping, aligning the center of the loop with the hairband. Make sure the ends of the hair meet (or pass) the hairband.

6 Grasp the looped hair in the middle, at the hairband, in one hand, and with the other wrap the 1" section of hair around the center of the loop. Wrap the 1" section as many times as needed, and try to end this piece on the underside of the ponytail.

7 Bobby pin the wrapped piece on the underside. You may want to cover the entire cadogan knot with a small hairnet. If you do, make sure to twist the excess hairnet on the underside, and bobby pin it to the underside of the knot.

8 Unclip one of the front sections. Make a 2" horizontal parting at the bottom of the section, and then clip the top portion out of the way.

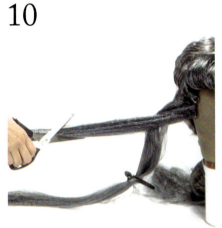

9 Part the lower section horizontally into two equal sections. Clip the top of these out of the way.

10 Trim the section of hair so that it is about 10" long.

11 Wrap the ends of this section around the roll form, rolling **up** to the top of the head.

12 Continue rolling up...

Finished Styles 283

13 ...until you reach the wig base at the ear. Remove the form carefully, and bobby pin, using Xed pins, the buckle to the wig.

14 Repeat steps 10-13 with the upper section of hair, creating the top buckle.

Repeat steps 8-14 on the other side.

15 Unclip the front top sections, combine them and comb them smooth. If you have added extra hair at the hairline, you will have a lot of hair to put into the front roll. I suggest parting a section in the center, near the back, and cutting it very short, simply to remove some of the bulk of the hair.

You can skip this step if you have not added any extra hair to the wig.

16 Twist the ends of the hair into a ponytail at the back of the head.

17 Fold the twist under, so that the twist is hidden under the front hair...

18 ... and bobby pin the front roll to the wig.

The height of the front section will be determined by how much hair is twisted under. If the front is higher than you would like, you can unpin the front section, cut the twisted tail slightly shorter, and then refold and pin the front. I suggest trimming the tail in short, 1" sections, and experimenting with the result.

Captain Robert
Bushy Style (1780s)

Finished Styles 285

*T*he Captain Robert is a bushy, heavily powdered style. It could be easily varied through the treatment of the queue: worn in a ponytail, in ringlets, wrapped with a ribbon in the Ramillies style, or any of the other styles show in the year-by-year section.

It appears that this style of wig was achieved through one of two methods. Some of the wigs appear cut to the desired length on the top and sides, while others are done by leaving the top/sides longer and tucking them under. This second method is demonstrated here, and it is a safer option for those who are nervous about cutting a wig. The same approach can be used on women's hairstyles of the 1780s.

Eighteenth-century visual sources occasionally show the wearer's own hair peeking out at the temples and along the sides and nape of the neck, so I suggest not worrying if the same happens to your model. You can powder the hair here to match the wig color. You may wish to trim the model's sideburns slightly, if he is agreeable.

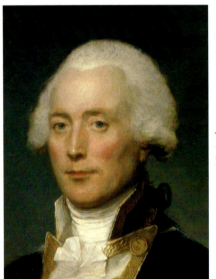

Abbott, Lemuel Francis. Detail from *Captain Robert Calder*. Oil on canvas, c. 1787-90. NGA.

I used the "Showgirl" wig by Lacey Costume Wigs in color #60 (silver/white), and powdered the wig lightly.

Supplies

Beyond the standard supplies required for all styles (listed on page 133):

- 1 **wig**, 26" or longer, straight or wavy
- **Foam rollers**: about 60 frames (you will be removing the foam piece, so diameter does not matter)
- 1 large **hairband** (covered rubber band)
- 1 tiny **roll form** (about 1/4" diameter)
- 1 **wig bag** (see page 286)

1 Block the wig. Part the hair from behind the ear, across the crown of the head, to behind the other ear.

2 Clip the back hair out of the way. Roll all of the front hair into tiny curls, by wrapping small pieces around the center plastic stick, without the foam piece, of a foam roller. Curl direction is not important.

Set the curls by pouring boiling water over the curled portion of the wig (see page 104). Allow the wig to dry.

3 Reblock the wig.

4 Comb the back hair smooth and tie it into a ponytail at the nape of the neck.

5 Untwist each individual curl.

6 Comb out each individual untwisted curl in order to frizz it.

Finished Styles 287

7 Part a section above the ear, about 1.5" high and 3" wide. Clip that section out of the way. Repeat on the other side.

Temporarily clip sections of the front hair back towards the crown.

8 Examine the feature photo to see where the frizzed section ends. Cut the frizzed hair about 2-4" past this point (we need that extra 2-4" to be able to roll the hair under).

9 Keep pushing more of the frizzed hair back towards the crown, cutting off any unnecessary length.

If this makes you nervous, you can try out step 10 to see if you need to trim more hair. Go slow, make small cuts.

10 Take all of the front hair and pull it back towards the crown of the head, rolling the ends under. Bobby pin, using Xed pins, the rolled-under hair to the wig.

Examine the silhouette of the frizzed hair. If it is fuller than you would like, you can 1. trim the ends of the hair a bit more, and/ or 2. pull the hair tighter before rolling it under.

11 Unclip the parted side section from step 7. Comb it out, and roll it **up**, towards the top of the head, on the roll form.

12 Carefully remove the roll form, and pin the buckle to the wig, using Xed pins on both sides.

13 For a quick and easy widow's peak, pinch a bit of hair at the center front hairline, and insert a bobby pin into the base of the pinch.

14 Tie the bag onto the ponytail, making sure that the hairband is hidden inside of the bag.

TO MAKE A WIG BAG

Supplies

- 1/4 yard black silk taffeta **fabric** (or scraps large enough for the pattern pieces plus the decorative bow or cockade)
- 1 yard narrow black **ribbon** (about 1/4" wide)
- **Sewing supplies**: black thread, scissors, hand needle or sewing machine
- Small **safety pin**
- **Awl**, if you are going to make the eyelets by hand

1 Calculate the size of your pattern:
- **Width** = desired width of finished bag x 2, plus seam allowance x 2
  Example: desired width of finished bag = 5" x 2 = 10"; seam allowance = .5" x 2 = 1"; 10" + 1" = 11"
- **Height** = desired length of finished bag, plus seam allowance x 3
  Example: desired length of finished bag = 10"; seam allowance = .5" x 3 = 1.5"; 10" + 1.5" = 11.5"

2 Cut a rectangle of fabric to the measurements created in step 1.

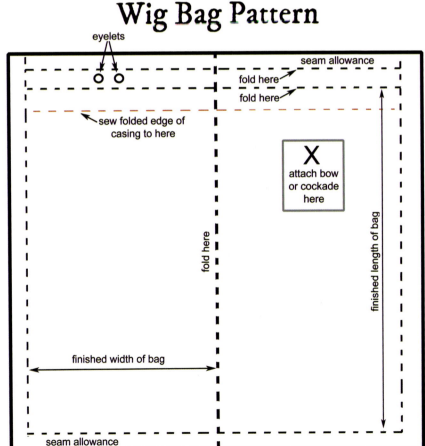

3 Fold the fabric in half along the fold line.

4 Wrong sides together, sew the bottom and side seams closed.

5 Make two eyelets where marked. If you are using a sewing machine, you can make two tiny buttonholes.

6 Fold the top edge under twice to make a casing, then sew the folded edge to the marked line.

7 Turn the bag right side out.

8 Make a decorative bow or cockade out of the same fabric.

9 Attach the bow or cockade to the marked position on the outside of the bag.

10 Use the safety pin to thread the ribbon through the casing, beginning by going in through one of the eyelets, around the width of the bag, and then out of the other eyelet.

11 To wear, insert the queue into the bag. Gather up the top edge of the bag using the ribbon. Tie the ribbon with a bow, and then tuck the bow inside of the bag.

Shopping Resources

Wigs & Hair Supplies

There are numerous wig/hair sellers online. Listed below are the companies that have served me well. Feel free to look beyond this list, but also remember, buyer beware! A nice website does not necessarily make a reputable company.

In my experience, it is more affordable to buy wigs online, while weaving and braiding hair is cheaper (and colors, lengths, and textures are more diverse) if purchased at a brick-and-mortar store. Check to see if you have any wig stores in your area and explore their options.

Wilshire Wigs
http://www.wilshirewigs.com/
Wigs, hairpieces, wig blocks & clamps, wig clips, styrofoam heads.

Cosplay Supplies
http://www.cosplaysupplies.com/
Wigs.

Doctored Locks
http://www.doctoredlocks.com/
Braiding and weaving hair.

Recommended Base Wigs

There are many long wigs that will work well for eighteenth-century styles. These are just a few that I have found to work well consistently:

"**Ashley**" by Giant (available at Wilshire Wigs). Long straight wig with a center part that comes in *many* colors.

"**Lioness**" by Wig America (available at Wilshire Wigs). Long, very curly wig with long layers and no strong part.

"**Naomi**" style by New Look (available at Cosplay Supplies). Long style with no layering and no strong part.

"**Showgirl**" by Lacey Costume Wigs (available at Wilshire Wigs as "Showgirl 340"). Long wavy wig with long layers and no strong part, which has a slightly larger cap size. Do not buy the "Deluxe Showgirl," as it has bangs. Limited colors.

"**Southern Belle**" by Lacey Costume Wigs (available at Wilshire Wigs). Short wavy layers on top, long ringlets underneath. Do not buy the bargain, it looks too cheap. Limited colors.

Hair Powder

Colonial Williamsburg Marketplace
http://www.williamsburgmarketplace.com/
White scented loose powders: Powder of Violets, Roses, Lavender, and Magnolia.

Bumble & Bumble
http://www.bumbleandbumble.com/
Colored aerosol spray powders: white, "a bit blondish," brown, black.

Little Bits
http://www.etsy.com/shop/LittleBits
Reproduction 18th century cosmetics, including hair powder in many colors (white, grey, blue, pink, etc.).

Supplies

Sally Beauty
http://www.sallybeauty.com/
Hairspray, bobby pins in many colors, hairnets, temporary color aerosol sprays, and more.

Sources & Further Reading

History

Amann, Elizabeth. "Blonde Trouble: Women in Wigs in the Wake of Thermidor." *Fashion Theory: The Journal of Dress, Body & Culture* 13, no. 3 (2009): 299-324.
— *Social and political aspects of the fashion for blonde wigs in Paris just after the Terror.*

Arnold, Janet. *Perukes & Periwigs.* London: H.M.S.O., 1970.
— *Focused on men's wigs in England.*

Baker, Malcolm. 2004. "'No Cap or Wig but a Thin Hair Upon It': Hair and the Male Portrait Bust in England Around 1750." *Eighteenth-Century Studies* 38, no. 1 (2004): 63-77.
— *The English trend for depicting men with little or no hair in portrait busts, thus making the subject appear classical and timeless.*

Bindman, David and Henry Louis Gates, Jr., eds. *The Image of the Black in Western Art.* Cambridge, Mass.: Belknap Press of Harvard University Press, 2010.
— *Artistic representations of people of African descent, including discussion of clothing and hairstyles.*

Blackwell, Caitlin. "'The Feather'd Fair in a Fright': The Emblem of the Feather in Graphic Satire of 1776." *Journal for Eighteenth-Century Studies* 36, no. 3 (2013): 353-376.
— *Criticism of feathered hairstyles in England.*

Buck, Anne. *Dress in Eighteenth-Century England.* New York: Holmes & Meier, 1979.
— *An excellent overview.*

Chico, Tita. *Designing Women: The Dressing Room in Eighteenth-Century English Literature and Culture.* Bucknell University Press, 2005.
— *The dressing room as a cultural symbol.*

Chrisman-Campbell, Kimberly. "The Face of Fashion: Milliners in Eighteenth-Century Visual Culture." *Journal for Eighteenth-Century Studies* 25, no. 2 (2002): 157-171.
— *Images and satires of milliners (dressmakers and fashion stylists).*

----. "Dressing to Impress: The Morning Toilette and the Fabrication of Femininity." In *Paris: Life & Luxury in the Eighteenth Century,* 53-74. Los Angeles: J. Paul Getty Museum, 2011.
— *The ritual of the* toilette, *including consumer items associated with it and its depiction in art.*

----. "French Connections: Georgiana, Duchess of Devonshire, and the Anglo-French Fashion Exchange." *Dress* 31 (2004): 3-14.
— *Georgiana's influence on fashion, including some brief descriptions of hairstyles.*

Corson, Richard. *Fashions in Hair: The First Five Thousand Years.* London: P. Owen, 1980.
— *Useful, although the broad time span makes it quite general.*

Cunnington, C. Willett and Phillis Cunnington. *Handbook of English Costume in the Eighteenth Century.* Boston Plays, 1972.
— *Useful information on hairstyles and wigs, but few sources are cited, and this work has been proven to have misconceptions. Use with care.*

Cross, Louisa. "Fashionable Hair in the Eighteenth Century: Theatricality and Display." In *Hair: Styling, Culture and Fashion,* 15-26. Oxford: Berg, 2008.

Delpierre, Madeleine. *Dress in France in the Eighteenth Century.* New Haven: Yale University Press, 1997.
— *An excellent overview, although light on visuals.*

Falakay, Fayçal. "From Barber to Coiffeur: Art and Economic Liberalisation in Eighteenth-Century France." *Journal for Eighteenth-Century Studies* 36, no. 1 (2013): 35-48.
— *How French coiffeurs framed themselves as artists in order to establish themselves as separate from the barber-wigmakers' guild.*

Le Faye, Deirdre. *Jane Austen's "Outlandish Cousin": The Life and Letters of Eliza de Feuillide*. London: British Library, 2002.

Festa, Lynn. "Personal Effects: Wigs and Possessive Individualism in the Long Eighteenth Century." *Eighteenth-Century Life* 29, no. 2 (2005): 47-90.
— *The social significance of wigs in Britain.*

Gayne, Mary K. "Illicit Wigmaking in Eighteenth-Century Paris." *Eighteenth-Century Studies* 38, no. 1 (2004): 119-137.
— *The organization of the wigmaker's guild and its response to illegal wigmaking by non-guild members.*

Haulman, Kate. *The Politics of Fashion in Eighteenth-Century America*. Chapel Hill: University of North Carolina Press, 2011.
— *Social/cultural aspects of fashion in the American colonies/United States.*

----. "A Short History of the High Roll." *Common-Place* 2, no. 1 (October 2001): http://www.common-place.org/vol-02/no-01/lessons/
— *Images and criticism of the high hairstyles of the 1770s in the American colonies/United States.*

Herzog, Don. "The Trouble with Hairdressers." *Representations* 53 (1996): 21-43.
— *The role of hairdressers historically in British culture.*

Hosford, Desmond. "The Queen's Hair: Marie-Antoinette, Politics, and DNA." *Eighteenth-Century Studies* 38, no. 1 (2004): 183-200.
— *The political significance of Marie-Antoinette's hairstyles, including some information about specific styles and her coiffeurs.*

Lanoë, Catherine. *La Poudre et le Fard: Une Histoire des Cosmétiques de la Renaissance aux Lumières*. Seyssel: Champ Vallon, 2008.
— *A history of cosmetics, including hair powder, from the Renaissance through the eighteenth century.*

Kwass, Michael. "Big Hair: A Wig History of Consumption in Eighteenth-Century France." *American Historical Review* 111, no. 3 (June 2006): 630-659.
— *The popularity of wigs, particularly as relates to issues of social class.*

Martin, Morag. *Selling Beauty: Cosmetics, Commerce, and French Society, 1750-1830*. Baltimore: Johns Hopkins University Press, 2009.

Modes et Révolutions : 1780-1804 : 8 février-7 mai 1989, Musée de la Mode et du Costume, Palais Galliera. Paris: Paris-Musées, 1989.
— *Exhibition on Revolutionary fashion. Includes an essay on hairstyles.*

Molineux, Catherine. "Hogarth's Fashionable Slaves: Moral Corruption in Eighteenth-Century London." *Elh* 72, no. 2 (2005): 495-520.
— *The symbolism of Black slaves in Hogarth's paintings and eighteenth-century art more generally, including portrayals of clothing and hair.*

Palmer, Caroline. "Brazen Cheek: Face-Painters in Late Eighteenth-Century England." *Oxford Art Journal* 31, no. 2 (2008): 195-213.
— *Attitudes towards cosmetics, particularly in portraiture, with some information about hair powdering.*

Patton, Tracey Owens. "Hey Girl, Am I More Than My Hair?: African American Women and Their Struggles with Beauty, Body Image, and Hair." *NWSA Journal* 18, no. 2 (2006): 24-51.
— *Includes some discussion of traditional African hairstyling practices, how those changed (or remained) when Africans were enslaved in America, and the resulting effects on African-American beauty and body image.*

Pointon, Marcia R. *Hanging the Head: Portraiture and Social Formation in Eighteenth-Century England.* New Haven, Conn.: Yale University Press, 1993.
— *Useful for a discussion of wigs, both their role in English culture and their representation in art.*

Powell, Margaret and Joseph Roach. "Big Hair." *Eighteenth-Century Studies* 38, no. 1 (2004): 79-99.
— *Philosophical debates about hairstyles and wigs in England, with a focus on the theater and the writings of Horace Walpole.*

Rauser, Amelia. "Hair, Authenticity, and the Self-made Macaroni." *Eighteenth-Century Studies* 38, no. 1 (2004): 101-117.
— *The extravagant wig styles, and their symbolic associations, worn by "Macaronis" (English fops).*

Ribeiro, Aileen. *The Art of Dress: Fashion in England and France, 1750 to 1820.* New Haven, Conn.: Yale University Press, 1995.
— *An excellent overview of the topic, although more focus on art than Dress in Eighteenth-Century Europe.*

----. 2002. *Dress in Eighteenth-Century Europe, 1715-1789.* New Haven: Yale University Press.
— *An excellent, detailed overview of the topic.*

Steele, Valerie. "The Social and Political Significance of Macaroni Fashion." *Costume* 19 (1): 94-109.
— *The social and political messages of Macaroni (English fop) fashion, including hair.*

Stevens-Cox, James. *An Illustrated Dictionary of Hairdressing & Wigmaking : Containing Words, Terms and Phrases (Current and Obsolete), Dialectal, Foreign, and Technical, Used in Britain and America Pertaining to the Crafts of Hairdressing and Wigmaking; Also Words Derived from These Crafts Having a Wider Use.* London: Batsford Academic and Educational, 1984.
— *Lots of fascinating, detailed information on eighteenth-century hairdressing, styles, and wigmaking in dictionary form.*

Stewart, Imogen. "Betsy Sheridan's Journal and her Attitude to Fashion." *Costume* 22(1): 39–43.
— *References to late eighteenth-century fashion in a well-to-do Englishwoman's diary.*

Styles, John. *The Dress of the People: Everyday Fashion in Eighteenth-Century England.* New Haven, Conn.: Yale University Press, 2007.
— *The dress, including hair and wigs, worn by more common people.*

Vincent, Susan J. *The Anatomy of Fashion: Dressing the Body from the Renaissance to Today.* Oxford: Berg, 2009.
— *Includes a detailed overview of wigs, hairstyles, and the styling of both in seventeenth- and eighteenth-century England.*

Waugh, Norah Waugh. *The Cut of Women's Clothes, 1600-1930.* New York: Theatre Arts Books, 1968.
— *Mostly focuses on patterns for clothing, but has some interesting historical quotations related to hair and wigs.*

White, Shane, and Graham White. "Slave Hair and African American Culture in the Eighteenth and Nineteenth Centuries." *Journal Of Southern History* 61, no. 1 (February 1995): 45.
— *Hairstyles worn by African American slaves and the role that hairstyling played in that culture.*

The Wigmaker in Eighteenth-Century Williamsburg: An Account of His Barbering, Hair-Dressing, & Peruke-Making Services, & Some Remarks on Wigs of Various Styles. Williamsburg, VA: Colonial Williamsburg, 1971.
— *Wigmaking and wear, particularly as it happened in the colonies.*

Winner, Viola Hopkins. 2001. "Abigail Adams and 'The Rage of Fashion.'" *Dress.* 28: 64-76.
— *Abigail Adams's impressions of French and English fashions during her travels of the 1780s, and her comparisons of them with American styles.*

Theatrical Wig Making & Styling

Baker, Patsy. *Wigs and Make-Up for Theatre, Television, and Film.* Oxford: Focal Press, 1993.
— *Only useful for information about building wigs from scratch, including ventilating (knotting individual hairs) and weaving wefts. No instructions for historical styles.*

Swinfield, Rosemarie. *Hair and Wigs for the Stage: Step-by-Step.* Cincinnati: Betterway Books, 1999.
— *Useful for techniques, like wearing and styling wigs, but not as much as* Wig Making and Styling *by Lowery & Ruskai.*

Lowery, Allison and Martha Ruskai. *Wig Making and Styling: A Complete Guide for Theatre & Film.* Burlington, Mass.: Focal Press, 2010.
— *Indispensable for wig techniques: styling, making, adapting, and wearing wigs.*

Lowery, Allison. *Historical Wig Styling: Ancient Egypt to the 1830s.* Burlington, Mass.: Focal Press, 2013.
— *Useful for styling demonstrations, although there are only three eighteenth-century female styles and three male, and the details of the styles are not historically accurate.*

Rennells, Lauren. *Vintage Hairstyling: Retro Styles with Step-by-Step Techniques.* Denver, Colo.: HRST Books, 2009.
— *A book on a different era, but still useful for its excellent demonstration of hair styling methods, especially pincurling.*

Stephens, Janet. "Papillote Curls: Historical Hairdressing Techniques." August 14, 2012. https://www.youtube.com/watch?v=lP9PJsY5__4
— *Demonstration of a reconstructed eighteenth-century technique for creating curls, using modern tools.*

18th Century Sources

Many of these are available online at Gallica (gallica.bnf.fr) and Google Books (books.google.com/).

Adams Family Papers (correspondence between John and Abigail Adams, and the Diary of John Adams): www.masshist.org/digitaladams/archive/index

Adams, Abigail. *Letters of Mrs. Adams: the Wife of John Adams.* Boston: C.C. Little and J. Brown, 1840.

Angelo, Henry. *Reminiscences with Memoirs of His Late Father and Friends, Including Numerous Original Anecdotes and Curious Traits of the Most Celebrated Characters that Have Flourished During the Last Eighty Years.* London: Henry Colburn and Richard Bentley, 1830.

Autié, Léonard. *Recollections of Léonard: Hairdresser to Queen Marie-Antoinette.* New York: Sturgis & Walton Company, 1909.

Bachaumont, Louis Petite de. *Memoirs Secrets.* London: J. Adamson, 1781.

Barry, Marie Jeanne, Countess du. *La Du Barry: De Lettres et Documents Inédits Tires de la Bibliotheque Nationale, de la Bibliotheque de Versailles, des Archives Nationales, et de Collections Particulieres.* Eds. Edmond de Goncourt & Jules de Goncourt. Paris: Bibliothèque-Charpentier, 1903.

Beaumont. *L'Enciclopédie Perruquiere. Ouvrage Curieux a l'Usage de Toutes Sortes de Têtes, Enrichi de Figures en Taille-Douce. Par M Beaumont, Coëffeur dans les Quinze-Vingts.* Amsterdam & Paris, 1757.

Buc'hoz, Pierre-Joseph. *The Toilet of Flora; or, A Collection of the Most Simple and Approved Methods of Preparing Baths, Essences, Pomatums, Powders, Perfumes, Sweet-Scented Waters, and Opiates for Preserving and Whitening the Teeth...* London: Printed for J. Murray and W. Nicoll, 1775.

Burney, Frances. *The Early Diary of Frances Burney, 1768-1778: With a Selection from her Correspondence, and from the Journals of her Sisters Susan and Charlotte Burney.* London: George Bell and Sons, 1889.

Delany, Augusta Waddington Hall Llanover, Lady. *The Autobiography and Correspondence of Mrs. Delany.* Boston: Roberts Brothers, 1879.

Depain. *Coiffures des Dames.* Paris, 1780.

Dictionnaire Universel François et Latin, Contenant la Signification et la Définition... Paris: Delaulne, Foucault, Clousier, Nyon, & Gosselin, 1721.

A Dissertation upon Head Dress: Together with a Brief Vindication of High Coloured Hair, and of Those Ladies on Whom It Grows; the Whole Submitted to the Connoisseur in Taste, By an English Periwig-Maker. London: printed for J. Williams, C. Moran, and Edward Macklew, 1767.

Encyclopédie, ou Dictionnaire Universel Raisonné des Connoissances Humaines. Ed. Fortuné Barthélemy de Félice. Yverdon, 1773.

Encyclopédie Méthodique, Arts et Métiers Mécaniques. Ed. Charles Panckoucke. Paris: Chez Panckoucke, 1785.

Fenton, Richard and Samuel Rogers. *Memoirs of an Old Wig.* London: Printed for Longman, Hurst, Rees, Orme, and Brown, Paternoster-Row, 1815.

Garsault, François-Alexandre Pierre de. *Art du Perruquier, Contenant la Façon de la Barbe, la Coupe des Cheveux, la Construction des Perruques d'Hommes et de Femmes, le Perruquier en Vieux et le Baigneur-Étuviste, par M. de Garsault.* 1767.

Frampton, Mary. *The Journal of Mary Frampton: From the Year 1779, Until the Year 1846. Including Various Interesting and Curious Letters, Anecdotes, &c., Relating to Events which Occurred During that Period.* London: S. Low, Marston, Searle, & Rivington, 1885.

Hamilton, Mary. *Mary Hamilton Dickenson, Mary Hamilton, Afterwards Mrs. John Dickenson, at Court and at Home.* London: J. Murray, 1925.

Hogarth, William. *The Analysis of Beauty: Written with a View of Fixing the Fluctuating Ideas of Taste.* London: Printed by J. Reeves, 1753.

Kalm, Pehr. *Kalm's Account of His Visit to England: On His Way to America in 1748,* trans. Joseph Lucas. London: Macmillan and Co., 1892.

Legros. *L'Art de la Coëffure des Dames Françoises, avec des Estampes Où Sont Représentées les Têtes Coeffées...* Paris: A. Boudet, 1768.

Legros. *Supplément de l'Art de la Coëffure des Dames Françoises, par le Sieur Legros.* Paris: A. Boudet, 1768.

Lennox, Lady Sarah. *The Life and Letters of Lady Sarah Lennox, 1745-1826, Daughter of Charles, 2nd Duke of Richmond...* London: J. Murray, 1901.

Moore, William. *The Art of Hair-Dressing: and Making it Grow Fast, Together, with a Plain and Easy Method of Preserving it; with Several Useful Recipes, &c.* Bath: Printed for the author by J. Salmon, in Stall-Street, 1780.

The New London Toilet: or, a Compleat Collection of the Most Simple and Useful Receipts for Preserving and Improving Beauty, Either by Outward Application or Internal Use... London: Printed for Richardson and Urquhart, under the Royal-Exchange, 1778.

Papendiek, Charlotte Louise Henrietta. *Court and Private Life in the Time of Queen Charlotte: Being the Journals of Mrs. Papendiek, Assistant Keeper of the Wardrobe and Reader to Her Majesty.* London: R. Bentley & Son, 1887.

Ritchie, David. *A Treatise on the Hair: Shewing Its Generation...* London: Printed for the author, and sold by him, at his shop in Rupert-Street, two Doors from Coventry-Street, Haymarket, 1770.

Pratt, Ellis. *The Art of Dressing the Hair: A Poem...* Bath: Printed by R. Cruttwell, 1770.

Recueil Général de Coeffures de Différents Gouts... Desnos, 1778.

Sheridan, Betsy, and W Le Fanu. *Betsy Sheridan's Journal: Letters from Sheridan's Sister, 1781-1786, and 1788-1790.* New Brunswick, N.J.: Rutgers University Press, 1960.

Stewart, James. *The Art of Hair Dressing: or, The Gentleman's Director...* London: Printed for and sold by the author, at his hair-dressing academy, No.12, Davies-Street, Berkeley-Square, 1788.

----. *The Art of Hair Dressing: or, the Ladies Director...* London: Printed for and sold by the author, at his hair-dressing academy, No.12, Davies-Street, Berkeley-Square, 1788.

----. *Plocacosmos: or the Whole Art of Hair Dressing...* London, 1782.

Vigée-Le Brun, Louise-Elisabeth. *Memoirs of Madame Vigée Lebrun.* Translated by Lionel Strachey. New York: Doubleday, 1903.

Magazines & Newspapers

Cabinet des Modes, ou les Modes Nouvelles (1785-1786)
Journal des Dames et des Modes (1797-1800)
Courier de la Mode (1768-1769)
Fashions of London & Paris (1799-1800)
Gallerie des Modes et Costumes Français (1778-1787)
Gallery of Fashion (1794-1800)
Journal de la Mode et du Goût (1790-1791)
Lady's Magazine (1770-1800)
Magasin des Modes Nouvelles, Françaises et Anglaises (1786-1789)

Image Collections

British Museum: www.britishmuseum.org/
Frick Collection: www.frick.org/
Lewis Walpole Library, Yale University: www.library.yale.edu/walpole/
Los Angeles County Museum of Art: collections.lacma.org/
Metropolitan Museum of Art: metmuseum.org/
Museum of Fine Arts Boston: www.mfa.org/
Museum of London: www.museumoflondon.org.uk/
National Gallery of Art: images.nga.gov/
Prints & Photographs, Library of Congress: www.loc.gov/pictures/
Réunion des Musées Nationaux: www.photo.rmn.fr
Rijksmuseum: rijksmuseum.nl/
Victoria & Albert Museum: images.vam.ac.uk/
Wellcome Library: wellcomeimages.org/
Wikimedia Commons: commons.wikimedia.org/
Yale Center for British Art: britishart.yale.edu/

Illustration Credits

Licensed images have specific credit information listed in their caption.

Abbreviations

CC0 BY 1.0
Photography specifically licensed under the Creative Commons CC0 1.0 Universal Public Domain Dedication. https://creativecommons.org/publicdomain/zero/1.0/

CC BY 2.0
Photography specifically licensed under a Creative Commons Attribution 2.0 Generic (CC BY 2.0) license. http://creativecommons.org/licenses/by/2.0/

CC BY 3.0
Photography specifically licensed under a Creative Commons Attribution 3.0 Unported (CC BY 3.0) license. http://creativecommons.org/licenses/by/3.0/

Getty
The Getty/The J. Paul Getty Trust, Los Angeles
Digital image courtesy of the Getty's Open Content Program. All selected artworks are in the public domain, and their photographs are specifically licensed "to be used for any purpose." https://www.getty.edu/about/opencontent.html

LACMA
Los Angeles County Museum of Art
All selected artworks are in the public domain, and their photographs are specifically licensed "for use without restriction." http://www.lacma.org/about/contact-us/terms-use

LoC
Library of Congress, Prints and Photographs Division, Washington D.C.
All selected artworks are in the public domain, and their photographs are specifically licensed as "no known restrictions on publication." http://www.loc.gov/rr/print/res/rights.html

LWL
Photography provided courtesy of the Lewis Walpole Library, Yale University. All selected artworks are in the public domain, and Yale University does not claim copyright of their photographs. http://www.library.yale.edu/walpole/research/rights_reproductions.html

MMA
Metropolitan Museum of Art
All select artworks are in the public domain, and their photographs are specifically authorized for use in scholarly publications, courtesy of the Metropolitan Museum's Open Access for Scholarly Content program. Scholarly publications are defined as "the dissemination of ideas and knowledge derived from study or research for educational/cultural purposes." The museum further clarifies, "Scholarly publication is not limited to academic institutions or university publishers, since commercial publishers/entities may also produce scholarly publications"; "self-published books" are included in the list of examples of scholarly publications. http://www.metmuseum.org/research/image-resources

NGA
National Gallery of Art, Washington, D.C.
All selected artworks are in the public domain, and their photographs are specifically licensed "for any use, commercial or non-commercial." https://images.nga.gov/en/page/openaccess.html

PD
Photography made available under a public domain license.

Rijksmuseum
Rijksmuseum, Amsterdam
All selected artworks are in the public domain, and their photographs are specifically licensed under a CC0 1.0 Universal Public Domain Dedication. http://creativecommons.org/publicdomain/zero/1.0/

Wellcome
Wellcome Library, London
All selected artworks are in the public domain, and their photographs are specifically licensed under the Creative Com-

mons-Attribution only (CC-BY) license. http://wellcomeimages.org/indexplus/page/News.html

WC/Yorck
Wikimedia Commons, the Yorck Project
All selected artworks are in the public domain, and their photographs are specifically licensed under the GNU Free Documentation License. http://commons.wikimedia.org/wiki/Commons:10,000_paintings_from_Directmedia

YBA
Yale Center for British Art
All selected artworks are in the public domain, and their photographs are specifically licensed "for use by anyone for any purpose." http://britishart.yale.edu/collections/using-collections/image-use